YALE JUDAICA SERIES

VOLUME XXXII

THE CODE OF MAIMONIDES
(*MISHNEH TORAH*)

BOOK TWO

YALE JUDAICA SERIES

The Code of Maimonides

BOOK TWO

The Book of Love

TRANSLATED FROM THE HEBREW BY
MENACHEM KELLNER

YALE UNIVERSITY PRESS
NEW HAVEN AND LONDON

Set in Granjon Roman type by Tseng Information Systems, Inc.
Printed in the United States of America.

Library of Congress Cataloging-in-Publicaton Data

Maimonides, Moses, 1135–1204.
[Sefer ahavah. English]
The code of Maimonides. Book two, The book of love / translated from the
Hebrew by Menachem Kellner.
    p.   cm. — (Yale Judaica series ; v. 32)
Includes bibliographical references and index.
ISBN 0-300-10348-4 (alk. paper)

1. Judaism—Customs and practices—Early works to 1800.   2. Judaism—
Liturgy—Early works to 1800.   3. Jewish law—Early works to 1800.
I. Kellner, Menachem Marc, 1946–   II. Title.   III. Series.
BM700.M23513   2004
296.1'812—dc22   2004048078

A catalogue record for this book is available from the British Library.

The paper in this book meets the guidelines for permanence and durability of
the Committee on Production Guidelines for Book Longevity of the Council
on Library Resources.

10   9   8   7   6   5   4   3   2   1

For
AVINOAM
who talked me into doing this

CONTENTS

ACKNOWLEDGMENTS

Ivan Marcus invited me to undertake this translation; Avinoam Kellner convinced me to accept the invitation; in addition, Ivan has been unfailingly helpful, supportive, and encouraging. My thanks to them both.

I have benefited from the detailed comments of Ya'akov Blidstein on the entire manuscript. Seth Kadish has been most helpful on specific points. Rebecca Temima Kellner has always been available, in the next room or at the other end of a phone line, for consultations on matters of translation, always putting her finger on precisely the right word or phrase. Paul Betz did a wonderful job of copyediting. I am pleased to acknowledge my debt to them here.

The illustrations appear courtesy of the Bodleian Library, University of Oxford (MS Huntington 80. Folios 122v, 123r, 131r, 131v).

Without Jolene S. Kellner none of this would have happened, and none of it would matter.

NOTE ON THE TRANSLATION

Maimonides cites biblical passages by the incipit only; in instances where there is no doubt whatsoever about the whole passage (such as in the case of the mezuzah or tefillin), I cite the beginning and end of the passage; in cases where customs may differ concerning where the passage ends (such as with many *haftarot*), I cite the incipit only.

Hebrew words and names which have been incorporated into standard English are treated as such and neither translated nor italicized. This leads to a certain amount of inconsistency (kaddish versus *qedushah*, for example) and to some oddities (*ḥamez*, but matzah; *'amidah*, but Shema, etc.). Holiday names which I judge to have passed into English are cited in that language; otherwise they are in Hebrew. This also leads to some inconsistency: Day of Atonement versus *Rosh ha-Shanah*, Passover versus *Sukkot*, and so on. There seems to be no good way of solving this problem.

TRANSLATOR'S INTRODUCTION

Maimonides calls the second of the fourteen books into which he divided the *Mishneh Torah* "The Book of Love" (*Sefer Ahavah*). This book contains six treatises or sections as follows:

Laws Concerning the Recitation of the Shema
Laws Concerning Prayer and the Priestly Blessing
Laws Concerning Tefillin, Mezuzah, and the Torah Scroll
Laws Concerning Fringes
Laws Concerning Blessings
Laws Concerning Circumcision

In the introduction to the *Mishneh Torah,* Maimonides explains that he included in the second book "all the commandments which we have been commanded to fulfill constantly so that we love God and be ever mindful of God, such as recitation of the Shema, prayer, phylacteries, and the priestly blessing.[1] Circumcision is included among them since it is a mark in our flesh serving as a constant reminder, even when there are no phylacteries or fringes, etc. I have called this book 'The Book of Love.'" "The Book of Love" includes those commandments which are fulfilled on a regular, continuing basis, and which both express and stimulate love of God.

This theme finds expression in the two places in which Maimonides discusses "The Book of Love" in the *Guide of the Perplexed*. In the first of these (III.35, p. 537)[2] he writes: "The ninth class [of commandments] comprises all the other practices of worship prescribed to everybody [i.e., Israelites as well as Priests and Levites] such as prayer and the recitation of the Shema and other things we have enumerated in the Book of Love. . . . The utility of this class is manifest, for it is wholly composed of works that fortify opinions concerning the love of the deity and what ought to be believed about Him and ascribed to Him."

In III.44 (p. 574), Maimonides characterizes the book in the following terms:

The commandments comprised in the ninth class are the commandments that we have enumerated in the Book of Love. All of them have manifest reasons and evident causes. I mean that the end of these actions pertaining to divine service is the constant commemoration of God, the love of Him and the fear of Him, the obligatory observance of the commandments in general, and the bringing about of such belief concerning Him, may He be exalted, as is necessary for everyone professing the Law. Those commandments are prayer, the recital of the Shema, the blessing after food and what is connected with it, the priestly blessing, phylacteries, mezuzah, acquiring a Torah scroll and reading it at certain times. All these are actions that bring about useful opinions.

These two texts tell us that "The Book of Love" includes practices of worship incumbent upon all Jews (and not just priests in the Temple);[3] that these practices strengthen love and awe of God and teach correct doctrines about God; and that instituting acts of worship with such ends in view makes excellent sense. The emphasis in these two passages is on worship, not as reflecting love of God, but as instilling it and as teaching true doctrines. It is noteworthy that all the sections of "The Book of Love" are alluded to in these two passages with the exception of "Laws Concerning Circumcision."[4]

Given what Maimonides does say in the *Guide of the Perplexed* about "The Book of Love," it is strange that he chooses as his motto for the book the verse *O how I love Your Torah! It is my study all day long* (Ps. 119:97) and not a verse such as *You shall love the Lord your God with all your heart and with all your soul and with all your might* (Deut. 6:5).[5]

A possible reason for this is that for Maimonides love of God is consequent upon knowledge of God, such knowledge, in turn, being consequent upon study of the Torah (in its fullest sense).

All Jews are commanded to love God: *You shall love the Lord your God with all your heart and with all your soul and with all your might* (Deut. 6:5). What is the nature of this love? Maimonides consistently connects love of God to knowledge of God, making love depend upon knowledge, but without reducing the former entirely to the latter. He raises the issue explicitly first in "Laws Concerning the Foundations of the Torah," II.1: "And what is the way that will lead to the love of Him and the fear of Him? When a person contemplates His great and wondrous works and creatures and from them obtains a glimpse of His wisdom which is incomparable and infinite, he will *immediately* love Him, praise Him, glorify Him, and long with an exceeding longing to know His great name."[6]

Maimonides tells us here that love of God is an immediate consequence of knowledge of God. The more knowledge, the more love: "One only loves God with the knowledge with which one knows Him. According to the knowledge will be the love: if the former be little or much, so will the latter be little or much."[7] Might it not appear that love of God and knowledge of God are the same thing, as Spinoza was later to claim?

A passage in the *Guide of the Perplexed* seems to support both possibilities: "As for the dictum of Scripture: *And thou shalt love the Lord with all thy heart* (Deut. 6:5)—in my opinion its interpretation is: with all the forces of your heart; I mean to say, with all the forces of the body, for the principle of all of them derives from the heart. Accordingly the intended meaning is . . . that you should make His apprehension the end of all your actions."[8] On the one hand, we are told here that in order to fulfill the scriptural command to love the Lord, one must use all the forces of one's body. On the other hand, we are further told here that the goal of using all the forces of one's body to love the Lord is to make knowledge of God the end of all our actions. Everything we do should serve the end of furthering our knowledge of God.[9] The points made here are expressed again toward the end of the *Guide* (III.28, 512–513): ". . . *with all thy heart, and with all thy soul, and with all thy might* (Deut. 6:5). We have already explained [10] . . . that this love becomes valid only through the apprehension of the whole of being as it is and through the consideration of His wisdom as it is manifested in it." In this passage, Maimonides seems to present love of God as a consequence of knowledge of God, and not as identical with it.

Near the end of the *Guide* (III.51, 621), Maimonides reiterates the relationship of dependence between love and knowledge: "Now we have made it clear several times that love is proportionate to apprehension." The more we know God, the more we love God.

What is the nature of this love we are commanded to have for God? Maimonides tells us in "Laws Concerning Repentance," X.5:

> What is the love of God that is befitting? It is to love God with a great and exceeding love, so strong that one's soul (*nafsho*) shall be knit up with the love of God such that it is continually enraptured by it, like love-sick individuals whose minds (*da 'atam*) are at no time free from passion for a particular woman, and are enraptured by her at all times . . . even intenser should be the love of God in the hearts of those who love Him; they should be enraptured by this love at all times.[11]

Maimonides reiterates the point again in X.6, "It is known and certain that the love of God does not become closely knit in a man's heart till he is continuously and thoroughly possessed by it and gives up everything else in the world for it." He makes much the same claim in some passages in the *Guide,* defining the passionate love of God (Arabic: *ishq*) as "an excess of love, so that no thought remains that is directed toward a thing other than the Beloved." [12]

Let us now look at the last passage in the *Guide* (III.52, 630) in which the issue comes up explicitly: "You know to what extent the Torah lays stress upon love: *With all thy heart, and with all thy soul, and with all thy might* (Deut. 6:5). For these two ends, namely love and fear, are achieved through two things: love, through the opinions taught by the Law, which include the apprehension of His Being as He, may He be exalted, is in truth; while fear is achieved by means of all actions prescribed by the Law, as we have explained." Maimonides' position here is tolerably clear: we achieve love of God through the apprehension of God's being to the greatest extent possible for humans.[13]

All this may help us to understand why "The Book of Love" follows "The Book of Knowledge" in the *Mishneh Torah:* love of God is dependent upon and follows from knowledge of God. Indeed, the last section of "The Book of Knowledge," "Laws Concerning Repentance" ends with a chapter devoted to love of God, providing an elegant transition to "The Book of Love." [14] As I understand him, Maimonides holds that knowledge (and hence love) of God alone does not constitute the highest possible form of human perfection. The *vita contemplativa* must be completed in the *vita activa,* and the one who truly knows and loves God will seek to imitate God, *Who acts with kindness, justice, and equity in the world* (Jer. 9:23). Knowledge of God must be followed by love of God, which, if true, finds expression in behavior ("the obligatory observance of the commandments in general," as above).[15]

Various scholars have sought to explain why the section "Laws Concerning Circumcision" is included in "The Book of Love." Boaz Cohen suggests that this is "because circumcision is associated in aggadic sources with phylacteries, mezuzah and fringes."[16] David Hartman, adopting Maimonides' own explanation as cited above, maintains that circumcision "serves as a sign upon our flesh that we must love God at all times."[17]

Howard Kreisel also focuses on the constancy (emphasized at the end of the "Laws Concerning Repentance") which "is an essential feature shared by the commandments which follow in the *Book of Love*. The goal of each of the commandments [in that book], and an integral part of their fulfillment, is awareness of God. Moreover, one is required to perform them constantly."[18] This is certainly true of circumcision.[19]

"The Book of Love" is, of course, first and foremost a halakhic work. "Laws Concerning the Recitation of the Shema" contains four chapters. The first describes and justifies the biblical passages which constitute the recitation of the Shema, the blessings which precede and follow its recitation, and the time of its recitation. The second chapter deals with how the Shema is to be recited, while the third details restrictions on where the Shema may be recited. The fourth and final chapter deals primarily with cases in which the Shema need not be recited.

"Laws Concerning Prayer and the Priestly Blessing" contains fifteen chapters. Of these, the last two deal with the priestly blessing, the others with various matters concerning prayer, the synagogue, and the reading of the Torah. In this context, "prayer" refers to the *'amidah*[20] only, not to the entire prayer services known today. Chapter 1 takes up the issue of the number of prayers to be recited each day, obligatory and voluntary. Chapter 2 discusses the blessing added to the *'amidah* cursing sectarians, the shortened *'amidah* known as "havinenu," and the order of prayers for the whole year. The third chapter details times for prayer, while the fourth lists matters which make prayer impossible, and also takes up the question of prayer while traveling. Eight matters which a person praying must do are listed in chapter 5. Chapter 6 takes up questions of deportment when praying outside of a synagogue, what may and may not be done before prayer, and who need not pray. Chapter 7 moves from the fixed prayers to the blessings which are to be recited every day. The eighth chapter takes up questions relating to communal prayer, the synagogue, and the prayer-leader ("cantor" in modern parlance). Recitation of communal prayers during the weekday and on Sabbaths, and deportment in the synagogue, are the main subjects of chapter 9. Chapter 10 takes up questions of when prayer is defective: due to lack of proper intention and due to skipped elements in the 'amidah. The structure of the synagogue is the focus of chapter 11, including issues of who must build a synagogue and proper disposal of a synagogue building. Chapter 12 details the order of Torah reading throughout the year and how it is to be done. This subject is continued in chapter 13. Chapter 14 takes up the number of times priests are to bless the congregation and how it is to be done; the priestly blessing in the synagogue is contrasted with that of the Temple. The fifteenth and final chapter deals with things which restrict a priest from blessing the community, and with the special problems of congregations made up entirely of priests, or in which there are no priests.

While Maimonides presents "Laws Concerning Phylacteries, Mezuzah, and the Torah Scroll" as one section of ten chapters, in practice it is often treated as three distinct sections: four chapters on phylacteries, two on mezuzah, and four on Torah scrolls. Maimonides' description of the kosher Torah scroll, and its division into paragraphs, has proven to be of great historical as well as halakhic interest and has enabled scholars to determine that he based his description on the celebrated Ben Asher codex.[21] Chapter 1 lists ten issues which render phylacteries unfit, the differences between the parchments necessary for phylacteries, mezuzot, and Torah scrolls, and the ways in which these are to be written. The second chapter takes up the question of the paragraphs from the Torah which constitute phylacteries, how they are to be written, and from whom phylacteries may be purchased. Chapter 3 deals with the order of these paragraphs, and with the straps which are used to bind the phylacteries to head and arm. In the fourth chapter Maimonides instructs the reader how and when to don phylacteries, the blessings made when putting them on, and who does not have to wear them. Turning to mezuzot, chapter 5 describes how they are to be written, affixed, and examined, while chapter 6 deals with the kinds of domicile and kinds of doorways which require a mezuzah. Chapter 7 opens the discussion of the Torah scroll by noting the obligation of every Jew (especially the king) to write a Torah scroll and describes how one goes about doing it. Open and closed paragraphs in the Torah scroll are the subject matter of chapter 8; the way in which lines are to be written is taken up as well. In chapter 9 Maimonides deals with the physical dimensions and attributes of a kosher Torah scroll, and how to handle one which has been torn. The last chapter emphasizes the sanctity of Torah scrolls, what renders them unsanctified, and how one is to treat them.

"Laws Concerning Fringes" contains three chapters. The first explains what fringes are and how they are to be made. Chapter 2 deals with the techniques of dying azure threads for the fringes and the special case of an azure tallit. The final chapter of this section deals with the kinds of garments on which fringes are to be tied.

"Laws Concerning Blessings" consists of eleven chapters. The first defines the rabbinic obligation to bless God before and after enjoying any food or drink, describes the standard forms of such blessings, and deals with the obligation to answer "amen" to blessings made by another. The second deals with the grace after meals, while the third details the kinds of grains over which one says the blessing "Who brings forth" before eating and the blessing ("grace after meals," as it is often called) after eating, in its longer and shorter versions. The circumstances under which the grace after meals is recited are discussed in chapter 4, including wedding meals, and various sorts of interruptions in the meal. Chapter 5 continues the discussion of wedding meals and generally deals with who is required to recite the grace after meals. In chapter 6 we are taught how one washes one's hands before eating bread and after a meal. Chapter 7 deals with rabbinic customs concerning meals. In chapter 8 we turn from grains to fruits, and the blessings appropriate to them. Chapter 9 deals with blessings over pleasant scents, and chapter 10 with a variety of other blessings over unusual occurrences. Chapter 11 discusses when blessings are made before an act and when after, and raises questions dealing with the language of blessings.

"Laws Concerning Circumcision" consists of three chapters. The first discusses the obligation of circumcision in general, on whom it falls, and when it is to be performed. Chapter 2 deals with those fit to circumcise and how it is done. The blessings of circumcision are discussed in chapter 3.

"The Book of Love" is poor in discussions of philosophical interest. "Laws Concerning the Recitation of the Shema," I.2 (which deals with a straightforwardly halakhic issue), is one of the few instances in which Maimonides' philosophical view of Judaism may insert itself into the book:

> What does one recite? The three paragraphs beginning with the words *Hear* (Deut. 6:4–9); *If, then, you obey* (Deut. 11:13–21); and *The Lord said* (Num. 15:37–41). The paragraph *Hear* is recited first because it contains commandments concerning God's unity, the love of God, and the study of God, which is the basic principle upon which all depends.[22] After it, *If, then, you obey* is recited since the passage commands obedience to all the other commandments. After that, the paragraph concerning the fringes is recited since it also contains a command to recall all the commandments.[23]

In the second sentence of this passage, the phrase "and the study of God" is a translation of the Hebrew word *ve-talmudo.* The interpretation of that word makes a tremendous difference to the meaning of the passage. The sentence could be translated as follows: "One recites the paragraph *Hear* first because it contains a commandment concerning God's unity, love of God, and study *of His Torah,*[24] which is the great principle upon which all depends."[25] A straightforward talmudist reads this sentence with great satisfaction: the study of Torah is made "the great principle upon which all depends," and it is in part because that study is found in the first paragraph of the Shema (*you shall teach them diligently to your children*—Deut. 6:7) that this paragraph is indeed the first of the paragraphs of the Shema.

The philosophically more alert reader of the *Mishneh Torah* finds something else here, different from, but by no means inconsistent with, what the talmudist finds. Such a reader must understand the key term, *ve-talmudo,* to mean the study of God, and not the study of God's Torah. The study of God, as is taught in the first four chapters of the *Mishneh Torah,* involves the study of physics and metaphysics, not the study of Talmud as ordinarily understood. Maimonides, of course, has nothing against the study of God's Torah as the talmudist understands it, but the obligation to undertake that study is not the issue here, at least for the reader of this passage who has carefully read the *Mishneh Torah* to this point.

Why do I say this? I take Maimonides to be teaching that we recite Deut. 6:4–9 first because of the first verse, *Hear, O Israel, the Lord, our God, the Lord is one.* This verse indeed teaches "the great principle upon which all depends," namely God's existence and unity. In "Laws Concerning the Foundations of the Torah," I.6, Maimonides uses the same exact expression, "the great principle upon which all depends," with reference to God's unity.[26]

One should not be confused by the reference to the love of God in the Maimonidean text before us. It calls to mind other passages in his writings in which Maimonides teaches us that love of God is proportionate to knowledge of God.[27]

Knowledge of God, of course, results from the study of physics and metaphysics (our knowledge of immaterial entities and our understanding of the limitations of what we can actually know about God). The student of Maimonides who has read and assimilated the *Guide of the Perplexed* knows that love of God finds its finest expression not in the study of Talmud but in the study of physics and metaphysics. This, too, is hinted at in the passage under discussion.

The greatest significance of "The Book of Love" in the Halakhah would appear to be the imprimatur given by Maimonides to the Ben Asher codex of the Pentateuch (discussed above).

"The Book of Love" has, of course, been published in all standard editions of the *Mishneh Torah.* All of these editions are unreliable to one extent or another, but we are in the happy situation of having a manuscript of the first two books of the *Mishneh Torah,* "The Book of Knowledge" and "The Book of Love," which bears the imprimatur of Maimonides himself. This manuscript, Oxford Huntington 80, was checked against the copy held by Maimonides himself, as is evidenced by his signature at the end of "The Book of Love" and was, moreover, designated as the manuscript against which all future copies of the *Mishneh Torah* should be checked. This manuscript has been published in a splendid facsimile edition by the Ofeq Institute (Jerusalem and Cleveland, 5757), and under the supervision of Professor Shlomo Zalman Havlin. Professor Havlin added an extremely valuable historical and bibliographical introduction.[28]

This manuscript served as the basis for the edition of and commentary on "The Book of Love" prepared by Rabbi Dr. Nachum L. Rabinovitch: *Rabbi Mosheh ben Maimon (Maimonides), Mishneh Torah According to the Bodleian Ms. Huntington 80 with a Comprehensive Commentary [Yad Peshuṭah].*[29] In his own edition of and commentary on the *Mishneh Torah,* Rabbi Joseph Kafiḥ took note of the Oxford manuscript and noted important variations from the Yemenite manuscript on which he based his edition: Rabbenu Mosheh ben Maimon, *Sefer Mishneh Torah Yozei le-Or Pa'am Rishonah al pi Kitvei Yad Teiman im Perush Makif.*[30] Both Rabbis Rabinovitch and Kafiḥ provide source notes and summaries of the halakhic literature surrounding "The Book of Love." Rabbi Rabinovitch also provides parallels to Maimonides' other writings.

"The Book of Love" has been translated into English twice. The first time by Moses Hyamson in *Mishneh Torah, The Book of Adoration by Maimonides* (Jerusalem: Boys Town Publishers, 1962). This book presents a transcription of the Oxford manuscript[31] with an English translation on facing pages. The translation, while certainly competent, errs in the direction of excessive literalness and occasional coyness (in places where Maimonides deals with matters offensive to the apparently exquisite, almost Victorian, sensibilities of the people to whom Hyamson addressed his translation). Moznaim Publishing Corporation of New York and Jerusalem has been issuing a translation of the *Mishneh Torah.* "The Book of Love" has come out in four volumes, the first, covering "Laws Concerning the Recitation of the Shema" and part of "Laws Concerning Prayer," was translated by Rabbi Boruch Kaplan (1988). The other three volumes—the rest of "Laws Concerning Prayer" (1989); "Laws Concerning Tefillin, Mezuzah, and Sefer Torah," and "Laws Concerning Fringes" (1991); and "Laws Concerning Blessings" and "Laws

Concerning Circumcision" (1991)—were all translated by Rabbi Eliyahu Touger. The thoroughly competent Kaplan-Touger translation is accompanied by the Hebrew text and an English-language halakhic commentary. The main deficiency of this edition (aside from a number of places in the commentary where the authors' apparent association with Habad Hassidism becomes evident) is that it is based upon the standard printed texts of the *Mishneh Torah* and ignores the many places where the Oxford manuscript preserves different (and because approved by Maimonides himself, superior) readings.

The present translation is based on the Oxford manuscript.[32] I have sought to be as literal as possible while remaining faithful to the canons of standard English. Hebrew and English are dramatically different languages. I have thus felt free to restructure sentences and to add words required by English but not found in the original Hebrew. In line with the style of Yale University Press, I have not enclosed these additions in parentheses.

Appended to the end of the Oxford manuscript is a brief description of the prayers to be recited throughout the year. This text is not a prayerbook in the full sense of the term, since it rarely provides the full text of any prayer. Although the text appears in the manuscript *after* the conclusion of "The Book of Love" and *after* Maimonides' signed attestation to the effect that the manuscript had been checked against his personal copy, most scholars agree that the order of prayer prescribed here was approved by Maimonides. It is also agreed by almost all scholars who have dealt with the issue that the rite found here more or less represents the form of prayer common in Egypt in Maimonides' day.[33]

Maimonides, in other words, simply appended to "The Book of Love" the order of prayers to which his Egyptian Jewish compatriots were accustomed. There is thus little of historical or halakhic significance to be learned from this text. For that reason, it was not translated here; a detailed description can be found in the appendix.

THE BOOK OF LOVE

In the Name of God, the Eternal Lord *

O how I love Your Torah! It is my study all day long
(Ps. 119:97)

Book Two, the Book of Love, comprises six treatises in the following order:

Laws Concerning the Recitation of the Shema
Laws Concerning Prayer and the Priestly Blessing
Laws Concerning Tefillin, Mezuzah, and the Torah Scroll
Laws Concerning Fringes
Laws Concerning Blessings
Laws Concerning Circumcision

Laws Concerning the Recitation of the Shema comprise one positive commandment: to recite the Shema twice a day.

Laws Concerning Prayer and the Priestly Blessing comprise two positive commandments: the first, to worship the Lord in prayer every day; the second, that the Priests bless Israel every day.

Laws Concerning Phylacteries, Mezuzah, and the Torah Scroll comprise five positive commandments, as follows: (a) that phylacteries be placed upon the head; (b) that they be tied upon the arm; (c) to affix a mezuzah to the openings of doorways; (d) that every man write a Torah scroll for himself; (e) that the king write a second Torah scroll for himself, so that he will have two Torah scrolls.

Laws Concerning Fringes comprise one positive commandment: to make fringes upon the corners of one's garment.

Laws Concerning Blessings comprise one positive commandment: to bless the Holy One, blessed be He, after eating.

Laws Concerning Circumcision comprise one positive commandment: to circumcise males on the eighth day after birth.

The total of all the commandments in this book is eleven positive commandments.

*Or, Lord of the Universe.

TREATISE I

Laws Concerning the Recitation of the Shema comprise one positive commandment, to recite the Shema twice daily. The clarification of this commandment will be found in these chapters:

CHAPTER ONE

1. The Shema is recited twice every day, once in the evening and once in the morning, as it is said: *Recite them when you stay at home and when you are away, when you lie down and when you get up* (Deut. 6:7). The time when people customarily lie down is evening and the time when people customarily get up is morning.[1]

2. What does one recite? The three paragraphs[2] beginning with the words *Hear* (Deut. 6:4–9);[3] *If, then, you obey* (Deut. 11:13–21);[4] and *The Lord said* (Num. 15:37–41).[5] The paragraph *Hear* is recited first because it contains commandments concerning God's unity, the love of God, and the study of God,[6] which is the basic principle on which all depends.[7] After it, *If, then, you obey,* is recited since the passage commands obedience to all the other commandments. After that, the paragraph concerning the fringes is recited, since it also contains a command to recall all the commandments.[8]

3. Even though the commandment concerning fringes is not fulfilled at night, the paragraph concerning it is recited at night since it contains a reference to the Exodus from Egypt, and there is a commandment to recall the Exodus from Egypt both in the daytime and at night, as it is said: *so that you may remember the day of your departure from the Land of Egypt all the days of your life* (Deut. 16:3).[9] The recitation of these three paragraphs in this order is what is called "the recitation of the Shema."[10]

4. When reciting the Shema, one quietly says, "Blessed be the name of His glorious majesty for ever and ever"[11] after the first verse, and then continues reciting *You shall love the Lord* aloud till the end. Why does one recite in this fashion? We have a tra-

dition to the effect that when our father Jacob's death was nigh
he gathered his sons together in Egypt and exhorted them to take
particular care concerning correct belief in God's unity and not to
stray from the path of God, on which his fathers Abraham and
Isaac had walked.[12] He then diligently inquired of them: "My sons,
perchance there is among you someone unworthy who does not
agree with me on the issue of the unity of the Master of all the Universe?"—as Moses our master said to us, *Perchance there is among
you some man or woman or some clan or tribe, whose heart is even now
turning away from the Lord our God to go and worship the gods of those
nations—perchance there is among you a stock sprouting poison weed
and wormwood* (Deut. 29:17).[13] They all replied: *Hear, O Israel! The
Lord is our God, the Lord alone* (Deut. 6:4), that is to say, "Hear us
say, our father Israel,[14] the Lord our God, the Lord alone." The old
man responded, "Blessed be the name of His glorious majesty for
ever and ever." It is therefore customary among all Jews to recite
the praise uttered by the elderly Israel after the first verse of the
Shema.[15]

5. When reciting the Shema, one recites blessings before it and
after it; in the morning,[16] two before and one after; in the evening,
two before and two after.[17]

6. The first blessing before it in the morning is "Who forms light,
etc."; the second is "with eternal love have You loved us." The blessing after is "true and certain." The first blessing before it in the
evening is, "Who brings on the evening," and the second is "You
have loved the house of Israel Your people with eternal love." The
first blessing after it is "true, trustworthy," and the second is "cause
us to lie down."[18]

7. The first blessing before it, whether morning or evening,
opens with "blessed" and closes with "blessed." Each of the rest
of the blessings closes with "blessed" but has no opening.[19] These
blessings, as well as all the others regularly recited by all Israel, were
instituted by Ezra and his court. No one has the authority to reduce the number of blessings or add to it. In a blessing where it was
instituted to close with "blessed," one is not permitted not to close
in this fashion, and in a blessing where it was not so instituted, one
is not permitted to close with "blessed." In a blessing where it was
instituted not to open with "blessed," one is not permitted to open

in this fashion, and in a blessing where it was instituted to open with "blessed," it is not permitted not to open with "blessed." The general rule is that anyone who changes the formula established by the Sages for blessings has erred and must repeat the blessing correctly. Whoever does not say "true and certain" in the morning prayer and "true, trustworthy" in the evening prayer has not fulfilled his obligation.[20]

8. A person who recites the second blessing before the first, whether during the day or the night, and whether before or after the Shema, has fulfilled his obligation since the blessings have no obligatory order. But if in the morning he opened with "Who forms light" and closed with "Who brings evenings," he has not fulfilled his obligation; if he opened with "Who brings evenings" and closed with "Who forms light," then he has fulfilled his obligation. Similarly, in the evening, if he opened with "Who brings evenings" and closed with "Who forms light," he has not fulfilled his obligation; but if he opened with "Who forms light" and closed with "Who brings evenings," then he has fulfilled his obligation, since all blessings follow their concluding formula.[21]

9. At what time does one recite the Shema in the evening? The obligation obtains from the time the stars come out till midnight.[22] If one transgressed and did not recite before midnight but recited before dawn,[23] he nonetheless fulfilled his obligation, since they[24] only said "until midnight" in order to distance one from transgression.[25]

10. One who recites the evening Shema after dawn but before sunrise did not fulfill his obligation, unless circumstances—such as being drunk or sick, etc.—prevented him from reciting it before dawn. One who is thus forced to recite the evening Shema at this time does not recite "cause us to lie down."[26]

11. At what time of the day is the Shema recited? Properly to observe the commandment one begins reciting long enough before sunrise so that he finishes the recitation and says the last blessing with the sunrise. The time thus required is one-tenth of an hour before the sun rises. If one delayed, and recited after the sun rose, he still fulfilled his obligation, since the permissible time for one who transgressed[27] and delayed its recital is till the end of the third hour of daytime.[28]

12. One who recites the morning Shema earlier than the appointed time but after dawn has fulfilled his obligation, even if he finishes before the sun rises. When constrained by circumstances, such as when one must leave early on a journey, one may recite from dawn even in the first instance.[29]

13. One who recites the Shema after the third hour of the day, even if circumstances constrained him to delay its recital, has not fulfilled his obligation to recite the Shema in its proper time; it is as if he were simply reading Scripture. Despite this, one still recites the blessings before it and after it throughout the day, even if he delayed and recited it after the third hour.[30]

CHAPTER TWO

1. One who recites the first verse of the Shema—*Hear, O Israel! The Lord is our God, the Lord alone*—without proper intention[31] has not fulfilled his obligation. But one who recites the other verses without proper intention has fulfilled his obligation. Even were he simply reading from the Torah or examining the text of these paragraphs in a Torah scroll[32] during the time the Shema is to be recited, he has fulfilled his obligation, so long as he had proper intention for the first verse.[33]

2. Every one may recite the Shema as is his wont, whether standing, walking, reclining, or riding on an animal. But it is forbidden to recite the Shema while lying prone with one's face flat on the ground, or lying on one's back, with one's face pointing upward. But one may recite while lying on one's side. One who is very fat, and cannot turn on his side, or one who is ill, should lean a bit toward his side and then recite.[34]

3. A person walking should stand still for the first verse, but he may recite the rest while continuing to walk. If one is asleep, he should be roused and awakened in order to recite the first verse. After that, if sleep overcomes him,[35] he is not to be disturbed.[36]

4. A person working interrupts his work to recite the entire first paragraph; so, too, hired craftsmen interrupt their work for the first paragraph so that their recitation not be haphazard.[37] Such a person may recite the rest of the Shema while engaged in his work.

Even if he is standing atop a tree or a wall, he should recite in that place, with the blessings before and after.[38]

5. A person engaged in the study of Torah when the time comes to recite the Shema should interrupt his study and recite with the blessings before and after. A person engaged in communal activities should not interrupt them, but finish them and then recite if time remains.[39]

6. A person who is eating, bathing, having a haircut, examining hides, or sitting in judgment finishes his task and then recites the Shema. But one who interrupts these activities to recite, out of concern that he might miss the appointed time, is praiseworthy.[40]

7. If a person who has immersed himself in a ritual bath can leave the bath, cover himself, and recite before the sun rises, he should do so. If he is concerned that the sun might rise before he could do all this, he should use the water he is standing in to cover himself. He should not cover himself in this fashion with water which has a bad odor, nor with water which has been used to soak flax, nor with clear water—because his nakedness is then visible. Rather, one may cover himself with cloudy water that does not have a bad odor and recite where he stands.[41]

8. While reciting the Shema one should not wink his eyes, or purse his lips, or point to things with his fingers, lest his recitation be haphazard.[42] One who does these things is blameworthy, but he has fulfilled his obligation. One must recite in such a way that he can hear his own recitation; if he did not, he has still fulfilled his obligation. One must take care to pronounce the letters clearly; if he did not, he has still fulfilled his obligation.[43]

9. How does one take care to pronounce the letters clearly? He should exercise care not to pronounce a stop as a spirant, nor a spirant as a stop, nor a quiescent shewa as a mobile shewa, nor a mobile shewa as a quiescent shewa. Therefore, he must pause between two similar letters, when one ends a word and the other begins the following word, as in *with all your heart*.[44] He must recite *bekhol,* pause, and then continue and recite *levavkha.* So also with *veavadetem meherah* (Deut. 11:17) and *ha-kanaf petil*[45] (Num. 15:38). One must pronounce the "zayyin" of *tizkeru* (Num. 15:40) clearly. One must extend the "dalet" of *ehad* (Deut. 6:4) sufficiently to pro-

claim God's sovereignty over the heavens, the earth, and the four corners of the world.[46] One must not cut the "ḥet" in the word *eḥad* short such that it sounds like *eiḥad*.[47]

10. One may recite the Shema in any language he knows. One who recites in any language other than Hebrew must also diligently avoid mistakes in that language, and must take care to pronounce the words properly in that language just as he must take care when reciting it in Hebrew.[48]

11. One who recites the Shema out of sequence has not fulfilled his obligation. To what does this apply? To the order of the verses. But if he rearranged the order of the paragraphs, even though it is not permitted, I say that he has fulfilled his obligation, since they are not adjacent to each other in the Torah.[49] Reciting a verse twice is blameworthy; but if one repeats a word—for example, if he recited "Hear, hear"—he is to be silenced.[50]

12. One who has paused during the recitation of the Shema has fulfilled his obligation, even if the pauses were long enough for him to have recited the whole of the Shema during them, on condition that he recited it in the correct order. One who recites in a state of drowsiness—that is, one is who neither fully awake nor fully asleep—has fulfilled his obligation, provided that he was awake for the first verse.[51]

13. One who is unsure whether he recited the Shema or not, recites it again, and makes the blessings before it and after it. But if he is sure that he recited, but is unsure whether or not he made the blessings before it and after it, he does not make the blessings again. One who recites and makes a mistake should begin again at the point of the mistake. One who loses track of the paragraphs and does not know which paragraph he completed and which he has to begin, should return to the first section, which is, *You shall love the Lord your God* . . . (Deut. 6:5).[52]

14. One who has made a mistake in the middle of a section, and does not know where he stopped, should return to the beginning of the section. One who recited *inscribe them* and does not know if it is the *inscribe them* of *Hear* (Deut. 6:4) or the *inscribe them* of *If, then, you obey,* (Deut. 11:13) returns to the *inscribe them* of *Hear*.[53] But if he was unsure after reciting *To the end that you and your children*

may endure (Deut. 11:21),[54] he does not return to the first section, relying on his habitual way of reciting.[55]

15. If, while reciting, a person met other people or was met by them — if he was between sections, he interrupts his recitation and greets those to whom he is obligated to show respect, such as his father, or his teacher, or anyone greater than he in wisdom, and responds to the greetings of all those who greet him.[56]

16. If he was reciting in the middle of a paragraph, he may only interrupt his recitation to greet those whom he fears, such as a king, or a violent man, and the like. But if one to whom he is obligated to show respect, such as his father or his teacher, greets him first, he interrupts his recitation and returns the greeting.[57]

17. These are the divisions between the sections: between the first and second blessing, between the second blessing and *Hear,* between *Hear* and *If, then, you obey,* and between *If, then, you obey* and *The Lord said.* But between *The Lord said* and *true and certain* is like the middle of the section, and one may not interrupt his recitation there except to greet from fear and to respond out of honor.[58]

CHAPTER THREE

1. One who recites the Shema should wash his hands with water before the recitation. If the time for the recitation has arrived and he has found no water, he should not delay the recitation in order to seek water, but should rub his hands with dust, with pebbles, with wood, and such and recite.[59]

2. One does not recite in the bathhouse, or in the privy, even if there is no excrement in it, or in the cemetery, or near a corpse.[60] But if he has moved four cubits from the grave or from the corpse, he may recite. Anyone who recites in an impermissible place must recite again.[61]

3. It is permissible to recite the Shema near, but not in, a new privy which has not yet been used. It is permissible to recite in a new bathhouse.[62] If there were two structures, and one was designated as privy, and about the other the builder[63] only said, "And this . . ." — about this second it is uncertain whether it has been des-

ignated as a privy or not; therefore, one does not recite in it in the first instance, but if one has recited in it, he has fulfilled his obligation. But if the builder said, "And this also . . . ," then both are designated privies and one does not recite in them. It is permissible to recite the Shema in the courtyard of the bathhouse, it being a place where people are clothed.[64]

4. No other sacred matter may be uttered in the bathhouse and the privy, even if not in Hebrew,[65] and not only the recitation of the Shema. Not only is it forbidden to utter Torah matters there, it is even forbidden to think about them in the privy, bathhouse, or any other filthy place, that is, a place with excrement or urine.[66]

5. Everyday matters may be spoken about in Hebrew in the privy, and so also epithets of God, such as "Merciful" and "Faithful," etc. But the specific names of God—that is, the names which may not be erased[67]—may not be mentioned in a privy or a bathhouse that has been used. But if the opportunity to dissuade one from doing something forbidden arose in a bathhouse or in privy, it should be done, even in Hebrew, and even if it concerns sacred matters.[68]

6. It is forbidden to recite the Shema near human excrement or near canine or swine excrement in which skins are soaking; similarly, it is forbidden to recite the Shema while near any foul-smelling excrement like these; so also while near human urine. But one may recite the Shema while near animal urine. One need not distance himself from the excrement and urine of a child who is incapable of eating an olive's worth of grain in the time that it takes an adult to eat three egg's worth of grain.[69]

7. It is forbidden to recite the Shema near excrement even if it is as dry as pottery. If it were drier than pottery, such that if thrown it would crumble, it is considered to be like dust, and one may recite the Shema near it. It is forbidden to recite the Shema near urine that has soaked into the ground but which can still moisten one's hand; but if the urine-soaked ground does not moisten the hand, it is permitted.[70]

8. How far must one move away from excrement and urine in order to recite the Shema? Four cubits. This is so when they are behind him or to his side; but if they are in front of him, he must move away till he no longer sees them, and then recite.[71]

9. When does this apply? When he is in a building with them

on the same level; if there is a level ten handbreadths higher or ten handbreadths lower than the excrement or urine in the building, he may sit there[72] and recite, so long as no foul odor reaches him, since they are separated from him. So also, if he has placed a vessel over the excrement or urine, they are considered as buried, and even though they are with him in the same building, he may recite.[73]

10. If a glass barrier separates him from the excrement, he may recite the Shema next to it even though he sees it through the glass. One may recite the Shema within four cubits of the urine of a single urination if it has been diluted with a quarter-*hin*[74] of water.[75]

11. If there is excrement in a depression in the ground, one may stand with one's shoe covering the depression and recite, provided that his shoe does not touch the excrement. If he is standing near a very small amount of excrement, about a drop's worth, he may expectorate thick spit to cover it and may then recite. If there is some liquid residue of excrement on his flesh, or his hands are soiled from the privy, but there is no foul odor because the remnants are so small or dry, it is permissible to recite because there is no odor. But if it is in its original place,[76] even if it is not visible when he stands, since it can be seen when he sits,[77] it is forbidden to recite until he cleans himself very well, since it is moist excrement and has an odor. Some of the Ge'onim ruled that it is forbidden to recite if one's hands are soiled; this is what ought to be done.[78]

12. One should move four cubits from a foul odor that has a concrete source and may then recite if the odor subsides. If it does not subside, he should keep moving till it does. But in the case of a foul odor that has no concrete source, as when someone breaks wind, one need only move far enough away for the odor to subside[79] and then recite. It is forbidden to recite the Shema near a chamber pot or a container of urine, even if they are empty and have no odor, since they are considered to be like privies.[80]

13. It is forbidden to recite near passing excrement, such as excrement floating by on water; the mouth of a pig is considered to be like passing excrement. It is forbidden to recite near passing excrement or the mouth of a pig until they pass four cubits beyond him.[81]

14. If one is reciting and has come to a filthy place, he should not

cover his mouth with his hand and continue reciting but should stop reciting until he passes that place. So also, if one is reciting and breaks wind, he should stop till its odor passes and then continue his recitation; so also with Torah study. But if another breaks wind, even though he interrupts the recitation of the Shema, he does not interrupt Torah study.[82]

15. If one is reciting the Shema in a building, and a question arises over whether or not there is excrement or urine in the building, it is permissible to recite. But if he were to recite at a garbage heap and a question arose of whether or not there is excrement there, he may not recite until he investigates the matter, since a garbage heap is presumed to be a filthy place. But if a question arises about urine, even at a garbage heap, it is permissible to recite.[83]

16. Just as it is forbidden to recite near excrement and urine, such that one must move away from them, so it is forbidden to recite facing exposed private parts; one must turn his face aside. Even with respect to a gentile or a child—it is forbidden to recite when facing their exposed private parts. Even were there an intervening barrier of glass, since the private parts are visible, it would not be permitted for one to recite until he turns his face aside. The entire body of a woman is considered an exposed private part, and one may therefore not look at the body of a woman while reciting. It is not even permitted to recite facing one's wife if a handbreadth of her body is exposed.[84]

17. Just as it is forbidden to recite facing the private parts of others, so is it forbidden to recite when one's own private parts are exposed; thus one may not recite while naked till one has covered his private parts. Were he to wear a sash of cloth, leather, or sacking on his loins, even though the rest of his body is exposed, he may recite, so long as his heel not touch his private parts.[85] One who was sleeping naked under a blanket should use the blanket to make a separation under his heart and recite. But he should not do so under his neck, for then his heart "sees" his private parts, and it is as if he recited without a sash.[86]

18. If two men have been sleeping under one blanket, neither may recite, even if each were to cover himself from below the heart, unless the blanket separates between them, so that the flesh of one does not touch the flesh of the other from the loins down. But if he

has been sleeping with his wife, or his children, or other minors in his household, their bodies are considered like his since they do not arouse him, and he may therefore turn his face aside, make a separation beneath his heart, and recite, even though his flesh touches theirs.[87]

19. Till what age are they considered minors with respect to this matter? With respect to boys, twelve years and one day, with respect to girls, eleven years and one day, if their physical form is that of adults, with *firm breasts and sprouted hair* (Ez. 16:7). From that time on he may not recite unless a blanket divide between him and them. But if they lack *firm breasts and sprouted hair,* he may recite with his flesh touching theirs without need of separation, until the boy becomes thirteen years and one day old, and the girl twelve years and one day old.[88]

CHAPTER FOUR

1. Although women, slaves, and children are exempt from the obligation to recite the Shema, children are to be taught to recite it in its proper time with the blessings before and after it, in order to train them in the observance of the commandments. One who is preoccupied with the fulfillment of any of the other commandments is exempted from reciting the Shema. Thus, a bridegroom who has married a virgin is exempt from the recitation of the Shema till he has relations with her, since he is distracted by concern that he may find her not to be a virgin. But if he delayed and did not have relations with her till Saturday night,[89] he is then obligated to resume the recitation of the Shema, since his mind has cooled and he is no longer aroused by her, even though he did not have relations with her.[90]

2. But one who marries a woman who is not a virgin, even though he is occupied with the fulfillment of a commandment,[91] is obligated to recite since nothing confuses his mind, and so with all similar cases.

3. One who has suffered the loss of a relative for whom he is obligated to mourn[92] is exempt from the recitation of the Shema until the funeral, since his mind is not clear enough to recite. If one is watching over the dead, even one for whom he is not obligated

to mourn,[93] he is exempt from the recitation of Shema. But if two have been watching, one watches while the second moves to another place in order to recite, returns and watches, and the other then moves to another place and recites. So also, one who digs a grave for the dead is exempt from the recitation of the Shema.[94]

4. The dead are not to be carried out for burial close to the time of the recitation of the Shema[95] unless the deceased were a great person. If a funeral has begun and the time for the recitation of the Shema has arrived, of those accompanying the dead person, only those who are needed—such as those who carry the bier, their replacements, and their replacements' replacements, whether they have been before or after the bier—are exempted.[96] But the rest of the funeral party, who play no necessary role, are obligated to recite.[97]

5. If the time for the recitation of the Shema arrives while eulogies are being said in the presence of the deceased, one after another of those present moves away in order to recite and then returns to the funeral. But if they are not in the presence of the deceased, then everyone present recites the Shema while the mourner sits by silently, since he is not obligated to recite until he buries his dead.[98]

6. If, after the dead have been buried, the mourners are ready to accept consolation, and those present have followed the mourners from the gravesite to the place where they stand in a row to receive consolation, then if those present can recite one complete verse of the Shema before they reach the row of mourners, they should begin the recitation; but if they cannot recite one complete verse, they should not begin, but first console the mourners, and, only after leaving them begin the recitation. Of those people standing at the row, only the innermost ones, who directly see the mourners, are exempt from the recitation of the Shema. Those on the outside, since they do not see the mourners, are obligated to recite the Shema where they stand.[99]

7. Anyone who is exempt from reciting the Shema may, if he wishes, be stringent with himself and recite, so long as his mind is settled. But if the person exempt from the recitation is frightened or confused, he is not permitted to recite till his mind settles.[100]

8. All those in a state of ritual impurity are obligated to recite the Shema and the blessings before and after it while in their state

of impurity. This is the case even when it is possible for them to purify themselves the same day, as is the case with those who have touched a creeping thing, a menstruant woman, a woman with vaginal discharge, or the bed of one of these,[101] and other things like them. Ezra and his court ordained that, of all those who are ritually impure, only a person who has had a seminal emission may not read[102] until he has immersed himself.[103] This ordinance was not accepted by all of Israel, since most of the community did not have the strength to observe it, and it therefore became null. All Israel have long since become accustomed to reading the Torah and reciting the Shema even after a seminal emission, since the words of the Torah do not become impure, and remain in their pure state forever.

Blessed be the Merciful One Who assists us
This section is ended[104]

TREATISE II

Laws Concerning Prayer and the Priestly Blessing
comprise two positive commandments: the first,
to worship the Lord in prayer[1] every day; the second,
that the Priests bless Israel every day. The clarification
of these two commandments is found
in the following chapters:

CHAPTER ONE

1. It is a positive commandment to pray[2] every day, as it is said, *You shall serve the Lord your God* (Exod. 23:25). Tradition teaches that this "service" is prayer. It is written, *serving Him with all your heart and soul* (Deut. 11:13), about which the Sages said, "What is service of the heart? Prayer."[3] The number of prayers is not fixed in the Torah, nor is their format, and neither does the Torah prescribe a fixed time for prayer. Women and slaves are therefore obligated to pray, since it is a positive commandment without a fixed time.[4]

2. Rather, this commandment obligates each person to pray, supplicate, and praise the Holy One, blessed be He, to the best of his ability every day; to then request and plead for what he needs; and after that praise and thank God for all that He has showered[5] on him.[6]

3. One who is articulate offers up many supplications and requests, while one who is inarticulate[7] prays to the best of his ability, whenever he wishes. With respect to the number of prayers, each prays according to his ability. There are those who pray once each day, and there are those who pray many times. All pray facing the Sanctuary,[8] wherever it may be. Such was the practice always, from Moses our Master until Ezra.[9]

4. After the Jews were exiled by the evil Nebuchadnezzar, they mingled with the Persians, Greeks, and other nations and gave birth to children in these foreign lands. These children spoke a confused language, composed of many languages, and could not speak

well in any single language, as it says, *their children spoke the language of Ashdod and the language of those various peoples and did not know how to speak Judean* (Neh. 13:24).

5. Because of this, when one of them prayed, he was unable to ask for what he needed or praise the Holy One, blessed be He, in Hebrew, without mixing in other languages. Seeing this, Ezra and his court ordained eighteen blessings in the following order.[10]

6. The first three consist of praises of God, the last three consist of thanksgiving, while those between consist of requests for the principal desires of individuals and the principal needs of the community. The prayers were thus well ordered for all, and learned by everyone. In this way, the prayers of the inarticulate could be as perfect as those of the eloquent. For this reason, all the blessings and prayers regularly recited by all Jews were ordained, so that the full meaning of the blessings be well expressed, even by the inarticulate.[11]

7. So also was it ordained that the number of *'amidah* prayers correspond to the number of sacrifices: two *'amidah* prayers every day corresponding to the two daily sacrifices. A third was ordained for every day on which there is an additional sacrifice, corresponding to that sacrifice. The *'amidah* prayer corresponding to the daily morning sacrifice is called the morning *'amidah* prayer; the prayer corresponding to the daily evening sacrifice is called the afternoon *'amidah* prayer;[12] and the *'amidah* prayer corresponding to the additional sacrifices is called the additional *'amidah* prayer.[13]

8. So also was it ordained that one *'amidah* prayer be recited at night, for the leftovers of the daily evening sacrifice were left to be consumed all night, as it is said, *This is the ritual of the burnt offering: The burnt offering itself shall remain where it is burned upon the altar all night until morning, while the fire on the altar is kept going on it* (Lev. 6:2). This is consistent with what is said, *Evening, morning and noon I speak and cry out* (Ps. 55:18). The evening *'amidah* prayer is not obligatory like the morning and afternoon *'amidah* prayers, but, despite that, all Jews in all their habitations have customarily recited the evening *'amidah* prayer and accepted it as an obligatory prayer.[14]

9. On fast days only, another *'amidah* prayer was also ordained after the afternoon *'amidah* prayer, near the time of the sun's set-

ting, in order to add supplication and petition on the fast. This is called *ne''ilah,* i.e., at the time that the gates of heaven are locked,[15] the sun then being hidden behind them; this *'amidah* prayer is only recited close to sunset.[16]

10. There are thus three *'amidah* prayers every day: evening, morning, and afternoon.[17] On the Sabbaths, festivals, and new moons, there are four: the three daily *'amidah* prayers and the additional *'amidah* prayer. On the Day of Atonement there are five: these four, and *ne''ilah.*

11. Although one may not reduce the number of these *'amidah* prayers, one may add to them; one who wishes to pray throughout the whole day may do so.[18] Such additional *'amidah* prayers are like free-will sacrifices.[19] Therefore, one must add something new relevant to each of the middle blessings, but if one adds something to only one of the blessings, that is sufficient in order to make it clear that the *'amidah* prayer is like a free-will sacrifice and not an obligatory one. But one is never to add to, detract from, or change anything in the first three and last three blessings.[20]

12. Congregations[21] do not offer free-will *'amidah* prayers since congregations do not bring free-will sacrifices. Nor may an individual recite the additional *'amidah* prayer twice—the obligatory one for the day and an additional free-will *'amidah* prayer—since there is no free-will additional sacrifice.[22] Some of the Ge'onim forbade the recitation of free-will *'amidah* prayers on Sabbaths and holidays since on those days free-will sacrifices are not brought, only the sacrifices obligatory on those days.

CHAPTER TWO

1. In the days of Rabban Gamaliel[23] sectarians multiplied among the Jews; they troubled them and enticed them to turn away from God. Seeing that faithfulness to God[24] was the greatest need of the people,[25] he and his court instituted a blessing which contained a petition to God to destroy the sectarians, and included it in the *'amidah,* so that it be regularly said by all; thus the number of blessings in the *'amidah* is nineteen.[26]

2. One should recite these nineteen blessings in their proper order in each of the three daily *'amidah* prayers. When does this

apply? When his mind[27] is properly directed and his speech fluent; but if he is preoccupied or rushed, or his speech not fluent, then he should recite [only] the first three blessings—one blessing which summarizes all the intermediate ones and the last three blessings—and in this way fulfill his obligation.[28]

3. This is the blessing which was instituted to summarize all the intermediate ones: "Give us understanding, O Lord, our God, that we may know Your ways, and circumcise our hearts to hold You in awe; be a Forgiver to us, that we may be redeemed; keep us far from pain; make us prosperous[29] and cause us to dwell in the pastures of Your land; gather those scattered from the four corners of the earth; may those who go astray be judged by Your mind;[30] raise Your hand over the wicked; let the righteous rejoice in the rebuilding of Your city, in the reestablishment of Your temple, in the flourishing of the horn of David Your servant, and in the rekindling of the light of David son of Jesse, Your anointed; before we call, You answer; before we speak, You hear, for You are He who answers in every time of trouble, redeems, and saves from all distress; Blessed are You Who hears prayer."[31]

4. When does this apply? In the summer. But one does not say the "Give us understanding" prayer in the winter because one must petition [for rain] in the blessing concerning prosperity. Similarly, on nights after the Sabbath and holidays one does not say the "Give us understanding" prayer because one must recite *havdalah*[32] in "You favor humans with knowledge . . ."[33]

5. On Sabbaths and holidays one recites seven blessings in each of the four *'amidah* prayers of that day: the first three, the last three, and a middle blessing expressing the substance of that day. On Sabbaths one concludes the middle blessing with "Who sanctifies the Sabbath," while on the festivals one concludes with "Who sanctifies Israel and the seasons." When the Sabbath and a festival coincide, one concludes with "Who sanctifies the Sabbath, Israel, and the seasons." On Rosh ha-Shanah one concludes it with "King over all the earth, Who sanctifies Israel and the Day of Remembrance"; if it is also the Sabbath, one concludes it with "Who sanctifies the Sabbath, Israel, and the Day of Remembrance."[34]

6. When does this apply? In the evening, morning, and afternoon *'amidah* prayers. But in the additional *'amidah* prayer of Rosh

ha-Shanah one recites nine blessings: the first three and the last three of every day, and three intermediate blessings—of which the first concerns God's sovereignty, the second remembrance, the third the shofar—and concludes each one with a reference to its content.[35]

7. On the Day of Atonement one recites seven blessings in each of the five 'amidah prayers: the first three, the last three, and an intermediate one expressing the substance of the day, concluding it with "King over all the earth, Who sanctifies Israel and the Day of Atonement."[36]

8. When does this apply? On the Day of Atonement[37] of normal years. But on the Day of Atonement of the Jubilee Year there are nine blessings in the additional 'amidah prayer just as in the additional 'amidah prayer on Rosh ha-Shanah; they are precisely the same blessings, without addition or diminution. They are recited on the Day of Atonement only when the Jubilee is in effect.[38]

9. Before the first blessing of each of the 'amidah prayers one says, *O Lord, open my lips, and let my mouth declare Your praise* (Ps. 151:17), and at the conclusion of the 'amidah prayer he says, *May the words of my mouth and the prayer of my heart be acceptable to You, O Lord, my rock and my redeemer* (Ps. 19:15), and then steps backward.[39]

10. On *Rosh Ḥodesh,* and on the intermediate days of the festivals, one recites nineteen blessings in the evening, morning, and afternoon 'amidah prayers, as on other days, and in the blessing concerning the Temple service adds, "Our God and God of our fathers. . . may remembrance of us . . . ascend and come." On the intermediate days of the festivals, the 'amidah prayer of the holiday itself is recited. On *Rosh Ḥodesh* one recites seven blessings, the first three, the last three, and an intermediate one expressing the substance of the new moon sacrifice, concluding it with "Who sanctifies Israel and the new moon."[40]

11. If a Sabbath falls in the intermediate days of a festival, and so also if *Rosh Ḥodesh* falls on a Sabbath, one recites seven blessings in the evening, morning, and afternoon services, as on other Sabbaths, and adds "ascend and come" in the blessing concerning the Temple service. In the additional 'amidah prayer, one begins the middle blessing with reference to the Sabbath, and so concludes it,

making reference to the special sanctity of the day in the middle of the blessing. On *Rosh Ḥodesh* one concludes with "Who sanctifies the Sabbath, and Israel, and the new moon," while on the intermediate days of the festival one concludes as one does on a holiday which falls on the Sabbath.[41] If a holiday falls on a Sunday, one adds to[42] the fourth blessing Saturday night as follows:

12. "You have made known to us Your righteous judgments and taught us to perform the statutes of Your will. You have given us, O Lord, our God, the sanctity of the Sabbath, the honor of the holiday, and celebration of the pilgrim festival. You have distinguished between the sanctity of the Sabbath and that of the holiday, and the great and holy seventh day have You sanctified. You have given us, O Lord, our God, festivals on which to rejoice . . ." But on the conclusion of a regular Sabbath or holiday,[43] one marks the separation of the sacred from the profane in "You have favored . . ."[44] even though one also performs *havdalah* over a cup [of wine].[45]

13. On Hannukah and Purim one adds "For the miracles" in the blessing of thanks. If the Sabbath falls on Hannukah or Purim[46] one includes "For the miracles" in the additional prayer as one does in the other prayers.[47]

14. On fast days, even a single individual who fasts[48] adds "Answer us, Our Father . . ." in "Who hears prayer."[49] The prayer leader recites it as a blessing in its own right between "redeems" and "heals"[50] and concludes with "Who answers in the time of trouble" and thus recites twenty blessings. On the Ninth of Av, in "Who builds Jerusalem," we add: "Have mercy upon us, O Lord, our God, and upon Israel Your people, and upon the destroyed and abandoned city . . ."[51]

15. During the winter one says in the second blessing, "Who causes rain to fall," and during the summer, "Who causes dew to fall." From when does one say, "Who causes rain to fall"? From the additional *'amidah* prayer of the last holiday of Sukkot through the morning *'amidah* prayer of the first holiday of Passover. From the additional *'amidah* prayer of the first holiday of Passover, one says, "Who causes dew to fall."[52]

16. From the seventh day of *Marḥeshvan*,[53] one asks for rain in the blessing concerning years;[54] this continues all the while that rain is

mentioned.[55] Where does this apply? In the Land of Israel. But in Shin'ar,[56] Syria, and Egypt, and in places near them and climatically similar to them, one asks for rain from the sixtieth day after the autumnal equinox.[57]

17. In places where rain is needed during the summer, such as the distant islands, one asks for rain when it is needed in "Who hears prayer."[58] In places where holidays are observed for two days,[59] one says "Who causes rain to fall" in the additional prayer of the first day of *Shemini 'Azeret*[60] and so continues for the rest of the winter.[61]

18. All year long one concludes the third blessing with "the holy God" and the eleventh blessing with "the King Who loves righteousness and justice." But in the ten days between Rosh ha-Shanah and the end of the Day of Atonement one concludes the third with "the holy King" and the eleventh with "King of justice."[62]

19. There are places where it is customary during these ten days to add in the first blessing "remember us for life . . ." and in the second "who is like unto You, merciful Father . . ." In the eighteenth blessing one adds "remember Your mercy and overcome . . ." and in the last "in the book of life . . ." There are also places where it is customary during these ten days to add to the third blessing "and so . . . and so . . ."[63] On Rosh ha-Shanah and the Day of Atonement, however, it is common practice [in all communities] to add "and so . . . and so . . ." to the third blessing.

CHAPTER THREE

1. The morning *'amidah* prayer is ideally recited at sunrise; it may, however, be recited until the end of the fourth hour, which is one-third of the day. But if one transgressed or was mistaken, and prayed after the fourth hour, but before midday, he has fulfilled his obligation to pray, but not his obligation to pray at the correct time; for while the commandment of prayer derives from the Torah, there is a separate rabbinic commandment to pray at the time ordained by the Sages and Prophets.[64]

2. We have already stated[65] that the time of the afternoon *'amidah* prayer was ordained to correspond with the time of the daily evening sacrifice. Since this sacrifice was brought daily at nine and one-half hours into the day, the time for the *'amidah* prayer was

ordained from nine and one-half hours; this is what is called "the lesser afternoon *'amidah* prayer." But since on a Passover eve which fell on a Friday,[66] the daily evening sacrifice was slaughtered six and one-half hours into the day, they said that one who prays after this time has fulfilled the obligation. At this hour the obligation [to recite the afternoon *'amidah* prayer] begins; this is what is called "the greater afternoon *'amidah* prayer."[67]

3. Many people customarily recite both the greater and lesser afternoon *'amidah* prayers, one of them being optional.[68] Some of the Ge'onim taught that it is appropriate to make only the greater afternoon *'amidah* prayer optional; this is reasonable, since it corresponds to something which is not done regularly every day. But if he has prayed the greater afternoon *'amidah* prayer as an obligatory service, he may only pray the lesser afternoon *'amidah* prayer as optional.

4. You have thus learned that the time for the greater afternoon *'amidah* prayer is from six and one-half hours through nine and one-half hours into the day. The proper time for the lesser afternoon *'amidah* prayer is from nine and one-half hours till one and one-quarter hours before the end of the day; but it may be recited until sunset.[69]

5. The proper time for the additional *'amidah* prayer is from after the morning *'amidah* prayer until the end of the seventh hour. One who recites the *'amidah* prayer after the seventh hour, even though he transgressed, has fulfilled his obligation, since it may be recited all day.[70]

6. The evening *'amidah* prayer, even though it is not obligatory, has a proper time; it should be recited from the beginning of night until dawn. The *ne'ilah 'amidah* prayer should be recited such that one completes it near sunset.[71]

7. One who recites an *'amidah* prayer before its proper time has not fulfilled his obligation, and he must recite it again in its proper time. But were one constrained to recite the morning *'amidah* prayer after sunrise, he will still have fulfilled his obligation. One may recite the Sabbath evening *'amidah* prayer on Friday before sunset and may also recite the Saturday night evening *'amidah* prayer while it is still the Sabbath. Since the evening *'amidah* prayer is optional, it is not necessary to be precise concerning its time, so

long as one recites the Shema in its time, after the stars have come out.

8. If one intentionally missed the proper time for an *amidah* prayer, there is no rectification and it may not be made up. If the omission was inadvertent, or one was constrained or preoccupied, he makes up the missed *amidah* prayer at the time of the next *amidah* prayer. First one recites the required *amidah* prayer, and then recites the makeup *amidah* prayer.[72]

9. How is this to be done? If one erred and did not say the morning *amidah* prayer before the end of the first half of the day, one should then say the afternoon *amidah* prayer twice; the first being the afternoon *amidah* prayer, the second, compensation for the morning *amidah* prayer. If one erred and did not say the afternoon *amidah* prayer until the sun had set, one should then say the evening *amidah* prayer twice; the first being the evening *amidah* prayer, the second making up for the afternoon *amidah* prayer. If one erred and did not say the evening *amidah* prayer before dawn, one should then say the morning *amidah* prayer twice; the first being the morning *amidah* prayer, the second making up for the evening *amidah* prayer.[73]

10. If one erred and did not say two *amidah* prayers in a row, one only makes up the last *amidah* prayer missed. How? If one erred and did not say either the morning or afternoon *amidah* prayers, one should then say the evening *amidah* prayer twice; the second making up for the afternoon *amidah* prayer. But there is no way to make up the morning *amidah* prayer, as its day has passed; and so with the other *amidah* prayers.[74]

11. If one has the obligation to say two *amidah* prayers, the afternoon *amidah* prayer and the additional *amidah* prayer, one first says the afternoon *amidah* prayer and then the additional *amidah* prayer. There are those who have taught that this is not done in a congregation, so that they not err.[75]

CHAPTER FOUR

1. The set time for prayer[76] having come, it should still be delayed for five reasons: purity of hands, nakedness, purity of the place of prayer, the pressure to rush, and correct intention.

2. What does purity of hands involve? One should wash one's hands in water up to the wrist and only then pray. If one is journeying when it comes time to pray and no water is available, if the closest water is less than four miles[77] distant—which is eight thousand cubits[78]—one should go to the water, wash, and then pray. But if the water is more distant than that, one should rub his hands with pebbles, dust, or wood and then pray.[79]

3. When does this apply? When the water is in the direction in which one is traveling. But, if the water is behind him, we do not require him to go back more than a mile:[80] thus, if he has gone more than a mile from the water, he is not required to return; rather, he rubs his hands and prays. When does the rule that one purifies only his hands for prayer apply? With respect to every 'amidah prayer but the morning 'amidah prayer. But for the morning 'amidah prayer one should wash one's face, hands, and legs, and only then pray. But if one is far from water, one may rub one's hands only and pray.[81]

4. A person in a state of ritual impurity washes his hands only, and he may then pray, just as those who are ritually pure. Even were it possible for him to immerse himself in a ritual bath and remove himself from the impure state, the need for immersion does not prevent prayer. We have already explained that Ezra ordained that the only person who should not read Scripture until he immerses himself is one who had a seminal emission and that a later court instituted this for prayer as well.[82] This has nothing to do with ritual impurity or purity, but, rather, was ordained so that scholars not be with their wives like roosters; it was for this reason that with respect to prayer it was ordained that, of all those in a state of ritual impurity, immersion was required only for a person who had had a seminal emission.[83]

5. Therefore, while this enactment was in force, even a man who had a seminal emission[84] while suffering from a flux from the sexual organ[85] and a menstruant woman who discharged semen,[86] and a woman who saw menstrual blood after having sexual relations, had to immerse themselves in order to recite Shema and pray, even though they were ritually impure. This makes sense since this immersion[87] has nothing to do with ritual purity but is a consequence of the decree that scholars not be with their wives all the

time. But this enactment has ceased to apply with respect to prayer, since it was not accepted by all Israel, and the public did not have the strength to adhere to it.[88]

6. It is customary throughout Spain and Shin'ar that one who has had a seminal emission not pray until he wash all his flesh in water; this is based on the verse *prepare to meet your God, O Israel* (Amos 4:12). When does this apply? In the case of a healthy man, or a sick man who has had sexual relations; but a sick man who has had an unintended seminal emission is exempt from the requirement to bathe, nor is there any custom requiring it. So also there is no custom concerning a man suffering from a flux from the sexual organ who has had a seminal emission, or a menstruant woman who has discharged semen, rather they wipe themselves off, wash their hands, and pray.[89]

7. How does one cover one's nakedness?[90] Even if one has covered his nakedness as it is to be covered in order to recite Shema,[91] he should not pray until he also covers his heart. But if he has not covered his heart, or if he is constrained by not having anything with which to cover his heart, then he ought not to pray in the first instance, but if he has prayed anyway, he has fulfilled his obligation by having covered his nakedness.[92]

8. What does purity of the place of prayer involve? One may not pray in a filthy place,[93] in a bathhouse, in a garbage dump, or in any place not presumed to be pure until it is checked. The general rule is this: one may not pray in any place where one may not recite the Shema;[94] just as one must move away from excrement, from urine, from a bad smell, from a dead body, and from seeing nakedness in order to recite the Shema, so must one move away from these in order to pray.

9. If one prayed and then found[95] excrement, since he sinned in not checking before he prayed, he must pray again in a pure place. If he was standing in prayer and saw excrement facing him, he should walk far enough forward so that it remains four cubits behind him if he can; if he cannot, he should move sideways; if he cannot do that, he should stop praying.[96] The greatest sages would not pray in a building housing beer[97] or in a building housing frothing brine because of its bad smell, even if the place was pure.[98]

10. What does the pressure to rush mean? If one has to relieve

himself, he should not pray. The prayer of one who has to relieve himself is an abomination;[99] one should first relieve himself and then pray. But, if one can restrain oneself for the amount of time that it takes to walk one *parsah*[100] and prays, one's prayer is considered prayer. Even so, in the first instance one ought not to pray before checking himself very carefully, relieving himself, removing phlegm and mucus and anything else that might distract him, and only then pray.[101]

11. One who yawns, burps, or sneezes during prayer voluntarily has done something blameworthy; but if he examined himself before praying and these then occurred involuntarily, they have no significance. Saliva which collects during prayer should be wiped away with one's prayer shawl or clothing. If this procedure would distress him, he should cast the saliva behind him with his hand, so that he not be distressed during prayer and thus distracted. One who inadvertently has broken wind during prayer ceases praying until the odor passes and then continues.[102]

12. One who feels the need to break wind during prayer, is in great discomfort, and cannot restrain himself, should move back four cubits, break wind and wait till the odor passes. He should then say, "Master of the Universe, You created us with orifices and cavities. Our shame and disgrace—shame and disgrace during our lifetimes, and worms and decay upon our death—is well known to you." One then returns to his place and prays.[103]

13. If, while praying, urine has dripped on one's knees, one must wait until it stops and then continue praying from where one stopped. If, however, he has waited long enough to have finished the *'amidah,* he must start again from the beginning.[104]

14. So, too, one who urinates before prayer should wait the time it takes to walk four cubits and only then pray. One who has prayed should wait the time it takes to walk four cubits before urinating, so that he can completely finish praying.[105]

15. What does correct intention involve? Any prayer recited without correct intention is not prayer. One who prays without correct intention must pray again with correct intention. One who is confused or preoccupied may not pray until he becomes tranquil. Thus, one who returns from a journey fatigued or distressed is for-

bidden to pray until he becomes tranquil. The Sages said that such a person must wait three days until he rests and his mind settles before praying.[106]

16. How does one achieve correct intention? One must free his mind[107] of all thoughts and see himself as standing before the divine Presence. Therefore, one should sit awhile before prayer in order to direct his mind, and then pray gently and beseechingly. One must not pray as if it were a burden to be cast aside before one continues on his way. Thus, one should sit awhile after prayer and only then leave. The early pietists would wait an hour before prayer, an hour after prayer, and spend an hour praying.[108]

17. One who is drunk may not pray, since he has no correct intention; if he has prayed, his prayer is an abomination. Therefore, he must pray again when he becomes sober. One who is slightly drunk should not pray, but if he has prayed, his prayer is considered prayer. Who is drunk? One who cannot speak before a king. The person who is slightly drunk is one who can speak without confusion before a king after drinking. Even so, one who has drunk a quarter-*hin* of wine should not pray until its influence passes.[109]

18. So, too, one ought not to stand up to pray directly after laughter, frivolity, conversation, argument, or anger, but after words of Torah. Even though a halakhic debate consists of words of Torah, one ought not stand up to pray directly after such a debate, lest one's mind be preoccupied with determining the halakhah. Rather, one should stand up to pray after studying words of Torah that do not demand concentration, such as already determined laws.[110]

19. Before reciting an *'amidah* prayer said only occasionally — such as the additional *'amidah* prayer for the New Moon or the festival *'amidah* prayers — one ought to review the prayer and only then stand to pray, so that he does not fail to pray properly.[111]

20. If one is in a dangerous place, for example, where there are wild animals or bandits, and the time for prayer arrives, one should recite only one blessing: "The needs of Your people Israel are great and their minds are limited. May it be Your will, Lord our God, that You give each of them sustenance and each body what it lacks, and do what is good in Your eyes. Blessed are You, O Lord, Who hears prayer." One may recite this while walking, but if one can

safely stand still, then one should do so. When he reaches a town and his mind settles, he should then recite the *'amidah* properly, all nineteen blessings.[112]

CHAPTER FIVE

1. One who says the *'amidah* prayer[113] must take care to do eight things; but if he was pressured, constrained by circumstances, or simply transgressed and did not do them, they do not render the *'amidah* prayer void. They are: standing, facing the sanctuary, correct posture, correct clothing, correct place, voice modulation, genuflection, and prostration.

2. What does standing involve? One may say *'amidah* prayer only when standing. If one is sitting in a boat or in a carriage and can stand, then he must stand; if one cannot, then he should remain seated in his place and pray. A sick person may say the *'amidah* prayer even while reclining on his side,[114] so long as he can concentrate. A person who is thirsty or hungry is considered sick; if such a one has the ability to concentrate, he should pray; but if not, he should not say the *'amidah* prayer until he eats and drinks. If one is riding on an animal, and even if he has someone who can hold it, he should not alight but sit in his place and say the *'amidah* prayer, so that his mind is settled.[115]

3. What does facing the sanctuary involve? Outside the Land of Israel, one should turn to face the Land of Israel and say the *'amidah* prayer. In the Land, one faces toward Jerusalem. In Jerusalem, one faces the sanctuary. In the sanctuary, one faces the holy of holies. A blind person, or one who cannot determine the direction, or one traveling in a boat[116] directs his mind to the Divine Presence and says the *'amidah* prayer.[117]

4. What does correct posture involve? While standing in prayer, one should place one's feet next to each other, and direct one's eyes downward, as if looking at the earth, but his heart should be directed upward as if he were standing in heaven. One should rest his hands on his heart, his right hand clasping the left, standing like a slave before his master, in dread, awe, and fear. He should not rest his hands on his hips.[118]

5. What does correct clothing involve? One should arrange one's

clothing before praying, dressing himself nicely, as it says, *Bow down to the Lord in the beauty of holiness* (Ps. 29:2). One should not stand up to pray in his undershirt, bareheaded, or barefooted—if it is the local custom to appear before important personages in shoes. One may never hold one's phylacteries in his hands, or a Torah in his arms, while praying, because they will distract him,[119] nor he should hold money or tools in his hands. But one prays on Sukkot with the lulav in his hand, since it is the commandment of that day. If a person is carrying a burden on his head when it comes time to pray, if it weighs less than four *kav*,[120] he should push it over his shoulder and pray. If it weighs four *kav*, he should place it on the ground and then pray. It was the custom of all the sages and all the students to pray wrapped in their prayer shawls.[121]

6. What does a correct place involve? One should stand in a low place facing a wall. It is necessary to open windows or apertures facing Jerusalem so that one may pray facing them, as it says, *When Daniel learned that it had been put in writing, he went to his house, in whose upper chamber he had windows made facing Jerusalem, and three times he knelt down, prayed and made confession to God, as he had always done* (Dan. 6:11). One should designate a permanent place for his prayer. One may not pray in a ruin, or behind the synagogue, unless one is facing the synagogue.[122] It is forbidden to sit to the side of one standing in prayer, or pass within four cubits in front of him.[123]

7. One ought not to stand to pray on a place that is more than three handbreadths high, such as a bed or a chair. With respect to a raised platform: if it is four cubits by four cubits, which is defined as a structure in and of itself, it is considered as an upper floor, and it is permissible to pray on it. So, also, should the structure be surrounded by a partition on all sides, even if it is less than four cubits square, it is permissible to pray on it; it does not stand out as a raised platform since it constitutes an independent area in and of itself.[124]

8. Artisans working on the top of a wall or the top of a tree when it comes time to say the *'amidah* prayer should descend, pray, and then return to their work. But if they are on the top of an olive tree or a date palm, they pray where they are, since the trouble to descend is considerable.[125] What do they recite? If they are working for their meals alone, they say each of the three prayers of nineteen

blessings. If they are working for a salary, they say the summary of the intermediate blessings.[126] In either case, they do not lead the congregation or bless the congregation.[127]

9. What does a modulated voice involve? One ought not raise one's voice in one's *'amidah* prayer, or pray silently, but, rather, express the words with his lips quietly. He should not raise his voice unless he is ill, or unless he cannot achieve correct intention without it; in such cases it is permissible, so long as he is not in public, when others would be distracted by his voice.

10. What does genuflection involve? One genuflects five times in each *'amidah* prayer: in the first blessing and in the thanksgiving[128] at their openings and conclusions, while at the end of the *'amidah* prayer one genuflects and takes three steps backward while bowed, then turns to the left and to the right,[129] and then stands upright. In the first four genuflections, one bows with the word "Blessed" and stands upright at God's name. When does all the above apply? With respect to a layperson. The high priest, however, genuflects at the beginning of each blessing and at its end. A king, after prostrating himself in the first blessing, does not raise his head until finishing his prayer.[130]

11. Why does one turn to the left first? Because his left is the right of one who faces him; in other words, when he stands before a king, one turns to the king's right and then to the king's left. It has been established that one withdraws from one's prayer as one withdraws from a king.

12. In all these genuflections it is necessary to bend oneself so that all the vertebrae in one's spine stand out and one arches over. One ought not to be concerned if, because it causes him strain, he can bow only a little bit, so long as he appears to be genuflecting as much as he can.[131]

13. What does prostration involve? After raising himself from the fifth genuflection, one lowers himself to the ground, falls on his face, and makes as many supplications as he wishes. "Genuflection" always means kneeling; "bowing" always means lowering one's face; "prostration" always means spreading one's arms and legs so that one is lying face down on the ground.[132]

14. There are those who, when falling on their faces after prayer,

bow, and there are those who prostrate themselves. Prostration on a stone floor is forbidden everywhere but in the Temple, as we made clear in "Laws Concerning Idolatry."[133] An important person may not lower his head[134] unless he knows himself to be as righteous as Joshua;[135] rather, he should bend his face slightly and not press it into the ground. It is permissible to pray in one place and lower one's head in another.[136]

15. It is customary in all of Israel not to lower one's head on Sabbaths and festivals; or on Rosh ha-Shanah, *Rosh Hodesh,* Hannukah, or Purim; or in the afternoon service on the eves of Sabbaths and holidays; or in the evening service of any day. But there are individuals who do lower their heads in the evening service. On the Day of Atonement alone one lowers his head in every prayer, since it is a day of supplication, petition, and fast.

CHAPTER SIX

1. One may not pass by[137] the entrance of a synagogue during the time of public prayer without entering unless one is carrying a burden, or if the synagogue has two entrances in two different directions so that someone seeing him might think that he is going to enter by the second entrance; so also, if there are two synagogues in the city, so someone seeing him might think that he is going to his regular synagogue. But, if he is wearing phylacteries on his head,[138] he may pass a synagogue without entering even if none of these conditions obtain since the phylacteries prove that he eagerly observes the commandments and is not to be counted among those who evade prayer.[139]

2. One who prays with a congregation should not prolong his *'amidah* prayer too much, but when praying alone he may. Even if he wishes to recite the confession of the Day of Atonement after his *'amidah* prayer, he may do so; so also, he may add to each blessing of the middle blessings matters relating to it, if he so wishes.[140]

3. How is this done? Should he be concerned about a sick person, he pleads for mercy for him in the blessing concerning the sick[141] to the extent that his linguistic ability allows. Were he in need of livelihood, he adds supplication and petitions to the blessing con-

cerning years;[142] and so with each of them. He may ask for any of his needs to be met in "Who listens to prayer."[143] But one may not make such requests in the first three or last three blessings.[144]

4. One may neither eat anything nor do any work after dawn without first reciting the morning *'amidah* prayer. So also, one should not approach another's home to greet him before reciting the morning *'amidah* prayer; nor should one begin a journey before praying. But one may eat something and work before the additional *'amidah* prayer and before the afternoon *'amidah* prayer, though he should not have a full meal near the time of the afternoon *'amidah* prayer.[145]

5. Once the time for the greater afternoon *'amidah* prayer has arrived, one may not enter a bathhouse, even if only to sweat, until one has prayed, lest he faint and be unable to pray; one may not eat, even if it is only a snack, lest he continue eating; one may not judge, even if only to render a verdict, lest the verdict be upset, the litigation continue, and he be unable to pray. So also, one may not go to a barber, even if it is for only a simple haircut,[146] until he prays, lest the scissors break. One may not enter a tannery near the time of the afternoon *'amidah* prayer until he prays, lest he see a deficiency in the work, get involved with it, and be delayed from praying. But if he has begun one of these, he need not interrupt himself, but may finish, and then say the afternoon *'amidah* prayer.[147]

6. When does a haircut begin? From when the barber's apron is placed on one's knees. When does a bath begin? From when one removes his undergarment. When does work in the tannery begin? From when one ties an apron between his shoulders in the manner of the craftsmen. When does eating begin? For inhabitants of the Land of Israel, from when one washes his hands; for inhabitants of Babylonia, from when one loosens his belt.[148] When does a court case begin? When the judges wrap themselves in their prayer shawls and sit; if they are already sitting, then from when the litigants begin presenting their cases.[149]

7. Even though the evening *'amidah* prayer is not obligatory, one may not come home from his work and say, "I will eat a bit, take a nap, and then pray," lest sleep overcome him, resulting in his sleeping through the night. Rather, one ought to recite the evening *'amidah* prayer, and then eat, drink, or sleep. It is permissible to have

a haircut and enter the bathhouse near to the time of the morning 'amidah prayer, since it was only decreed not to do these things near to the time of the afternoon 'amidah prayer, when they are ordinarily done, since most people enter barber shops and bathhouses during the daytime; but since entering them in the morning is unusual no decree was enacted.[150]

8. One who is studying Torah when it comes time to say the 'amidah prayer stops studying and prays. But should Torah study be his craft, and he does no other work at all, and if he is involved in Torah at the time of prayer, he does not stop, since the commandment of Torah study is greater than the commandment of prayer. All those dealing with the needs of the many are considered as if they were dealing with matters of Torah.[151]

9. A person saying the 'amidah prayer may interrupt his prayer only if his life is endangered. Even a Jewish king greets him, he may not respond. But one interrupts his prayer for a gentile king, lest the latter kill him. One standing in prayer who sees a Gentile king or violent person coming toward him should shorten his prayer; if he cannot shorten it,[152] he stops. So also, if one sees snakes or scorpions coming toward him: when they reach him, if they are deadly, he interrupts his prayer and flees; but if they are not deadly, he does not.[153]

10. Women, slaves, and minors are obligated to pray. Everyone exempt from reciting Shema is exempt from prayer. All who accompany the dead, even those who fulfill no necessary purpose, are exempt from prayer.[154]

CHAPTER SEVEN

1. When the Sages ordained these 'amidah prayers, they also ordained other blessings to be recited every day as follows. When going to bed to sleep at night, one makes the blessing: "Blessed are You, Lord our God, King of the Universe, Who causes the ropes of sleep to fall upon my eyes and illumines the eye.[155] May it be Your will, Lord, my God, to save me from the evil inclination and from injury. Do not dismay me with bad dreams or bad thoughts. May my bed be perfect before You and may You raise me from it to peace and life. *Restore the luster to my eyes, lest I sleep the sleep*

of death (Ps. 13:4). Blessed are You, Lord, Who gives light to the universe."[156]

2. One then recites the first paragraph of Shema and goes to sleep. But if sleep overcomes him, he may recite only the first verse, or verses expressing God's mercy, and then sleep.[157]

3. On waking up, one makes the following blessing while still in bed: "My Lord, the soul with which You have inspirited me is pure. You created it, You formed it, You inspirited it in me, You preserve it in me, and You will take it from me and in the future return it to me. All the while the soul is within me, I thank You, my God, Master of all creation. Blessed are You, Lord, Who returns souls to dead bodies."[158]

4. When one hears the cock crow, he makes the blessing: "Blessed are You, Lord our God, King of the Universe, Who gives the rooster discernment to distinguish between day and night." As one dresses, he makes the blessing: "Blessed are You, Lord our God, King of the Universe, Who clothes the naked." While putting on his turban, he makes the blessing: "Blessed are You, Lord our God, King of the Universe, Who crowns Israel in glory." When rubbing one's eyes with his hands, he makes the blessing: "Blessed are You, Lord our God, King of the Universe, Who gives sight to the blind." When sitting up on his bed, he makes the blessing: "Blessed are You, Lord our God, King of the Universe, Who frees the imprisoned." On lowering one's feet from the bed and placing them on the ground, he makes the blessing: "Blessed are You, Lord our God, King of the Universe, Who stretches forth the earth upon the water." On standing up, one makes the blessing: "Blessed are You, Lord our God, King of the Universe, Who straightens the bent over." Before washing his hands, he makes the blessing: "Blessed are You, Lord our God, King of the Universe, Who has sanctified us with His commandments and commanded us to wash our hands." When one washes his face, he makes the blessing: "Blessed are You, Lord our God, King of the Universe, Who removes sleep from my eyes and drowsiness from my eyelids.[159] May it be Your will, Lord, my God and God of my fathers, that You accustom me to fulfill the commandments and not accustom me to violate them, that You cause the good inclination to rule over me and not let the evil inclination rule me, and strengthen me in Your commandments, and

let my portion be in Your Torah, and let me be viewed with grace, lovingkindness, and mercy by You and by all who see me, and may You favor me with acts of lovingkindness. Blessed are You, Lord, who bestows acts of lovingkindness."[160]

5. Whenever a person enters a privy, he should first say, "Be honored, O honorable and most holy servants of the Most High! Guard me, guard me while I enter and until I leave, for this is the way of human beings." After leaving, one makes the blessing: "Blessed are You, Lord our God, King of the Universe, Who formed humans with wisdom, creating in them orifices and cavities, such that if even one of them were to become blocked or opened, they could not continue to live for even a short time. Blessed are You, Lord, Who heals all flesh and acts wondrously."[161]

6. When putting on one's belt, one makes the blessing: "Blessed are You, Lord our God, King of the Universe, Who girds Israel with strength." On putting on one's shoes, he makes the blessing: "Blessed are You, Lord our God, King of the Universe, Who has supplied all my needs." On leaving home, one makes the blessing: "Blessed are You, Lord our God, King of the Universe, Who supports a man's footsteps." One should make the following blessings every day: "Blessed are You, Lord our God, King of the Universe, Who has not made me a Gentile"; "Blessed are You, Lord our God, King of the Universe, Who has not made me a slave"; and "Blessed are You, Lord our God, King of the Universe, Who has not made me a woman."[162]

7. These eighteen blessings have no set order; one makes them as appropriate. How is this done? If one puts on his belt while still in bed, he makes the blessing "Who girds Israel . . ." at that time. If he hears the cock crow after that, he then makes the blessing, "Who gives the rooster discernment . . ." If one is not obligated to make any of these blessings, he does not.

8. How is this done? If one has slept in his clothing, he does not make the blessing "Who clothes the naked" when he gets up. On the Day of Atonement and on the Ninth of Av, when one does not wash, he does not make the blessing "to wash our hands," nor "Who removes sleep . . ." One who does not use a privy does not make the blessing "Who has formed humans . . . ," and so with the other blessings.

9. The people in most of our cities customarily recite these blessings one after the other in the synagogue whether they are obligated to recite each of them or not. This is a mistake, and it is not proper to act in this way: one ought not to make a blessing unless actually obligated to do so.

10. One who gets up early to read in the Written or Oral Torah before reciting the Shema should wash his hands, make three blessings, and only then read. These are the blessings:

"Blessed are You, Lord our God, King of the Universe, Who has sanctified us with His commandments and commanded us concerning the words of Torah. Lord, our God, make the words of Your Torah sweet in our mouths and in the mouths of Your people, the entire House of Israel; may we, and our descendents and the descendents of Your people, the entire House of Israel, be among those who know Your name and study Your Torah for its own sake. Blessed are You, Lord, Giver of Torah."

"Blessed are You, Lord our God, King of the Universe, Who chose us from among all the nations and gave us His Torah."

"Blessed are You, Lord, Giver of Torah." [163]

11. One is required to recite these three blessings every day and then read some words of Torah. People customarily also read the priestly blessing and there are places in which *Command the Israelite people. . .* (Num. 28:1–8) is read instead; there are also places in which both are read. One then reads chapters or laws from the Mishnah or from the *baraitot*. [164]

12. The early Sages praised those who read certain psalms every day, they being from *A Song of Praise. Of David* (Ps. 145) to the end of the book. The people have established the custom of reading certain verses before and after these psalms. The Sages ordained a blessing to be recited before reading these psalms, "Blessed be He who spoke . . . ," and a blessing to be recited after reading them, "May Your name be praised . . ." After that, one makes the blessings of the recitation of the Shema and recites the Shema.

13. There are places in which it is customary to read the "Song at the Sea" (Exod. 15:1–18) every day after the blessing "May Your name be praised . . ." and before the blessings on the Shema. There are other places in which the poem *Give ear . . .* (Deut. 32:1–43) is read. Some individuals read both poems; it is all a matter of custom.

14. A person is required to make one hundred blessings in every twenty-four-hour day. What are these hundred blessings?

The twenty-three blessings which we enumerated in this chapter.

The seven blessings before and after the recitation of the evening and morning Shema.

When one wraps himself in fringes, he makes the blessing: "Blessed are You, Lord our God, King of the Universe, Who has sanctified us with His commandments and commanded us to wrap ourselves with fringes."

When one puts on phylacteries, he makes the blessing: "Blessed are You, Lord our God, King of the Universe, Who has sanctified us with His commandments and commanded us to don phylacteries."

Three 'amidah prayers, each of which contains eighteen blessings.

These come to eighty-six blessings. When one eats his two daily meals, he makes fourteen blessings, seven at each meal: one, when he washes his hands before the meal, four over the food—one before and three after—and one each before and after drinking water; this comes to seven altogether.[165]

15. At the present time, with the institution of the blessing concerning sectarians in the 'amidah prayer and the addition of "Who is good and beneficent" in the grace after meals, we have five additional blessings. On Sabbaths and holidays, when the 'amidah prayer has seven blessings, and also on other days if one is not obligated to make all these blessings, as in the case of one who has had a sleepless night, or slept without loosening his belt, or did not use the privy, and so on, one must make up the hundred blessings with blessings on the eating of produce.

16. How is this done? One eats some vegetable and makes the blessing before it and after it. One then eats some fruit, and makes the blessings before it and after it, and then eats of another fruit, and makes the blessings before it and after it. If one drinks wine, he makes the blessings before it and after it. He should keep track of the blessings he makes until he makes up the hundred daily blessings.

17. The order of blessings is as follows. One gets up in the morn-

ing and makes these blessings; reads the Psalms and makes the blessings before and after them; recites the Shema and makes the blessings before and after it. One skips the *qedushah*[166] in the first blessing before the Shema since a single individual does not recite *qedushah*.[167] On concluding the blessing "Who redeemed Israel," one immediately rises to recite the *'amidah* prayer so as to link redemption and prayer.[168] He then prays standing, as we have described.[169] When he finishes, he sits down and lowers his face, offers supplication, raises his face and offers a bit more supplication, sitting and reciting the words of supplication. After that he recites *A Song of Praise. Of David* (Ps. 145), offers supplications to the extent of his ability, and then leaves to go about his business.

18. One begins the afternoon service by reciting *A Song of Praise. Of David* (Ps. 145) while seated. One then rises and recites the afternoon *'amidah* prayer. When he finishes it, one must lower his face and offer supplication. One then lifts his head, offers a bit more supplication, and then leaves to go about his business.

19. In the evening service, one recites the Shema, recites the blessings before it and after it, links redemption to prayer, and says the *'amidah* prayer standing. When one finishes, he should sit a bit and only then leave. One who offers supplications after the evening service is praiseworthy. Even though the blessing "Cause us to lay down" is made after "Who redeems Israel," there is no pause between redemption and prayer since these two blessings are like one long blessing.

CHAPTER EIGHT

1. Communal[170] prayer is always heard by God. The Holy One Blessed be He never rejects the prayers of the many, even if there are sinners among them. Therefore, a person should always participate with a congregation and never pray alone whenever he can pray with a congregation. One should always pray in the synagogue, morning and evening, since a person's prayer is accepted every time only if it is made in a synagogue. Anyone who has a synagogue in his city and does not enter to pray is called an evil neighbor.[171]

2. It is a commandment to hurry to the synagogue, as it says, *Come, let us know, let us pursue knowledge of God* (Hosea 6:3); but

when leaving the synagogue one must not take big strides, but walk slowly. On entering a synagogue one goes in the distance of two doorways and then says prayers, to fulfill *Happy is the man who listens to me, coming early to my gates each day, waiting outside my doors* (Prov. 8:34).[172]

3. A study hall is more important than a synagogue. The greatest sages would only pray in a place where Torah was studied, even if there were many synagogues in their cities, on condition that congregational prayer took place there.[173]

4. How is congregational prayer conducted? One person prays aloud, and the others listen. This is not done with fewer than ten free [174] adults, the prayer leader [175] being counted among them. Even if some of them had already prayed and fulfilled their obligation, they can make up the ten, so long as most of the ten have not yet prayed. Without a quorum of ten, *qedushah* is not recited, the Torah is not read with the blessings before and after, nor is a portion read from the prophetic books.[176]

5. So, also, only with a quorum of ten does the prayer leader read the blessings of the Shema, the others listening and responding, "Amen." This is called "reading Shema aloud." [177] Kaddish is recited only with a quorum of ten.[178] The priestly blessing is only performed in a quorum of ten, counting the priests. This, because ten Jews are called a community,[179] as it says, *How much longer will that wicked community keep muttering against Me? ...* (Num. 14:27), and they were twelve, excluding Joshua and Caleb.[180]

6. Sacred proceedings may only be done in a congregation of ten Jews, as it says, *You shall not profane My holy name, that I may be sanctified in the midst of the Children of Israel ...* (Lev. 22:32). If any of these things were begun with ten people, and some of the ten have left — even though they should not have — the rest may finish.

7. All of the ten, including the prayer leader, must be together in one place. In a case where a small courtyard opens in its entirety into a larger courtyard, and there are nine people in the larger and one in the smaller, they may be counted together. But if the nine are in the smaller courtyard and one in the larger, they may not be counted together. If the congregation are in the larger, and the prayer leader in the smaller, they have fulfilled their obligation. But if the congregation are in the smaller, and the prayer leader in

the larger, they have not fulfilled their obligation, since he is separated from them and not with them in the same place. This is so
because the larger courtyard has walls on each side of the opening
to the smaller courtyard and is thus separated from it, while the
smaller courtyard which opens in its entirety into the larger one is
not separated off from it, but is like a corner of it.[181]

8. So, also, if there is excrement in the larger courtyard, it is forbidden to pray or recite the Shema in the smaller. But if there is
excrement in the smaller courtyard, it is permissible to pray and
recite the Shema in the larger, provided there is no offensive odor,
since it is separated from the smaller courtyard.

9. How does the prayer leader fulfill the obligation of the many?
If they listen to his prayer, and answer, "Amen," after each blessing, it is as if they prayed themselves. When does this apply? In the
case of one who does not know how to pray. But one who knows
fulfills his obligation only through his own prayer.[182]

10. When does this apply? In every case but that of Rosh ha-
Shanah and the Day of Atonement of a Jubilee Year. On these two
days the prayer leader fulfills the obligation of one who knows how
to pray just as he fulfills the obligation of the one who does not
know how to pray, because the blessings on those days are long
and even those who know them cannot concentrate their minds
concerning them as can a prayer leader. Therefore, even one who
knows how to pray may rely on the prayer of the prayer leader on
those two days in order to fulfill his obligation.

11. The person appointed prayer leader must be the individual
in the congregation greatest in wisdom and good deeds; it is most
praiseworthy if he is also an older person. An effort should be made
to find a prayer leader whose voice is pleasant and who is accustomed to reading the Torah. Even a very wise person who does not
have a fully grown beard should not be a prayer leader, out of respect for the congregation. But such a one may read Shema aloud
if he is thirteen years old and is physically mature.[183]

12. So, also, an inarticulate person, such as one who confuses 'ayin
and *aleph,* or anyone who cannot pronounce the letters properly,
may not be appointed prayer leader. A teacher may appoint one of
his students to lead the congregation in prayer in his presence.[184]

13. A blind person may read Shema aloud and be made a prayer

leader. But a person whose shoulders are exposed, even though he may read Shema aloud, cannot be a prayer leader until he is wrapped in a prayer shawl.[185]

CHAPTER NINE

1. The order of public prayer is as follows: In the morning, everyone sits and the prayer leader descends before the ark,[186] standing in the midst of the people. He begins by reciting Kaddish, all the people responding, "Amen, may His great name be blessed," with all their strength, and answering, "Amen," at the end of Kaddish. After that he says, "Bless the blessed Lord!" and they respond: "Bless the eternally blessed Lord!" He then begins to go over Shema aloud, and they respond, "Amen," after each blessing. One who knows how to make the blessings and to recite the Shema reads with him until he makes the blessing "Who redeemed Israel." [187]

2. Everyone immediately stands and recites the 'amidah prayer quietly; he who does not know how to pray stands in silence and waits while the prayer leader prays quietly with the rest of the people. When each person in the congregation finishes his prayer, he takes three steps backward and remains in that place.

3. After the prayer leader takes three steps backward, he begins to pray aloud from the beginning of the blessings[188] in order to fulfill the obligation of those who did not pray. Everyone stands, listens, and answers, "Amen," after each blessing, both those who have not already fulfilled their obligation and those who have.

4. The prayer leader says qedushah [189] in the third blessing. When the prayer leader reaches qedushah, it is permissible to return to the place in which one stood while praying.[190] When the prayer leader reaches "We thank" [191] and genuflects, the people all bow themselves slightly, but not too much, and say, "We thank You, Lord our God, and God of all flesh, Who formed us, He Who formed all at the beginning. Blessings and thanks are due Your great and holy name for Your having given us life and for sustaining us; so may You continue to grant us life, be gracious to us, and gather our exiles to Your holy courtyards, in order to observe Your laws, serve You, and do Your will with a perfect heart, for our giving

thanks to You." Anyone who says, "We thank You, we thank You," is silenced.[192]

5. After completing the *'amidah* prayer, the prayer leader and the rest of the public sit, lower their heads, lean over slightly, and offer supplications with lowered heads. They then sit up, raise their heads, and offer aloud a small amount of further supplications while seated.

6. The prayer leader then stands by himself and recites Kaddish a second time, while the others respond as they did before. He then says, *He is merciful* (Ps. 78:38), *A Song of Praise. Of David* (Ps. 145) while standing, the others sitting, reciting with him. After that he says, *As a Redeemer shall He come to Zion to those in Jacob who turn back from sin, declares the Lord* (Isa. 59:20), *But You are the Holy One . . .* (Ps. 22:4), *And one would call to the other . . .* (Isa. 6:3), and completes the *qedushah;* the rest respond with *Holy, holy, holy!* (Isa. 6:3) three times.[193] The prayer leader then repeats the *qedushah* in Aramaic. He next says, *Then a spirit carried me away . . .* (Ez. 3:12), and reads it in Aramaic. He then says, *The Lord will reign for ever and ever* (Exod. 15:18), and reads it in Aramaic so that the people will understand it. These verses before and after the *qedushah,* with their Aramaic translations, are called "the order of the day."[194] After that he offers supplications and recites verses of mercy and says Kaddish. The people respond as is their wont, and depart.

7. One is silenced if, in his supplications, he says things like "May He Who had mercy on the bird's nest, forbidding the taking of the mother and her chicks[195] [have mercy on us]," or "[May He who had mercy] and forbade the slaughter of an animal and its calf on the same day[196] have mercy on us." This is because these commandments are scriptural decrees, not expressions of mercy; if they had been motivated by mercy, no slaughtering whatsoever would have been permitted us.[197] Similarly, one ought not to add sobriquets for God, such as "The Lord, great, mighty, awesome, potent, courageous, and powerful," since no human has the power to enumerate all of God's praises. Instead of this, one should say what Moses our master said.[198]

8. In the afternoon service the prayer leader says:[199] *He is merci-*

ful, Happy are those who dwell in Your house . . . (Ps. 84:5), *Happy the people who have it so* . . . (Ps. 144:15), and *A Song of Praise. Of David* (Ps. 145). The prayer leader then stands and recites Kaddish, the people standing behind him, responding as is their wont, and then they all say the *'amidah* prayer silently. The prayer leader then recites the entire *'amidah* prayer again, aloud, as he did in the morning service. He then sits, and they all lower their heads and offer supplications. He and they then raise their heads, adding a little more supplication while seated, as in the morning service. He then stands and recites Kaddish. The people respond as is their wont, and depart to attend to their affairs.

9. In the evening the people all sit, while the prayer leader stands and says, *He is merciful,* (Ps. 78:38) and "Bless the blessed Lord," to which they respond: "Blessed is the blessed Lord for ever and ever." The prayer leader then begins to go over the Shema aloud. He then says Kaddish and after that all stand and say the *'amidah* prayer silently; when they finish, the prayer leader says Kaddish and they leave. He does not repeat the evening *'amidah* prayer aloud since the evening *'amidah* prayer is not obligatory. Since there is no one there who has to fulfill the obligation of reciting the blessings of the *'amidah* prayer, making these blessings [200] would be to utter wasted blessings.[201]

10. On Sabbath eve after the prayer leader finishes saying the *'amidah* prayer silently with the congregation, he prays aloud, not reciting seven blessings but rather one blessing which expresses the substance of the seven; this is what he says:[202]

11. "Blessed are You, Lord our God, God of our fathers, God of Abraham, God of Isaac, and God of Jacob, the great, mighty, and awesome God, highest God, Possessor of heaven and earth, Who repays good deeds and possesses all, Who shields the patriarchs with His word and resurrects the dead with His speech, the uniquely holy King, Who gives rest to His people on His holy Sabbath, for He took pleasure in them to give them rest. We will worship before Him in awe and fear and give thanks to His name every day without fail with this summary blessing, He Who is Master of peace, Who blesses the seventh day and sanctifies the Sabbath and causes a people satiated with delight to rest in holiness as a remem-

brance of the creation. God, and God of our fathers, find our rest desirable. . . . Blessed are You, Lord, Who sanctifies the Sabbath." The prayer leader then says Kaddish and all the people leave.

12. Why did the Sages ordain this?[203] Because most of the people come to the synagogue to say the evening *'amidah* prayer on the Sabbath eve and if a person should come late, not finish his prayer in time, and thus remain alone in the synagogue, he might come into danger.[204] For that reason the prayer leader repeats the prayer to delay the people, so that the one who came late can leave with them.

13. It is for this reason that when a holiday falls on the Sabbath, or when the Day of Atonement or *Rosh Ḥodesh* fall on the Sabbath, the prayer leader who leads the evening prayer does not mention that day[205] in this blessing, but concludes with "Who sanctifies the Sabbath" alone because there is no obligation on that day to say this prayer.[206]

14. On Sabbaths and holidays when the prayer leader completes the audible recitation of the morning *'amidah* prayer, he says Kaddish, reads *A Song of Praise. Of David* (Ps. 145), and says Kaddish again.[207] Everyone then says the *'amidah* prayer of the additional service quietly, and the prayer leader repeats the *'amidah* prayer aloud, as he does for the morning *'amidah* prayer, and says Kaddish after the *'amidah* prayer of the additional service. The people then leave. *Qedushah* and supplications are not said after the morning *'amidah* prayer as on other days;[208] rather, they are said before the afternoon service. How is this done? The prayer leader reads *A Song of Praise. Of David* (Ps. 145) and says the "order of the day"[209] and words of supplication and says Kaddish. They all then say the afternoon *'amidah* prayer, and the prayer leader repeats it aloud and says Kaddish.

15. On *Rosh Ḥodesh,* and on intermediate days of festivals, the "order of the day" is recited after the *'amidah* of the additional service. After the Sabbath one also says "the order of the day" after the evening *'amidah* prayer, recites Kaddish, and then makes *havdalah.*[210]

CHAPTER TEN

1. One who says the *'amidah* prayer without correct intention[211] must pray again with correct intention. But if he had correct intention during the first blessing, he does not have to repeat the *'amidah* prayer. One who makes a mistake in one of the first three blessings of the *'amidah* prayer must return to the beginning. One who makes a mistake in one of the last three blessings returns to the blessing concerning the Temple service.[212] One who makes a mistake in one of the middle blessings returns to the beginning of that blessing and continues in order. So also a prayer leader who made a mistake while praying aloud corrects his mistake in the manner described here.[213]

2. But if the prayer leader has made a mistake during his silent prayer, I say that he does not say the *'amidah* prayer again silently, so as not to burden the congregation,[214] but relies on the *'amidah* prayer he recites aloud; but if he made a mistake in that *'amidah* prayer he must always correct it as an individual does.

3. A prayer leader who makes a mistake while saying the *'amidah* prayer aloud and becomes confused, not knowing from where to begin, and thus tarries a while, is to be replaced. If he has made a mistake in the blessing concerning sectarians, we do not wait for him to correct the mistake but replace him immediately, since he may have been infected with sectarianism. This on condition that he not have begun the blessing; if he has, we wait a little while.[215]

4. The person asked to replace the prayer leader should not refuse in such a case.[216] From which point does the substitute begin? If the first prayer leader erred in one of the middle blessings, the substitute begins from the beginning of that blessing; if he erred in one of the first three blessings, the substitute begins from the beginning [of the *'amidah* prayer]; if he erred in one of the last blessings, the substitute begins from the blessing concerning the Temple service.

5. One who says, "I will not lead the service[217] because my clothing is colored," may not lead that service if he changes into white clothing; one who says, "I will not lead the service because I am wearing shoes," may not lead even if he then goes barefoot.[218]

6. One who is unsure whether or not he had said the *'amidah* prayer does not pray again unless the prayer is offered as volun-

tary, since an individual may offer voluntary *'amidah* prayers all day long. One who is standing in prayer and remembers that he has already prayed, stops, even in the middle of a blessing. But if it is the evening *'amidah* prayer, he does not stop, since it is in any event said in the knowledge that it is not obligatory.[219]

7. One who mistakenly says the weekday *'amidah* prayer on the Sabbath has not fulfilled his obligation.[220] If one remembers while saying the prayer, one finishes the blessing he has begun and then says the *'amidah* prayer for the Sabbath. When does this apply? In the evening, morning, or afternoon services; but in the additional *'amidah* prayer one stops even in the middle of a blessing. So, also, if one has completed the weekday *'amidah* prayer intending it as the additional *'amidah* prayer for the Sabbath, a holiday, or *Rosh Ḥodesh,* he must go back and say the additional *'amidah* prayer.[221]

8. If one has erred in the wintertime and failed to say, "Who causes rain to fall" and "Who causes dew to fall," he starts again from beginning; but if he has mentioned the dew, he does not start again. In one has erred in the summertime and said, "Who causes rain to fall," he has to begin again. But if one has failed to mention dew in the summertime we do not make him go back since dew is never withheld and there is thus no need to ask for it.[222]

9. If one forgets the petition[223] in the blessing concerning the year,[224] but remembers it before "Who hears prayer,"[225] he should ask for rain in the blessing of "Who hears prayer." But if he remembers after concluding the blessing of "Who hears prayer," he must then go back to the blessing concerning the year. If one only remembers after completing the *'amidah,* he must pray a second time.[226]

10. One who forgets to say, "[Our God, and God of our fathers, may remembrance of us . . .] arise and come [before You],"[227] but remembers it before completing his prayer, goes back to the blessing concerning the Temple service;[228] but if he remembers it after completing the *'amidah* prayer, he must go back to the beginning. But in such a case, one who has customarily recited supplications after the *'amidah* prayer, and who remembers before moving his legs at the end of the *'amidah* prayer, only goes back to the blessing concerning the Temple service.[229]

11. When does this apply? On the intermediate days of a festi-

val, or in the morning and afternoon services of *Rosh Ḥodesh;* but one who has not said, "[Our God, and God of our fathers, may remembrance of us . . .] arise and come [before You]," in the evening service of the day of the new moon does not repeat the *'amidah* prayer.[230]

12. In every case where an individual has to repeat his prayer, the prayer leader must also repeat his *'amidah* prayer, if the mistake has occurred while he was saying the *'amidah* prayer aloud, with the exception of the morning service of *Rosh Ḥodesh.* If the prayer leader in that instance has forgotten to say, "[Our God, and God of our fathers, may remembrance of us . . .] arise and come [before You]" and has remembered only after completing his *'amidah* prayer, he is not made to go back, so as not to be a burden to the congregation, since *Rosh Ḥodesh* will be mentioned in the additional *'amidah* prayer, which still remains to be said.[231]

13. If one errs during the ten days between Rosh ha-Shanah and the Day of Atonement and concludes the third blessing with "the Holy God,"[232] he must start again from the beginning. If he errs, and concludes the eleventh blessing with "Who loves righteousness and justice,"[233] he returns to the beginning of the blessing, concludes it with "the King of justice," and continues praying in the regular order. But if he only remembers[234] after having completed the *'amidah* prayer, he must start again from the beginning; this applies both to an individual and to the prayer leader.[235]

14. One who has forgotten to say *havdalah* in "Who graciously grants knowledge"[236] completes his prayer and does not have to repeat it. So also, one who has failed to say "for the miracles" on Hannukah and Purim,[237] or "answer us" in the *'amidah* of a fast day,[238] does not say the *'amidah* prayer again; this applies both to an individual and to the prayer leader. But if one remembers[239] before he moves his legs, he says: "Answer us, our Father, answer us . . . for You are He Who answers prayer, redeems, and saves in every time of distress. May the words of my mouth [and the thoughts of my heart be acceptable to You, Lord, my Rock and Redeemer]."[240]

15. If one forgot to say the afternoon *'amidah* prayer on Friday, he says the evening *'amidah* prayer for the Sabbath twice. So also with a holiday. If one has forgotten to say the afternoon *'amidah* prayer on a Sabbath or holiday, he says the weekday evening *'amidah* prayer

twice after the conclusion of the Sabbath or holiday. He says *havdalah* in the first, not the second. But if he has said *havdalah* in both or neither of them, he has still fulfilled his obligation.[241] But if he has said *havdalah* in the second and not in the first, he must pray a third time, since the first one did not count, as it came before the evening prayer.[242] Everyone who says two *'amidah* prayers together, even the morning service and the additional service,[243] should not say them one right after the other, but should tarry a while between the *'amidah* prayers, so that he will be in a supplicatory frame of mind for the second *'amidah* prayer.[244]

16. It is forbidden for one praying with the public to say his *'amidah* prayer in advance of the others.[245] If one enters a synagogue and finds the public saying the *'amidah* prayer silently, he should pray with them if he can begin and finish before the prayer leader reaches *qedushah;*[246] otherwise he should wait till the prayer leader begins praying aloud and pray with him silently, word for word, until the prayer leader reaches *qedushah;* he answers the *qedushah* with the public and then says the rest of the *'amidah* prayer by himself. If one has begun to pray in advance of the prayer leader, when the prayer leader reaches *qedushah* he does not interrupt his prayer to respond to *qedushah* with the public. So, also, if one is in the midst of the *'amidah* prayer, he may not answer, "Amen, may His great name be blessed."[247] This is certainly the case with respect to answering, "Amen," to other blessings.

CHAPTER ELEVEN

1. In every place where ten Jews live,[248] they must prepare a building in which to assemble for prayer at its proper time; this is called a synagogue.[249] The inhabitants of a city may force each other to build a synagogue,[250] and to purchase scrolls of the Torah, the Prophets, and Hagiographa.[251]

2. A synagogue should only be built on the highest place of the city, as it says, *Wisdom cries aloud in the streets, raises her voice in the squares. At the highest point of the busy streets she calls; at the entrance of the gates, in the city, she speaks out* (Prov. 1:21). The synagogue should be the highest building[252] in the city, as it says, *to raise [again] the house of our God* (Ezra 9:9). The synagogue's doors

must open toward the East, as it says, *Those who were to camp before the Tabernacle in front—before the Tent of Meeting, on the East . . .* (Num. 3:38). A shrine is constructed in the synagogue,[253] in which the Torah scrolls are placed. It is placed in the direction toward which people in that city pray, so that they face the shrine when they stand up to pray. A dais is placed in the synagogue, so that all may hear when the Torah is read and sermons preached. When an ark containing the Torah scroll is used, it is placed in the middle,[254] such that its back faces the shrine, and its front faces the people.[255]

3. How do the people sit in the synagogue? The elders sit facing the people, their backs toward the shrine. The rest of the people sit in rows, one behind the other, so that all the people face the shrine,[256] the elders, and the ark. When the prayer leader stands to pray, he stands on the ground in front of the ark, facing the shrine like the rest of the people.[257]

4. Synagogues and study halls are to be treated with respect. They are to be swept, and water is to be sprinkled on their floors.[258] All the Jews of Spain, the Maghreb, Babylonia, and the Holy Land[259] light lamps in the synagogue and sit on mats spread on the floor. In the Christian cities they sit on chairs.[260]

5. Frivolity, such as laughter, joking, and idle talk, is not permitted in a synagogue or study hall; one is not to eat or drink in them, or adorn oneself in them,[261] or stroll about in them. One does not enter a synagogue in the summer to escape the heat, or in the winter to escape the rain. Scholars and their students are allowed to eat and drink in them in cases of special need.[262]

6. One does not make computations in synagogues, unless it is connected to the fulfillment of a commandment, such as when it relates to the charity fund, redemption of captives, and so on. Only eulogies for or by public figures, such as the greatest scholars of the city, to which all the people come, may be made in a synagogue or study hall.[263]

7. If a synagogue or study hall has two entrances, one may not use it as a short cut, since it is forbidden to enter them except for something connected to the fulfillment of a commandment.[264]

8. If one has to enter a synagogue to call a child or a friend, he should enter and read from Scripture a bit or recite a traditional teaching, and only then call his friend, so that he does not enter

only for his own purposes. If he does not know how to do this, he should call over one of the children and say to him, "Recite for me the verse you are studying"; alternatively, he should tarry awhile in the synagogue, and only then leave, since simply sitting there is considered doing something connected to the fulfillment of a commandment, as it says, *Happy are those who dwell in Your house* (Ps. 84:5).[265]

9. One who enters through one doorway to read or pray may leave through the opposite doorway to shorten his route. One may enter a synagogue with his staff and shoes, and in his undershirt; if one must spit, he may do so in the synagogue.[266]

10. Ruined synagogues and study halls retain their sanctity, as it says, *I will lay your cites in ruin and make your sanctuaries desolate* (Lev. 26:31) — even though they are desolate, they retain their sanctity. They are to be treated in their ruined state as they are treated when they are in use, with the exception of sweeping and sprinkling which need not be done. If grass grows in them, it is to be plucked and left in its place so that it is seen by the people and they are prompted to attempt to rebuild them.[267]

11. One may not tear down a synagogue in order to build another on its site or at another site; rather, first the new synagogue is built and then the old one torn down lest the construction of the building be prevented.[268] Even with respect to only one wall of the synagogue: first the new is built next to the old, and only then is the old wall torn down.[269]

12. When does this apply? When the foundations have not been destroyed. But if the foundations have been destroyed, or if the walls are in danger of collapse, they are to be torn down immediately. The synagogue is then rebuilt, quickly, working day and night, lest the matter be delayed and it remain a ruin.

13. It is permissible to convert a synagogue into a study hall, but one may not convert a study hall into a synagogue, since the sanctity of a study hall is greater than the sanctity of a synagogue, and we raise things in sanctity, but do not lower them. So also, if the inhabitants of a city sell a synagogue, they may use the money to purchase an ark. If they sell an ark, they may use the money to purchase vestments or a case for a Torah scroll. If they sell vestments or a case, they may use the money to purchase books of the Penta-

teuch.[270] If they sell books of the Pentateuch, they may purchase a Torah scroll. But if they sell a Torah scroll, they may only use the money to purchase another Torah scroll, since there is no sanctity higher than that of a Torah scroll. The same principle applies to money left over from the sale.[271]

14. So, too, if money has been collected from the people to build a study hall or a synagogue, or to buy an ark, or vestments, or a case, or a Torah scroll, and it is then decided to change the purpose for which all the money has been collected, it may only be changed from a lesser sanctity to a greater sanctity. But if they have used the money for the purpose for which it was collected, and there are funds left over, these may be used for any purpose. Synagogue equipment is considered akin to the synagogue with respect to sanctity. The curtain over the cabinet[272] in which the scrolls are kept is like the vestment of the scrolls. But if conditions were made concerning them, the conditions obtain.[273]

15. When does the statement that it is permissible to sell a synagogue apply? In the case of a village synagogue built only so its inhabitants have a place to pray; if they all have decided to sell it, they may. But a synagogue in a city, built so that anyone coming to the country may pray in it, is considered as belonging to all Israel, and may never be sold.[274]

16. Villagers who wish to sell their synagogue and use the money to build another synagogue, or to purchase an ark, or to purchase a Torah scroll, must stipulate with the buyer that he not convert it into a bathhouse or a tannery—a place in which skins are worked —or a mikveh, or a laundry. But if seven of the city leaders in the presence of the other people in the city stipulate at the time of the sale that the buyer may do these things, then he may.[275]

17. So also, if seven of the city leaders in the presence of the other people in the city stipulate that excess funds[276] lose their sanctity, the money becomes profane. Thus, when they take the money[277] and build another synagogue, or purchase an ark or a vestment and case, or books of the Pentateuch, or a Torah scroll, what remains is profane as they stipulated and they may do with it as they see fit.[278]

18. So, too, if all the inhabitants of the city, or most of them, accept the authority of one man,[279] what he does is done. He may sell or give away or stipulate as he sees fit.[280]

19. Just as it is permissible to sell a synagogue, it may be given away, for if the public had had no benefit from the present they would not have given it away. But it may not be rented out or used as security. So, when synagogues are torn down in order to rebuild them, it is permissible to sell, exchange, or give away their bricks, timbers, and earth; but it is forbidden to loan them, since their sanctity can only be removed by money[281] or some benefit which is like money.[282]

20. Even though the people pray in the main street of the city on fast days and on days when the watches gather,[283] because there are too many of them to fit in the synagogue, it has no sanctity, because prayer in it is a temporary expedient, and it has not been designated for prayer. So, also, other buildings and courtyards in which the people gather for prayer temporarily, have no sanctity, since they were not designated specifically for prayer; one prays in them as a man prays in his home.[284]

CHAPTER TWELVE

1. Moses our teacher ordained that the Torah be read publicly on Sabbath, Monday, and Thursday mornings so that three days never pass without one's hearing the Torah. Ezra the scribe ordained that it also be read publicly in the afternoon service of every Sabbath for the benefit of the common people.[285] He also ordained that three people read from the Torah on Mondays and Thursdays[286] and that at least ten verses be read.[287]

2. These are the days when the Torah is read publicly: on Sabbaths, festivals, *Rosh Ḥodesh,* fast days, Hannukah, Purim, and Monday and Thursday of every single week. A passage from the prophetic writings is only read on Sabbaths, festivals, and the Ninth of Av.[288]

3. The Torah may be read publicly only if there are ten free adult males present. One never reads fewer than ten verses, including verses beginning with *And [the Lord/God] spoke . . . ,*[289] and there must be at least three readers.[290] If the reader begins a new section,[291] at least three verses from it must be read. One may not finish the reading within three verses of the end of a section.[292] A person called to the Torah must read at least three verses.[293]

4. Where three people read [a total of] ten verses, two read three verses and the third reads four verses. It is equally praiseworthy if the person who reads four verses is called first, second, or third.[294]

5. Each one who reads opens the Torah scroll, looks at the place he is to read from, and then says: "Bless the blessed Lord." All the people respond: "Bless the eternally blessed Lord!" He then continues and makes the following blessing: "Blessed are You, Lord our God, King of the Universe, Who has chosen us from among all the nations and given us His Torah. Blessed are you, Lord, Giver of the Torah." All the people respond with "Amen." He then reads till he finishes, rolls the scroll closed, and makes the following blessing: "Blessed are You, Lord our God, King of the Universe, Who gave us the Torah of truth; eternal life has He planted among us. Blessed are you, Lord, Giver of the Torah."[295]

6. One who reads from the Torah must wait till the public has finished saying, "Amen." If one errs in his reading, even with respect to the correct pronunciation of only one letter, he is to be made to repeat it so that he pronounces it correctly. Only one person should read from the Torah at a time. If one has begun reading and loses his voice, another person should replace him, begin where he began, and make the blessing at the end.[296]

7. One may not begin reading until the most important person in the public tells him to do so. Even the synagogue's Ḥazzan or leader does not read on his own initiative until the public or the most important person among them tells him to do so. Another must stand with him while he reads, as the Ḥazzan does with other readers.[297]

8. The reader may skip from place to place provided he keeps to the same subject, such as skipping from *The Lord spoke to Moses after the deaths of the two sons of Aaron . . . Tell your brother Aaron that he is not to come at will into the Shrine behind the curtain . . . thus only shall Aaron enter the shrine . . .* (Lev. 16:1–3) to the passage *Mark, the tenth of this seventh month is the Day of Atonement* (Lev. 23:27) which is in the weekly reading beginning with *Speak to the priests . . .* (Lev. 21:1),[298] and provided that he reads nothing by heart; it is forbidden to read even one word which is not from the written text. When skipping, one should wait only long enough for the translator to finish translating the verse.[299]

9. It is forbidden to speak, even about matters of halakhah, once the reader has begun to read from the Torah; rather, everyone should be quiet, listen, and pay attention to what he is reading, as it says, *The ears of all the people were given to the Torah scroll* (Neh. 8:3). It is forbidden to leave the congregation while the reader reads, but it is permitted to leave between people called to the Torah. One who is constantly occupied with Torah, and whose calling is Torah, may engage in Torah study while the readers read in the Torah.[300]

10. Since the time of Ezra it has been customary to have a translator translate for the people what the reader reads in the Torah so that they understand its meaning. The reader reads one verse and remains silent while the translator translates it and then reads the next verse. The reader may not read more than one verse at a time to the translator.

11. The reader may not raise his voice above that of the translator, nor should the translator raise his voice above that of the reader. The translator may not translate until the reader has finished reading the verse, and the reader may not read the next verse until the translator has finished the translation of the last verse. The translator may not lean on a column or a beam, but stands in awe and fear. The translator is not to translate from a written text, but must do so orally. The reader may not assist the translator, lest someone think that the translation is written in the Torah. Whereas a minor may translate for an adult, it is disrespectful to an adult if he translate for a minor.[301] Two should not translate together at the same time; rather one person reads and one person translates.

12. Not all of Scripture is to be translated in public. Reuben's deed,[302] the priestly blessing,[303] and the story of the golden calf from *Moses said to Aaron* (Exod. 32:21) to *Moses saw that the people were out of control* (Exod. 32:25), and one other verse, *The Lord sent a plague upon the people* (Exod. 32:35) are read but not translated. In the incident concerning Amnon, the verse which says, *This happened sometime afterward: Absalom son of David had a beautiful sister named Tamar, and Amnon son of David became infatuated with her* (2 Sam. 13:1), is neither read nor translated.[304]

13. One who reads a portion of the prophetic writings after the Torah reading[305] must read at least three verses from the Torah first. He may repeat what the person before him read. The Torah

scroll should be rolled up before reading from the prophets. One should not read fewer than twenty-one verses, unless an entire subject is completed in fewer. But if he has read ten verses, and the translator has translated them, that is sufficient, even if an entire subject is not completed. With respect to the prophets, one reads, but two may translate. One may skip from subject to subject, but not from prophet to prophet, except in the twelve minor prophets,[306] so long as one does not skip from the end of a book back to its beginning. When skipping, one may not wait between sections more time than it takes the translator to translate.[307]

14. When reading from the prophets, one should read three verses to the translator; the translator then explains them one after the other. But if the three verses are three paragraphs, he must read them to the translator one at a time.[308]

15. One who reads a portion of the prophetic writings after the Torah reading makes one blessing before, "Blessed are You, Lord our God, King of the Universe, Who chose the prophets . . . ," and four after. He concludes the first of these with "the Lord Who is faithful in all His words"; the second with "Who builds Jerusalem"; the third with "Shield of David"; and the fourth with a reference to the special sanctity of that day, as he does in the 'amidah. Thus, if Rosh Ḥodesh fell on the Sabbath, he who reads from the prophetic writings mentions the new moon in this blessing as he does in the 'amidah. How many people read? On Sabbath, in the morning service, seven; on the Day of Atonement, six; on holidays, five. Fewer may not be called than this, but more may be. On the day of the new moon and on the intermediate days of festivals, four read. Three read in the afternoon service of the Sabbath and the Day of Atonement, in the morning service on Mondays and Thursdays of every week, on Hannukah and Purim, and in the morning and afternoon services of fast days. This number may be neither reduced nor augmented.[309]

16. Women do not read publicly out of respect for the congregation. A minor who knows how to read and understands to whom the blessings are addressed can count as one of the readers. The person who reads from the prophets can also be counted, since he read from the Torah.[310] But if the prayer leader has intervened between the last person called to the Torah and the prophetic reading

by reciting Kaddish, then the person who reads from the prophets cannot be counted among those who are called to the Torah. If only one person knows how to read from the Torah in a congregation, he ascends and reads, descends, sits, and reads again and again until finishing the number of readers for that day.[311]

17. In each of these readings,[312] a priest reads first, after him a Levite, and an Israelite last. It is customary today that even a priest who is an ignoramus be called before an Israelite who is a great sage. In general, whoever is greater in wisdom reads first. The last one called, who rolls the Torah scroll, receives a reward as great as all the others together, so that even the greatest person in the congregation may be called last.[313]

18. If there is no priest, an Israelite ascends, but a Levite should not ascend after him. If there is no Levite, the priest who read first reads again in place of the Levite, but in such a case another priest should not read after him, lest people think that the first was unfit and therefore a second priest ascended. So, too, a Levite should not read after a Levite, lest it be thought that one of them was unfit.[314]

19. How is the Torah read in a prayer service? On a day which has an additional *'amidah,* after the prayer leader completes the morning service, he says Kaddish, takes out a Torah scroll and calls members of the congregation one after the other to ascend and read from the Torah. When they finish, he returns the Torah scroll to its place, recites Kaddish, and then the additional service is recited. On days when there is both a prophetic reading and an additional service, it is customary to recite Kaddish before the person reading from the prophets ascends, but there are places where it is customary to recite it after the prophetic reading.[315]

20. In the afternoon service of the Sabbath and the Day of Atonement, after the prayer leader finishes *A Song of Praise. Of David* (Ps. 145) and the order of the day, he recites Kaddish, takes out a Torah scroll, reads in it, returns it, recites Kaddish, and recites the afternoon *'amidah.* So also on fast days: the Torah is read in the afternoon service, Kaddish recited, and the afternoon *'amidah* prayed. But it is not customary on holidays to read the Torah in the afternoon service.

21. On a day when there is no additional service, when the morning service is completed, the prayer leader recites Kaddish, takes

out a Torah scroll, reads in it, returns it, recites Kaddish, and then says *A Song of Praise. Of David* (Ps. 145) and the order of the day as is done every day, recites Kaddish, and the people leave.

22. Books of the Pentateuch are not read in synagogues out of respect for the congregation. So, also, a Torah scroll is not rolled while the congregation waits so that the people are not troubled to have to wait till it is rolled. Thus, if it is necessary to read from two different places, two Torah scrolls are taken out. But one man should not read the same text from two Torah scrolls, lest it be thought that the first scroll was unfit and that is why he reads from the second.[316]

23. One rolls a Sefer Torah from the outside, but ties it inside;[317] the stitching should be in the center.[318] In places where the Torah scroll is taken after the reading to another building for safekeeping, the congregation may not leave before the Torah; they must accompany it, following behind it, until the place where it is put for safekeeping is reached.[319]

CHAPTER THIRTEEN

1. The custom in all Israel is to complete the reading of the Torah in one year. We begin on the Sabbath after the holiday of Sukkot and read the portion *In the beginning...* (Gen. 1:1);[320] on the second Sabbath, *These are the generations...* (Gen. 5:9); on the third Sabbath, *God said to Abraham* (Gen. 12:1); we continue to read in this order until we finish the Torah on the holiday of Sukkot. There are those who complete the Torah in three years, but it is not a generally accepted custom.[321]

2. Ezra ordained that the Jews should read the curses in the book of Leviticus[322] before Shavuot and those in Deuteronomy[323] before Rosh ha-Shanah. The generally accepted custom is to read *The Lord spoke to Moses in the wilderness of Sinai* (Num. 1:1) before Shavuot; *I pleaded* (Deut. 3:23) after the Ninth of Av; *You stand this day, all of you* (Deut. 29:9) before Rosh ha-Shanah; *Command Aaron and his sons* (Lev. 6:2) before Passover in a non–leap year. There are, therefore, some Sabbaths on which we read two portions in the morning service, such as *When a woman at childbirth* (Lev. 12:1) and *This shall be the ritual for a leper* (Lev. 14:1); or, *If you follow*

my laws (Lev. 26:3) and *The Lord spoke to Moses on Mt. Sinai* (Lev. 25:1),[324] and so on, so that the reading of the entire Torah will be completed in a year and those portions listed above will be read in their proper seasons.[325]

3. The reading in the afternoon service of the Sabbath takes up where the reading left off in the morning service, and so also on Monday, Thursday, and the following Sabbath. How is this done? If, on the first Sabbath the portion *In the beginning* (Gen. 1:1)[326] was read, then in the afternoon service ten or more verses are read from *This is the line of Noah* (Gen. 6:9), and so also on Monday and on Thursday. So, too, on the following Sabbath, in the morning service, the reading begins with *This is the line of Noah* and continues to the end of that portion.[327] This is the way the reading is done throughout the year. On every Sabbath we also read a passage from the prophetic writings which is related to the subject matter of the Torah reading.[328]

4. On *Rosh Ḥodesh* the first person called to the Torah reads three verses from the paragraph *The Lord spoke to Moses, saying: Command the Israelite people and say to them* (Num. 28:1). The second person repeats the third verse read by the first person and the two succeeding verses, so that three verses remain in the paragraph. The third person reads the three verses left over by the second person and also the verse "On the Sabbath day" (28:9). The fourth person reads "On your new moons" (28:11).[329] If *Rosh Ḥodesh* falls on the Sabbath, two Torah scrolls are taken out in the morning service; from one the portion of that Sabbath is read while the last person called up reads *On your new moons* from the second scroll. It is acceptable if the person called up to read the passage from the prophetic writings is the seventh called to read from the Torah portion of that Sabbath.[330] The prophetic reading is taken from *And new moon after new moon* (Isa. 66:23).[331] When *Rosh Ḥodesh* of the month of Av falls on the Sabbath, the prophetic reading is taken from *Your new moons and fixed seasons fill me with loathing* (Isa. 1:14). When *Rosh Ḥodesh* falls on Sunday, the prophetic reading for the preceding Sabbath is *Jonathan said to him: Tomorrow will be the new moon* (1 Sam. 20:18).[332]

5. All who ascend to read from the Torah should begin with something positive and end with something positive. Despite this,

in the reading *Give ear* (Deut. 32:1), the first person reads until *Remember the days of old* (32:7); the second begins with *Remember the days of old* and continues until *He set him atop the highlands* (32:13); the third begins with *He set him atop the highlands* and continues to *The Lord saw and was vexed* (32:19); the fourth begins with *The Lord saw and was vexed* and continues to *Were they wise* (32: 29); the fifth begins with *Were they wise* and continues to *Lo, I raise my hand to heaven* (32:40); the sixth begins with *Lo, I raise my hand to heaven* and continues through the end of the poetry (32:43). Why are the stops made at these junctures?[333] Because the entire passage is a rebuke to induce the people to repent.[334]

6. The eight verses at the end of the Torah may be read in the synagogue even if there are fewer than ten people present. Even though they are part of the Torah and were said by Moses on the basis of what he heard from the Almighty,[335] they are different from the rest of the Torah since their content refers to what happened after Moses' death, and they may be read by an individual.[336]

7. No breaks are made in the curses in Leviticus;[337] rather, one person reads them all. He begins with the verse before them and finishes with the verse after them. While it is permissible to make breaks in the curses in Deuteronomy,[338] it has become customary not to; rather, one person reads them all.[339]

8. Interruptions in the cycle of Torah readings are made for the festivals and for the Day of Atonement;[340] the reading is drawn from the subject matter of the festival, and not from the portion of that Sabbath. Moses our teacher ordained that the Jews read from the Torah on each festival concerning the festival and discourse and expound on it.[341] What is read? On Passover, the section concerning the festivals in Leviticus.[342] It has become customary to read *Go, pick out lambs for your families* (Exod. 12:21) on the first holiday and to take the prophetic reading from the account of Passover in Gilgal.[343] On the second holiday,[344] *When an ox or a sheep or a goat is born* (Lev. 22:26) is read and the prophetic reading is taken from Josiah's Passover.[345] On the third day, *Consecrate to Me every firstborn* (Exod. 13:1) is read. On the fourth day, *If you lend money to My people* (Exod. 22:24) is read. On the fifth day, *Carve two tablets of stone like the first* (Exod. 34:1) is read. On the sixth day, *Let the Israelite people offer the Passover sacrifice at its set time* (Num. 9:1)

is read. On the final holiday, *Now, when Pharaoh let the people go* (Exod. 13:17) till the end of the song (15:19) is read, and the prophetic reading is taken from *David addressed the words of this song to the Lord* (1 Sam. 22:1). On the eighth day, *All male firstlings* (Deut. 15:19) is read and the prophetic reading is taken from *This same day at Nob he shall stand and wave his hand* (Isa. 10:32).[346]

9. On Shavuot, *You shall count off seven weeks* (Deut. 16:19) is read. But it is a widespread custom to read instead *On the third new moon* (Exod. 19:1) on the first holiday. The prophetic reading is taken from the account of the chariot (Ez. 1:1–28). On the second day of the holiday the passage concerning the festivals is read,[347] and the prophetic reading is taken from Habakkuk.[348]

10. On Rosh ha-Shanah, *In the seventh month, in the first day of the month* (Num. 29:1) is read. But, it is a widespread custom to read instead *Now the Lord took note of Sarah* (Gen. 21:1). The prophetic reading is taken from *There was a man from Ramathaim* (1 Sam. 1:1). On the second day of Rosh Ha-Shanah, *Some time afterward God put Abraham to the test* (Gen. 22:1) is read; the prophetic reading is taken from the passage including *Truly, Ephraim is a dear son to Me* (Jer. 31:20).[349]

11. In the morning service of the Day of Atonement *After the death of the two sons of Aaron* (Lev. 16:1) is read; the prophetic reading is taken from *For thus said He Who high aloft forever dwells* (Isa. 57:15). In the afternoon service, the passage concerning forbidden sexual relations in the weekly portion *After the death of the two sons of Aaron* is read,[350] so that anyone who has faltered with respect to one of these will recall it, be humiliated, and repent. The third person called to the Torah reads the Book of Jonah as the prophetic reading.[351]

12. On the first two days of Sukkot the reading is taken from the section concerning the festivals.[352] On the first day, the prophetic reading is taken from *Lo, a day of the Lord is coming* (Zech. 14:1); on the second day, it is taken from *All the men of Israel gathered before King Solomon* (1 Kings 8:2). On the last holiday, *All male firstlings* (Deut. 15:19) is read and the prophetic reading is taken from *When Solomon finished* (1 Kings 8:54). On the following day,[353] the portion beginning *This is the blessing* (Deut. 33:1) is read and the prophetic reading is taken from *Then Solomon stood* (1 Kings 8:22).

But there are those who take the prophetic reading *After the death of Moses* (Josh. 1:1). On the other days of the festival, the passages concerning the sacrifices pertinent to it are read.[354]

13. How is this done? On each of the intermediate days of the festival, three sections are read. On the third day of Sukkot, which is the first of the intermediate days, the priest[355] reads *Second day* (Num. 29:17), the Levite reads *Third day* (29:20), the Israelite reads *Third day* (29:20), while the fourth person called to the Torah goes back and reads *Second day* and *Third day*. So also, on the fourth day of Sukkot, which is the second of the intermediate days, *Third day* and *Fourth day* (29:23) are read in this manner.

14. Two Torah scrolls are taken out during the morning service of every single holiday, and so also on the Day of Atonement and on the seven days of Passover. From one we read what we have described,[356] and from the second, the sacrifice for that day from the Book of Numbers.[357] The person who reads the passage concerning the sacrifice is also the person who reads from the prophetic writings.

15. On any day when two or three Torah scrolls are taken out, if they are taken out one after the other,[358] then, after the first is returned, Kaddish is recited, and the second then taken out. When the latter is returned, Kaddish is again recited. We have already stated[359] that the generally accepted custom is always to recite Kaddish after the last reader and then to read the passage from the prophetic writings.

16. If the Sabbath falls on the intermediate days of a festival, whether Passover or Sukkot, *See, You say to me, Lead these people forward* (Exod. 33:12) is read. On Passover, the prophetic reading is taken from the vision of the dry bones,[360] and on Sukkot, from *When God sets foot* (Ez. 38:18).[361]

17. On the first day of Hannukah, the priestly blessing[362] is read to the end of the description of the sacrifice brought by the one responsible for the sacrifice on the first day.[363] On the second day, the description of the sacrifice of the notable who brought a sacrifice on the second day is read,[364] and so till the eighth day, when the passage describing the sacrifice of the eighth day through all the sacrifices to the end of the weekly portion is read.[365] The prophetic reading of the Sabbath of Hannukah is taken from the candelabrum of

Zechariah;[366] if there were two Sabbaths, the prophetic reading of the first Sabbath is taken from the candelabrum of Zechariah, and the second from the candelabrum of Solomon.[367] He who reads the Hannukah reading[368] reads the passage from the prophetic writings.[369]

18. In the morning service of the Ninth of Av, *When you have begotten children* (Deut. 4:25) is read, while the prophetic reading is taken from *I will make an end of them* (Jer. 8:13). During the afternoon service, *But Moses implored* (Exod. 32:11) is read, as is done on other fast days. On other days, when we fast in remembrance of that which befell our ancestors, we read the Torah both in the morning and afternoon services. The first person called reads four verses from *But Moses implored.* The second and third read from *Carve two tablets of stone like the first* (Exod. 34:1) through *which I will perform for you* (Exod. 34:10). But, on fast days which are decreed by a community because of calamities, such as droughts, plagues, and so on, blessings and curses are read, so that the people repent, and abase their hearts when they hear them.[370]

19. All Jews customarily take the prophetic readings on the three Sabbaths before the Ninth of Av from passages containing rebukes. On the first Sabbath, the prophetic reading is taken from *The words of Jeremiah* (Jer. 1:1); on the second, from *The prophecies of Isaiah* (Isa. 1:1); and on the third, *Alas, she has become a harlot* (Isa. 1:21). On the Sabbath after the Ninth of Av, the prophetic reading is taken from *Comfort, oh comfort* (Isa. 40:1). On the Sabbaths from the Ninth of Av till Rosh ha-Shanah, it is the accepted custom in our cities to take the prophetic readings from Isaiah's prophecies of consolation. On the Sabbath between Rosh ha-Shanah and the Day of Atonement, the prophetic reading is taken from *Return, O Israel* (Hos. 14:2).

20. If *Rosh Ḥodesh* of the month of Adar falls on the Sabbath, the passage concerning the shekel is read,[371] while the prophetic reading is taken from the passage concerning Yehoyada the Priest.[372] So also, if *Rosh Ḥodesh* of the month of Adar falls in the middle of the week, even on Friday, we anticipate it by reading the passage concerning the shekel on the Sabbath preceding it. On the second Sabbath, *Remember what Amalek did* (Deut. 25:17) is read and the prophetic reading is taken from *Thus saith the Lord of Hosts: I am*

exacting the penalty (1 Sam. 15:2). Which is the second Sabbath? It is the Sabbath ending the week in which Purim falls, even if it falls on a Friday.[373] On the third Sabbath, the passage concerning the red heifer is read and the prophetic reading is taken from *I will sprinkle clear water upon you* (Ez. 36:25). Which is the third Sabbath? — the one closest to the fourth.[374] On the fourth Sabbath, *This month shall mark for you* (Exod. 12:1) is read and the prophetic reading is taken from *On the first day of the first month* (Ez. 45:18). Which is the fourth Sabbath? — the one ending the week in which *Rosh Hodesh* of the month of Nisan falls, even if it falls on a Friday.[375]

21. It thus turns out that sometimes there may be a break between the first and second Sabbaths, or between the second and third Sabbaths, and sometimes there may be two breaks, between the first and second Sabbaths and between the second and third Sabbaths, but no interruption is made between the third and fourth Sabbaths.[376]

22. Each of these four sections is read from a second Torah scroll, after that week's has been read from the first Torah scroll. If *Rosh Hodesh* of the month of Adar falls in the week of the portion *You shall further instruct the Israelites* (Exod. 27:20), six are called to read, from *You shall further instruct the Israelites* until *Make a laver of copper* (Exod. 30:18), while the seventh person called to the Torah goes back and reads from *When you take a census* (Exod. 30:12) till *Make a laver of copper*. But if the regular portion of that Sabbath is *When you take a census* itself, then six are called to read from *When you take a census* till *Moses convoked* (Exod. 35:1), while the seventh goes back and reads, from a second Torah scroll, from *When you take a census* till *Make a laver of copper*.[377]

23. If *Rosh Hodesh* of the month of Adar falls on the Sabbath, three Torah scrolls are taken out. From one, the portion of that day is read; from the second, the passage concerning the new moon; and, from the third, *When you take a census*. So also, if *Rosh Hodesh* of the month of Nisan falls on the Sabbath, the regular portion of that day is read from one Torah scroll, the passage concerning the new moon from the second, and *This month shall mark for you* (Exod. 12:1) from the third.[378]

24. If *Rosh Hodesh* of the month of Tevet[379] falls on the Sabbath, three Torah scrolls are taken out. From the first, the regular por-

tion of that day is read; from the second, the passage concerning the new moon; and from the third, the passage describing the dedication.[380] If it falls in the middle of the week, three read from the passage concerning the new moon, while the fourth reads from the passage describing the dedication.[381]

25. Even though one hears the entire Torah read publicly every year, he must still read the portion of each and every week for himself, reading the scriptural text twice and its Aramaic translation once—if a verse has no translation, it should be read three times. This must be done each week, so that one's private reading keeps pace with the weekly public reading.[382]

CHAPTER FOURTEEN

1. The priests bless the congregation[383] during the morning, additional, and *ne'ilah 'amidah* prayers.[384] But there is no blessing of the congregation during the afternoon *'amidah* prayer since by the afternoon *'amidah* prayer everyone has eaten and it is therefore possible that the priests have imbibed wine, and a person who is drunk may not bless the congregation. Even on a fast day, there is no blessing of the congregation during the afternoon *'amidah* prayer, following the practice of the afternoon *'amidah* prayer on a regular day.[385]

2. When does this apply? On a fast day when both the afternoon and *ne'ilah 'amidah* prayers are recited, such as the Day of Atonement and a public fast.[386] But since the afternoon *'amidah* prayer of a fast day on which *ne'ilah* is not recited, such as the Ninth of Av or the Seventeenth of Tammuz, is recited near sunset, it appears to be like *ne'ilah* and will not confused with the afternoon *'amidah* prayer of a regular day; therefore the priests bless the congregation. A priest who has transgressed and ascended the platform during the afternoon *'amidah* prayer of the Day of Atonement may go ahead and bless the congregation. Since all know that there is no drunkenness that day, we do not require him to come down,[387] lest it be said about him that he was disqualified by some blemish and therefore required to step down.[388]

3. How is the priestly blessing conducted outside the temple precincts? When the prayer leader gets to the temple service in

the repetition of the *'amidah* prayer and recites, *May You find favor . . . ,*[389] all the priests standing in the synagogue leave their places and ascend the platform. They stand there, facing the shrine, with their backs to the people, with their fingers bent into their hands,[390] until the prayer leader finishes the blessing of thanks.[391] They then turn to face the people, stretch out their fingers, raise their hands to the level of their shoulders and begin, *The Lord bless you . . .* The prayer leader dictates each word to them, and they repeat it, as it says, *The Lord spoke to Moses: Speak to Aaron and his sons: Thus shall you bless the people of Israel. Say to them:*[392] (Num. 6:23), continuing in this fashion till they finish the first verse, at which point the people all respond, "Amen." The prayer leader then dictates the second verse to them word by word and they repeat after him, till the second verse is completed, at which point all the people respond, "Amen," and so with the third verse.[393]

4. After the priests complete the three verses, the prayer leader begins the last blessing of the *'amidah* prayer, "Give peace . . ." The priests then turn to face the sanctuary[394] and then close their fingers and stand there on the platform until the prayer leader completes the blessing, at which point they return to their places.[395]

5. The one who calls out, "Priests!"[396] may not do so until the congregation has finished saying, "Amen."[397] The priests may not begin their blessing until the one who prompts them has finished doing so. The congregation may not answer, "Amen," until the priests finish reciting their blessing. The priests may not begin the next blessing until the congregation has finished saying, "Amen." Unlike the rest of the people, the prayer leader is not permitted to answer, "Amen," to the priests lest he become confused and not know which blessing he is dictating to them, the second verse or the third verse.[398]

6. The priests may not turn away from the congregation until the prayer leader begins "Give peace . . ." They may not move from their places until the prayer leader finishes "Give peace . . ." They may not bend the knuckles of their fingers before turning away from the congregation. Rabban Yoḥanan ordained that the priests not ascend the platform with their shoes on, but, rather, that they should stand barefoot.[399]

7. The priests may not stare at the people while blessing them or

let their minds wander; rather, they should look down, as is done while standing in prayer. One is not permitted to look at the priests while they are blessing, so that his mind does not wander;[400] rather, all the people direct their intentions to hear the blessing, while facing the priests without looking at their faces.[401]

8. If there was only one priest blessing, he begins the blessing by himself,[402] and the prayer leader dictates each word to him, as we have said. But if there are two or more, they do not begin the blessing until the prayer leader first prompts them and says to them, "Priests!" They then respond and recite "The Lord bless you. . . ." He then dictates the rest of the blessings to them word by word according to the order that we have stated.[403]

9. How is the priestly blessing conducted in the Temple? The priests ascend the platform after completing the regular morning worship.[404] They lift their hands above their heads, with their fingers widespread — with the exception of the high priest, who does not raise his hands above the frontlet.[405] The blessing is dictated to them word by word, as it is done outside the Temple, until they complete the three verses. In the Temple, the people do not respond, "Amen," after each verse; rather, it is treated as one blessing. When the priests finish it, all the people respond: "Blessed is the Lord, God of Israel, forever and ever."[406]

10. They recite the divine name as it is written, that is, the letters *yod, heh, vav,* and *heh* are pronounced. This is what is universally called "the explicit name." Outside the Temple, they use its appellation, that is, *aleph dal,*[407] since the name is expressed as it is written only in the Temple. When Simeon the Righteous died, the priests ceased blessing with the explicit name even in the Temple so that unworthy people would not learn it. The early Sages taught it to their worthy students and sons only once every seven years. All this out of esteem for the great and awesome name.[408]

11. The priestly blessing is never recited in any language but Hebrew, as it says, *The Lord spoke to Moses: Speak to Aaron and his sons: Thus shall you bless the people of Israel* (Num. 6:23), and thus was it learned by tradition from Moses:[409] ***Thus shall you bless*** — standing; ***Thus shall you bless*** — with raised hands; ***Thus shall you bless*** — in Hebrew; ***Thus shall you bless*** — face to face; ***Thus shall you bless*** —

aloud; *Thus shall you bless* — with the explicit name, if they are in the Temple, as we said.[410]

12. The priests may never add a blessing to the three verses, such as *May the Lord, the God of your fathers, increase your numbers a thousandfold, and bless you as He promised you* (Deut. 1:11), and so on, neither aloud nor quietly, since it says: *You shall not add anything to what I command you or take anything away from it, but keep the commandments of the Lord your God that I enjoin upon you* (Deut. 4:2). When each priest begins ascending the platform, he says, "May it be Your will, God our Lord, that this blessing, with which You have commanded me to bless Your people Israel, be a perfect blessing. May there be neither obstacle nor sin in it, now and forever more." Before turning to bless the people, he makes the blessing: "Blessed are You, God our Lord, King of the Universe, Who has sanctified us with the holiness of Aaron and has commanded us to bless His people Israel with love." He then faces the congregation and begins the blessing. When he turns away for the congregation after finishing the blessing, he says: "We have done what You have decreed upon us, do with us as You have promised: look out from Your heavenly abode of sanctity and bless Your people Israel."[411]

13. When the priests turn to face the congregation to bless it, and when they turn away after they have blessed, they must always turn to their right. So, also, every time a person turns, it should be to the right.[412]

14. In the Temple the priestly blessing is said once a day. After the daily morning sacrifice the priests stand on the steps of the porch[413] and bless as we have described. But outside the Temple the blessing is made after every *'amidah* but that of the afternoon service, as we have said.[414] An effort should always be made to have an Israelite[415] dictate the blessings to the priests, as it says, *Speak to Aaron and his sons,* from which it is learned that the one speaking to them is not one of them.[416]

CHAPTER FIFTEEN

1. Six matters prevent the priestly blessing: articulation, deformities, sin, age, wine, and ritual impurity of the hands. How does

articulation prevent it? Inarticulate people, who cannot pronounce the letters properly—such as those who pronounce *aleph* like *'ayin* or vice versa, or who pronounce *shibbolet, sibbolet,* and so on—may not perform the priestly blessing. So, too, those whose mouths and tongues are heavy such that their words are not clearly understood by all[417] may not perform the priestly blessing.[418]

2. How do deformities prevent it? A priest with deformed hands, face, or legs, such as one whose fingers are twisted inward or side-wise, or whose hands are covered with dull white spots,[419] may not perform the priestly blessing, because the people will stare at him.[420] One may not perform the priestly blessing if his spit drib-bles down his beard when he speaks, or if he is blind in either of his eyes. But if he is well known in his town, and all are accustomed to his being blind in one eye or to his spit dribbling down, it is per-mitted, since the people will not stare at him. So, too, one should not perform the priestly blessing if his hands are stained blue or red, but it is permitted if most of the people in that town worked with such dyes, since no one would stare at him.[421]

3. How does transgression prevent it? A priest who killed some-one, even if inadvertently, and even if he had repented, may not give the priestly blessing, since it says, *Your hands are stained with crime,* and it also says, *And when you lift up your hands.*[422] A priest who has performed idolatry, even if under compulsion or inadver-tently, and even if he has repented, may never perform the priestly blessing, since it says, *The priests of the shrines, however, did not as-cend the altar of the Lord in Jerusalem, but they ate unleavened bread along with their kinsmen* (2 Kings 23:9); and performing the bless-ing is like performing the temple rites, as it says, *At that time the Lord set apart the tribe of Levi to carry the Ark of the Lord's Cove-nant, to stand in attendance upon the Lord, and to bless in His name, as is still the case* (Deut. 10:8). So also a priest who has apostatized and become an idolater may never perform the priestly blessing, even if he repents. Other transgressions, however, do not restrain one from performing the priestly blessing.[423]

4. How does age prevent it? A young priest may not perform the priestly blessing until his beard comes in. How does wine pre-vent it? A person who imbibed a quarter-*hin* of undiluted wine at one swallow may not perform the priestly blessing until the effects

of the wine wear off, because of the connection made between the priestly blessing and the Temple rite.[424] But if he has imbibed a quarter-*hin* in two sips, or has diluted it with a bit of water, it is permitted. If he has drunk more than a quarter-*hin,* even if it is diluted, and even if in several sips, he may not perform the priestly blessing until the effects of the wine wear off. How much is a quarter-*hin?* It is the volume contained in a space two fingers by two fingers by two and seven-tenths fingers.[425] The "finger" used as a measurement throughout the Torah is the thumb, that is, the one called *the thumb of his right hand* (Lev. 8:23).[426]

5. How does impurity of the hands prevent it? A priest may not perform the priestly blessing if he has not washed his hands;[427] he must wash his hands with water up until the wrist in the way in which priests sanctify themselves for the Temple rites, and only then perform the blessing, as it says, *Lift your hands toward the sanctuary and bless the Lord* (Ps. 134:2). A ritually unfit priest[428] does not perform the priestly blessing because he does not have the status of priest.[429]

6. Any priest who does not suffer from these restrictions which prevent him from blessing the community, does so, even if he is neither wise nor punctilious in the observance of the commandments, or even if people speak slightingly of him, or even if his business dealings are not just. He is not prevented from blessing the community since it is a positive commandment incumbent on every single priest fit to bless the community, and we do not tell a wicked man to be more wicked, and refrain from fulfilling commandments.

7. Do not wonder and say, "Of what benefit can this common person's blessing be?"—since the receipt of the blessing is dependent on God, not on the priests, as it says, *Thus they shall link My name with the people of Israel, and I will bless them* (Num. 6:27). The priests fulfill the commandment they were commanded to do while the Holy One, blessed be He, blesses Israel as He wants.[430]

8. People standing behind the priests are not included in the blessing, while those standing to the side of the priests are. If there were to be a partition between the priests and those being blessed, even were it a wall of iron, they would be included in the blessing, since they and the priests face each other.[431]

9. The priestly blessing is to be conducted only when there are ten present, including the priests. In a synagogue made up entirely of priests, all bless the congregation. Whom do they bless? Their brethren to the North and South.[432] Who answers, "Amen," to them? The women and children. If there are enough priests such that ten can remain in the congregation after the others ascend the platform,[433] then the ten should answer, "Amen," and the rest bless.[434]

10. If the only priest in a congregation is the prayer leader, he does not bless the community. But if he can be sure that he can perform the blessing and return to his prayer without becoming confused, he may do so. If there is no priest at all, when the prayer leader gets to "Grant peace,"[435] he says: "God, God of our Fathers! Bless us with the threefold blessing in the Torah, which was said to Aaron and his sons, the priests, Your holy nation, as follows: 'The Lord bless you and protect you! The Lord deal kindly and graciously with you! The Lord bestow His favor upon you and grant you peace! Thus they shall link My name with the people of Israel, and I will bless them.'" The people do not answer, "Amen." He then says, "Grant peace."[436]

11. If a priest who has blessed the community in one synagogue goes to another and finds a congregation of people praying who have not yet reached the priestly blessing, he blesses them, and may do this even several times a day. A priest who did not move from his place to ascend the platform when the prayer leader said, "May You find favor . . . ," may not ascend anymore in that prayer service. But if he did move from his place in order to ascend, but only reached the platform after the completion of the blessing concerning the Temple rite,[437] he still ascends and blesses.[438]

12. Even though a priest who fails to ascend the platform has violated only one positive commandment, it is as if he had transgressed three positive commandments: *Thus shall you bless the people of Israel, Say to them,* and *Thus they shall link My name.* Any priest who does not bless is not blessed, and any priest who blesses is blessed, as it says, *I will bless those who bless you And curse him that curses you; And all the families of the earth shall bless themselves by You* (Gen. 12:3).[439]

TREATISE III

Laws Concerning Tefillin, Mezuzah, and the Torah Scroll comprise five positive commandments, as follows: (a) that tefillin be placed on the head; (b) that they be tied on the arm; (c) that a mezuzah be affixed to the openings of doorways; (d) that every man write a Torah scroll for himself; (e) that the king write a second Torah scroll for himself, so that he may have two Torah scrolls. The clarification of all these commandments is found in the following chapters:

CHAPTER ONE

1. Four passages—*Consecrate to Me every first-born*... (Exod. 13: 1–10); *And when the Lord has brought you into the land of the Canaanites* (Exod. 13: 11–16), from the Book of Exodus;[1] *Hear* (Deut. 6:4–9); and *If, then, you obey* (Deut. 11:13–21)[2]—when written individually and wrapped in leather are called tefillin.[3] They are to be placed on the head and tied on the arm. According to the Torah,[4] a mistake in the tip of only one of the letters in the four passages renders the whole unfit; they must all be written perfectly as they are supposed to be.[5]

2. So also, with respect to the two passages in the mezuzah— *Hear* (Deut. 6:4–9) and *If, then, you obey* (Deut. 11:13–21)—if even a single letter in one of these passages is missing its tip, the whole is rendered unfit according to the Torah; both must be written perfectly. So also, a Torah scroll missing only one letter is unfit.[6]

3. There are ten matters in tefillin, which are all laws transmitted by Moses from Sinai[7] and which are all necessary; if one of them is done differently than required, the tefillin are unfit. Two relate to the writing, and eight to the wrapping and the tying of the straps. The two relating to the writing are that they be written in ink and on *qelaf*.[8]

4. How is the ink prepared?[9] The soot of burning oils,[10] or of tar, or of wax, and the like, is collected and kneaded with tree sap and a little honey; it is then drenched, crushed, formed into the shape of thin pancakes, dried out, and put aside. When it is needed for writing, it is soaked in gallnut extract or something like it, and then used for writing. Such ink can be thoroughly erased.[11] This ink is the choicest for the writing of Torah scrolls, tefillin, and mezuzot. But if any of the three were written with gallnut extract or with vitriol, even though such writing is permanent and cannot be erased,[12] it is fit.[13]

5. If so, what does the law transmitted by Moses from Sinai, that they[14] be written in ink, exclude? It excludes other colors, such as red and green, and the like, for if even one letter in Torah scrolls, or tefillin, or mezuzot were written in another color or in gold, they are rendered unfit.[15]

6. There are three kinds of parchment:[16] *gevil, qelaf,* and *dukhsustus.* How are they prepared? The hide of a domesticated or wild animal is taken, and after the hair is removed, it is salted, worked with flour and then with gallnut or other substances which strengthen the leather and cause it to contract. At this stage it is called *gevil.*

7. If, after the hair was removed, the hide was split through its thickness into two, as the leatherworkers know how to do, so that it became two pieces of leather, one thin, on the hair side, and a thicker one on the flesh side, and if these were worked first with salt, then with flour and then with gallnut or other similar substances, then the hair side is called *dukhsustus* and the flesh side is called *qelaf.*

8. It is a law transmitted by Moses from Sinai that a Torah scroll be written on *gevil,* on the hair side; that tefillin be written on *qelaf,* on the flesh side; and that the mezuzah be written on *dukhsustus,* on the hair side. Anything written on *qelaf* on the hair side, or on *gevil* or *dukhsustus* on the flesh side, is unfit.[17]

9. Even though this is the law from Sinai, a Torah scroll written on *qelaf* is fit. *Gevil* was specified only to exclude *dukhsustus,* for a Torah scroll written on it is unfit. So also, if one has written a mezuzah on *qelaf* or on *gevil,* it is fit; *dukhsustus* was only specified as being preferred.

10. It is forbidden to write Torah scrolls, tefillin, or mezuzot on the hide of any non-kosher domesticated or wild animal, or fowl; rather, they should be written on the hides of a kosher domesticated animal, wild animal, or fowl, even if the animal died or was killed.[18] Nor are they written on the skin of even a kosher fish, since fish skins contain contaminants,[19] which cannot be removed by tanning.

11. *Gevil* to be used in a Torah scroll, and *qelaf* to be used for tefillin or for a Torah scroll, must be processed for that purpose. If they were processed with some other purpose in mind, they are unfit. Thus, if they were processed by a Gentile, they are unfit, even if we had directed him to process a particular hide for use in a Torah scroll or tefillin, since a Gentile intends his own ends, not those of the person who hires him. Therefore, anything which must be prepared for a particular purpose is unfit if prepared by a Gentile. But a mezuzah does not need to be processed for the express purpose of fulfilling the commandment.[20]

12. It is a law transmitted by Moses from Sinai that a Torah scroll and a mezuzah must be written on a ruled surface,[21] but tefillin do not need ruling since they are covered.[22] It is permissible to write tefillin and mezuzot without consulting a written exemplar,[23] since everyone studies those passages.[24] But not even one letter of a Torah scroll may be written without consulting a written exemplar.[25]

13. Torah scrolls, tefillin, or mezuzot written by a sectarian must be burned. But if written by a Gentile, an apostate Jew, a traitor,[26] a slave, a woman, or a minor, they are unfit and must be put away,[27] since it says, *Bind them as a sign on your arm and let them serve as a symbol on your forehead; inscribe them on the doorposts of your house and on your gates* (Deut. 6:8–9)—only he who is obligated to bind them[28] and who believes in it[29] may write them. If found in the possession of a sectarian, and it is not known who wrote them, they must be put away; but if found in the possession of a Gentile, they are fit. One may not purchase Torah scrolls, tefillin, and mezuzot from Gentiles for more than they are worth, so as not to get them used to stealing or robbing them.[30]

14. Torah scrolls, tefillin, and mezuzot written on the hides of non-kosher domesticated animals, wild animals, or fowl, or on untanned hides, are unfit, as are Torah scrolls or tefillin written on

hides not processed for the purpose of fulfilling the commandment.

15. A Torah scroll, tefillin, or mezuzah written without correct intention, that is, such that the divine names are written without proper intention, is unfit. Thus, while writing the divine name, one must not respond even if greeted by a king of Israel. But if he is writing two or three names in a row,[31] he may interrupt himself between them and reply.[32]

16. If one dips his pen to write God's name, he must not begin with that name, but with the letter before it.[33] If the scribe forgot to write God's name, he may insert it between the rows, but if part of the name is on the row, and part between them, then the scroll is unfit. But if he forgot other words, he may write part of them on the row and part of them above it. When does this apply? In the case of a Torah scroll; but not even a single letter may be inserted between the rows in mezuzot and tefillin. With respect to these, if he forgot even one letter, he must put away what he has written and write another. It is permissible to write God's name in them all in places where the writing had been scraped away or erased.[34]

17. Those who write Torah scrolls, tefillin, and mezuzot may not turn the sheet of parchment over;[35] rather, they may cover it with a cloth or fold it.[36]

18. If, after writing a Torah scroll, tefillin, or mezuzah, the scribe says, "I did not write God's names for the express purpose of fulfilling the commandment,"[37] he is not believed so far as to render them unfit, but he is believed so far as to lose his remuneration. Why is he not believed to render them unfit? We suspect him of trying to cause a loss to the purchaser of the item, or to the person who hired him, thinking that all he would lose by making this statement is that portion of the remuneration due him for the names. Therefore, if he says, "This Torah scroll or tefillin was written on hides not expressly prepared for the fulfillment of the commandment,"[38] since he is believed in this case so far as to lose his remuneration, he is also believed so far as to render them unfit, since everyone knows that if the hides were not prepared for the express purpose of fulfilling the commandment, he deserves no remuneration at all.[39]

19. Tefillin and mezuzot may only be written in Assyrian script.[40]

It was permitted to write Torah scrolls in Greek as well, but in no other script. But Greek has sunk into oblivion, become corrupted, and lost. Today, therefore, all three are only written in Assyrian script. Care must be taken that no letter touches another, since any letter not surrounded on four sides by parchment is unfit. A letter which cannot be read by a normal child [41] is unfit. Therefore care must be taken with the forms of the letters, so that *yod* and *vav* not look like each other, nor *ḳaf* and *bet*, nor *dal* and *resh*, and so forth, so that the reader can read easily. [42]

20. One should not write across a hole if the parchment is perforated. But if the ink passes across the hole, it is not considered a hole and it is permitted to write across it; it is therefore permitted to write on the tanned skins of fowl. If a hole appeared in the parchment after it was written on, if the hole is in the open part of the letter — in *heh* or *mem*, and the like — it is fit. If the hole appeared in one of the limbs of the letter, dividing it, it is fit if what remains is itself a complete, if smaller, letter and if it does not resemble any other letter; [43] but if a complete even though smaller letter did not remain, it is unfit. [44]

CHAPTER TWO

1. How are the tefillin for the head written? The four paragraphs are written on four pieces of *qelaf;* each is individually rolled up and they are then placed in four separate compartments made of one hide. [45] With respect to the tefillin for the arm, the four paragraphs are written in four columns on one piece of parchment and are rolled like a Torah scroll, from the end to the beginning, and placed in one compartment. [46]

2. Care must be taken with the paragraphs; writing a closed paragraph as open or an open paragraph as closed makes the tefillin unfit. [47] The first three paragraphs are all open, and the last paragraph, *If, then, you obey,* is closed. [48]

3. Care must be taken with plene and defective words; [49] all four paragraphs must be written as they are in a carefully examined Torah scroll. A defective word spelled plene makes the tefillin unfit until the extra letter is erased; but if a plene word is written defectively, the tefillin are unfit, and there is no way to repair it.

Here follows a list of the defective and plene words in the four paragraphs:

4. In the first paragraph, *Consecrate to Me: beḵhor* is plene, *zaḵhor* is plene, *be-ḥozeq* is defective, *hozi* is plene, *yozim* is without a *vav*, *yevi'aḵha* is plene, *ve-ha-emori* is defective, *ve-ha-yevusi* is plene, *le-avoteḵha* is without a *vav*, *ha-'avodah* is defective, *mazot* is defective, *ha-shevi'i* is plene, *mazot* is plene, *se'or* is defective, *gevulḵha* is defective, *ba-'avor* is full, *le-ot* is full, *u-li-ziḵḵaron* is full, *'eineḵha* is full, *torat* is full, *hozi* is without a *yod*, *ha-huḵḵah* is defective, *le-mo'adah* is full.

5. In the second paragraph, *And when: yevi'aḵha* is defective, *u-le-avoteḵha* is without a *vav*, *ḥamor* is defective, *beḵhor* is plene, *be-ḥozeq* is defective, *hozi'anu* is plene, *va-yaharog* is defective, *beḵhor* is plene, *mi-beḵhor* is defective, *ve-'ad beḵhor* is plene, *zove'aḥ* is defective, *ve-ḵhol beḵhor* is plene, *le-ot* is plene, *yadeḵhah* is written with a *heh*, *u-le-totafot* is without the second *vav*, *eineḵha* is plene, *be-ḥozek* is defective; *hozi'anu* is plene.

6. In the third paragraph, *Hear. . . : me'odeḵha* is defective, *levaneḵha* is plene, *be-veteḵha* is without the second *yod*, *u-ve-qumḵha* is plene, *le-ot* is plene, *yadeḵha* is without the second *yod*, *le-totafot* is without the two *vavs*, *eineḵha* is plene, *mezuzot* is without the first *vav*, *beteḵha* is without the second *yod*, *u-ve-sh'areḵha* is plene.

7. In the fourth paragraph, *If, then, you obey: shamo'a* is defective, *mizvotai* is written with one *vav*, *yoreh* is plene, *u-malḵosh* is plene, *ve-tiroshḵha* is without a *vav*, *ve-hishtahavitem* is plene, *yevulah* is plene, *ha-tovah* is defective, *noten* is defective, *otam* is defective, *le-ot* is plene, *le-totafot* is written without the second *vav*, *'eineḵhem* is plene, *otam* is defective, *be-veteḵha* is without the second *yod*, *u-ve-qumeḵha* is plene, *mezuzot* is plene, *beteḵha* is without the second *yod*, *u-ve-she'areḵha* is plene, *la-avoteḵhem* is without a *vav*.

8. Care must be taken with the crowns on the letters: these being like upright *zayins* on the letters which have them, as written in a Torah scroll. These are the crowned letters in the four paragraphs:

9. The first paragraph has only one such letter, it being the final *mem* of *miyamim*, which has three *zayins* on it. The second paragraph has five such letters, each of them being a *heh*, with four *zayins* on each one: the *heh* of *unetanah*, the first and last *heh* of *hiḵshah*, the *heh* of *va-yaharog*, and the *heh* of *yadeḵhah*.

10. The third paragraph has five such letters: the *qof* of *u-ve-qumekha* has three *zayins* on it, as does the *qof* of *u-qeshartem;* with respect to the *tet, tet* and *peh* of *le-totafot,* there are four *zayins* on each of these three letters.

11. The fourth paragraph has five such letters: the *peh* of *ve-asafta* has three *zayins,* the *tav* of *ve-asafta* has one *zayin;* with respect to the *tet, tet* and *peh* of *le-totafot,* there are four *zayins* on each of these three letters. Altogether, there are sixteen crowned letters. If one did not write in the crowns, or added to their number or detracted from it, the tefillin are not thereby rendered unfit.

12. Tefillin acquired from someone who is not an expert in their preparation must be carefully examined. If one hundred units were acquired, three must be examined, either two tefillin of the head and one of the arm, or vice versa. If they are found to be fit, the scribe achieves a presumption of competence and the rest need not be examined. But if they were acquired in separate lots, each lot must be examined separately, since it is presumed that the seller acquired them from many different people.[50]

13. Tefillin which a person wrote for himself, or which were acquired from an expert, or from any other person, after they are examined and returned to their leather cases, do not need to be examined again, even if several years go by: so long as their covers are undamaged they retain their presumption of being fit, and there is no need to be concerned lest one of the letters be erased or split. Hillel the Elder used to say, "These belonged to my mother's father."[51]

CHAPTER THREE

1. There are eight laws concerning the manufacture of tefillin;[52] they are all laws transmitted by Moses from Sinai and therefore can in no way be waived; if even one of them is done improperly, the tefillin are unfit. They are that the tefillin be square, sewn as to remain square, and with squared diagonals, so that they have four equal angles; that on the leather of the tefillin of the head the letter *shin* be embossed on the right and left; that the passages be wrapped in cloth covers; that the cloth covers be tied closed with hair and then placed in their compartments; that they be sewn with liga-

ments; that the leather covering be shaped into a loop such that the strap can pass freely through its eye; that the straps be black; that the knot in the straps should have the well-known knot, shaped like a *dal*.[53]

2. How are the tefillin of the head made? One takes a cube-shaped piece of wood, having equal length, height, and width — but it is not important if the height is greater or less than the width, since it is only necessary that its length and width be equal. Three grooves are carved in it, so that it has four protrusions [see figure 1].

The wood is then covered with water-soaked leather, which is pushed down into each groove. The wet leather is tweaked to produce the shape of a three-tined *shin* to the wearer's right and a four-tined *shin* to the wearer's left.

3. The leather is left on the wood till it dries, and then removed from the wooden mold. The leather will then have four empty compartments. The appropriate passage is then inserted in each compartment. The leather on the bottom is folded over and sewn from its four corners. Enough leather is left on the bottom like a circular band so that the strap can slide through it; this is called the loop.[54]

4. And how are the tefillin of the arm made? One takes a cube-shaped piece of wood having equal length and width, and the height of a finger, more or less, and covers it with wet leather, and leaves the leather on the mold until it dries. One then removes the leather, inserts the four passages in place of the wood, and folds over the leather on the bottom and sews it from its four corners. Enough leather is left over to form a loop for the strap.

5. What is the order of the passages? In the tefillin of the head, one inserts the last passage, *If, then you obey,* in the compartment to the wearer's right, *Hear* next to it, *And when the Lord has brought you* in the third compartment next to *Hear,* and *Consecrate to Me* in the fourth compartment, which is to the wearer's left, such that if one facing the wearer were to read them, he would read them in this order [as shown in figure 2].[55] If this order were changed, the tefillin would be unfit.[56]

6. The tefillin of the arm is written in four columns on one long piece of leather, like a Torah scroll, in their order in the Torah, thusly: [as shown in figure 2].

פרק שלישי

Figure 1. Laws Concerning Tefellin, Mezuzah, and the
Torah Scroll, III.2.

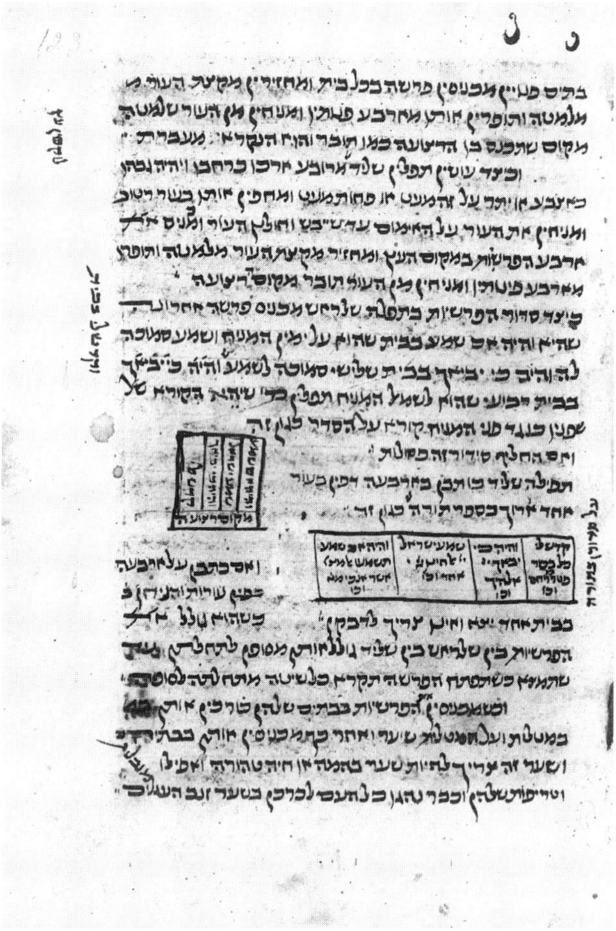

Figure 2. Laws Concerning Tefellin, Mezuzah, and the
Torah Scroll, III.5–6.

But if he has written them on four separate pieces of parchment and put them in one compartment, he has fulfilled the obligation, and they need not be connected together.[57]

7. When rolling the passages, whether of the head or of the arm, they should be rolled from the end to the beginning, so that one opening a passage can read every line of it from its beginning to its end.

8. Before the passages are placed in their compartments they are wrapped in cloth covers and bound with hair. The hair must be from a kosher domesticated or wild animal, even one which has died or been killed.[58] It is a universally accepted custom to bind them with the hair of a calf's tail.

9. Tefillin may only be sewn with sinews from a kosher domesticated or wild animal, even from those which have died or been killed. The sinew is taken from the heel of the domesticated or wild animal; these are white. If they are stiff, one softens them[59] with rocks and the like until they become like flax; they are then spun and twisted. Tefillin and the sections of a Torah scroll are sewn together with this thread.[60]

10. Tefillin are sewn so as to come out square. It is the widely accepted norm[61] for there to be three stitches on each side, so that there are twelve stitches in all, both on the tefillin of the arm and on that of the head. But if one made ten or fourteen stitches, so be it. Each stitch should be such that its thread passes through from each side.

11. The groove between the compartments of the tefillin of the head should reach the stitches. But if the groove is sufficient to make it clear that there are four sections, even though it does not reach the stitches, the tefillin are fit; but if the groove were not clearly visible, the tefillin would be unfit. One should pass through each groove in the leather a thread or cord to distinguish the compartments one from the other. It is a widespread custom to pass one of the sinews used for sewing through each of the three grooves.[62]

12. How are the straps made? One takes a strap of leather the width of a barleycorn; if it is wider than this measure, it is still fit. The length of the strap for the head should be sufficient to encircle the head, tie the knot, and extend on both sides down to the navel, or a bit above it. The length of the strap for the arm should be suf-

ficient to encircle the arm, tie the knot, and extend on one side[63] to the middle finger, where it is wound three times and tied. Straps longer than these measures are fit.[64]

13. The strap for the head is introduced into its loop, enough is left to encircle the head, and a square knot[65] like a *dal* is tied. Every scholar must learn this knot, as it is impossible to indicate its shape through written description; it must be seen. Similarly for the arm, one ties a knot like a *yod*,[66] such that the strap for the arm passes through the knot so that the strap can be loosened or tightened when one ties the tefillin to his arm.[67]

14. The outer side of the tefillin straps, both of the head and of the arm, are to be black; this is a law transmitted by Moses from Sinai. But the inner side of the straps, since they are inside, are fit if they are green or white.[68] One should not make them red, lest the strap turn over and he be disgraced.[69] The back of the strap must in every case be the same color as the leather box of the tefillin; if the box is greenish, the backs of the straps should be greenish, and if it is whitish, the back of the straps should be whitish. Tefillin which are entirely black — leather boxes and straps both — are considered the most beautiful.[70]

15. The leather with which the tefillin are covered and from which the straps are made should be taken from the hide of a kosher domesticated or wild animal, or fowl, even those which have died or been killed. If they were made from the hides of unkosher animals, or if they were glazed with gold, they would be unfit. The leather of the straps must be made for the express purpose of fulfilling the commandment,[71] while the leather with which they are covered[72] need not be processed at all; even if made of matzah[73] they are fit. Indeed, in many places it is customary to cover them with matzah hide.[74]

16. Tefillin are to be made by Jews only: because of the *shin* in the leather, discussed above,[75] making the cases is like writing the tefillin. Thus if a Gentile covered them[76] or sewed them, they would be unfit. Similarly, anyone who is unfit to write tefillin[77] may not make their cases.[78]

17. Tefillin for the head may not be converted into tefillin for the arm, but tefillin for the arm may be converted into tefillin for the head, since the status of an object should not be lowered from a

greater degree of holiness to a lesser degree of holiness.[79] Similarly, a strap taken from the tefillin for the head may not be used for the tefillin for the arm. When does this apply? When they have been worn. But if one wishes to convert a tefillin for the head which has never been worn to a tefillin for the arm, it is permissible. How is it to be done? One patches it with a piece of leather so that it becomes one,[80] and then ties it to his arm.[81]

18. Tefillin are rendered unfit if the stitches become undone as follows: two stitches next to each other, or a total of three stitches, even if not contiguous. When does this apply? With respect to old tefillin. But with respect to new ones, so long as the leather of their base remains unimpaired, they are fit. Tefillin are considered new if one can lift them by the flap of leather where a stitch broke and the leather does not tear; if they were to tear when thus lifted they would be considered old.[82]

19. If a strap breaks, it is not to be tied or sewn together, but is removed, put away,[83] and replaced. Remnants of torn straps are unfit unless their length and width satisfy the minimum measurements. One must always take care that the outer side of the leather of the straps face outward when they are tied on the arm and the head.[84]

CHAPTER FOUR

1. Where are the tefillin to be placed? The tefillin of the head is placed on the top of the head, at the hairline; this is the place of an infant's fontanel. It should be situated in the middle, between the eyes; the knot should be at the nape of the neck, where the skull ends.[85]

2. The tefillin of the arm is to be tied on the left biceps between the elbow and shoulder, such that when one's arm touches one's ribs the tefillin will be opposite the heart, thus fulfilling, *Take to heart these instructions with which I charge you this day* (Deut. 6:6).[86]

3. Wearing the tefillin of the arm on the palm of the hand or the tefillin of the head on the forehead is the way of the sectarians.[87] One who makes his tefillin round as a nut does not fulfill the commandment at all. A left-handed person places his tefillin on his right arm, which is to all intents and purposes his left. One who is ambidextrous places it on his left arm since this is the left arm

of a typical person. We know the positioning of the tefillin on the arm and on the head from tradition.[88]

4. Fulfillment of the commandment of the tefillin of the arm does not depend on fulfillment of the commandment of the tefillin of the head, and vice versa, since they are two independent commandments. What blessing does one make on them? On the tefillin of the head: "Who has sanctified us with His commandments, and commanded us concerning tefillin"; on the tefillin of the arm: "Who has sanctified us with His commandments, and commanded us to put on tefillin."[89]

5. When does this apply? When he puts on one of them; but if he puts on both of them, he makes one blessing, "to put on tefillin." One ties on the tefillin of the arm first and then puts on the tefillin of the head. When he removes them, he removes the tefillin of the head first and then removes that of the arm.

6. Having made the blessing "to put on tefillin," and having tied on the tefillin on the arm, it is forbidden for one to speak, even to respond to his teacher's greeting, until the tefillin of the head is put on. If one speaks, it is a transgression, and one must make the second blessing, "and commanded us concerning tefillin," and then put on the tefillin of the head.[90]

7. Every time one puts on tefillin one makes the blessing, even if he has taken them off and put them on a hundred times. Since with respect to all commandments one makes the blessing before their performance, one must make the blessing on the tefillin of the arm after placing it on the biceps, but before tying it, since tying it is the performance of the commandment.[91]

8. When one takes tefillin off and puts them in a receptacle he should not put the tefillin of the arm under the tefillin of the head, since when he wants to wear them again he will encounter the tefillin of the head first and put it aside and take out the tefillin of the arm—because one does not put on the tefillin of the head before that of the arm—and it is forbidden for one to put aside a commandment and pass on to another one, but one must fulfill commandments as the opportunity arises. Thus, one must place the tefillin of the arm on top, so it is encountered first, and put it on in the proper order.[92]

9. If a receptacle has been prepared for the storage of tefillin,

and used for that purpose, it has become sanctified and may not be used for profane purposes. If it was prepared, but not used, or used in a temporary fashion without having been prepared for that purpose, it is not sanctified and remains as profane as it was. It is forbidden to hang tefillin, whether by the strap or by the tefillin itself, but one may hang a bag in which tefillin are placed.[93]

10. Tefillin are to be put on during the daytime, not at night, as it says, *And this shall serve you as a sign on your arm and as a reminder on your forehead — in order that the Teaching of the Lord may be in your mouth — that with a mighty hand the Lord freed you from Egypt. You shall keep this institution at its set time from year to year* (Exod. 13:9–10);[94] "this institution" refers to the commandment of tefillin. So, too, tefillin are not worn on Sabbaths and holidays, as it says, *And this shall serve you as a sign* (Exod. 13:9), and Sabbaths and holidays are themselves a "sign." From what time may they be put on? From the time when one can recognize one's friend at a distance of four cubits till sunset.[95]

11. It is permitted to put on tefillin before sunset and keep them on after dark — even the whole night. This is not taught publicly; rather, everyone is taught not to leave their tefillin on but to remove them before sunset.[96] Anyone who puts on tefillin in the first instance after sunset violates a negative commandment, as it says, *You shall keep this institution at its set time from year to year* (Exod. 13:10).

12. One who returned from a trip wearing the tefillin of the head when the sun set should cover them with his hand till he gets home and then take them off. If one was sitting in the study hall with tefillin on his head when the Sabbath began, he should cover them with his hand till he reaches his home; if there is a house near the city wall[97] where they can be safely stored, they should be left there. If he did not remove the tefillin at sunset because there was no safe place to keep them, it is permitted to wear them to keep them safe.[98]

13. Anyone exempt from the obligation to recite the Shema is exempt from the obligation of tefillin.[99] A father should obtain tefillin for his son from the time he is able to take care of them, in order to educate him in the fulfillment of the commandments. Anyone suffering from an intestinal illness, and anyone who cannot control his orifices without pain, is exempt from the obligation

of tefillin. The ritually impure are obligated to put on tefillin, as are the ritually pure.[100] Anyone in distress, or a person in a disturbed state of mind, is exempt from the obligation of tefillin, since a person putting on tefillin must concentrate on them. Priests performing the Temple service, Levites when chanting on the platform, and Israelites during the time of their watch in the Temple, are all exempt from prayer and from tefillin.[101]

14. One must touch one's tefillin continuously while wearing them, so that his attention is not diverted from them even for a moment, their sanctity being greater even than that of the High Priest's frontlet,[102] since on the frontlet God's name is written only once, while the tetragrammaton occurs twenty-one times in the tefillin of the head, and similarly in the tefillin of the arm.[103]

15. Tefillin require a clean body, and one must take care not to break wind while they are on him. It is therefore forbidden to sleep while wearing them, whether in deep sleep or during a nap. But if one has covered them with a cloth kerchief and there is no woman with him, he may nap while wearing them. How ought one to behave? He may put his head between his knees and sleep while thus sitting. But if the tefillin have been wrapped within his hand, he may sleep deeply.[104]

16. One may only snack while wearing tefillin; before sitting down to a regular meal, however, one must remove the tefillin, place them on his table till he washes his hands, put them back on, and make the blessings over his food while wearing the tefillin.[105]

17. One who needs to relieve himself while wearing tefillin should not leave them in holes in the wall near the public domain and enter the privy, lest passersby take them. What should he do? Even if he only has to urinate, he takes his tefillin off four cubits from the privy, wraps them in his clothing like a Torah scroll, holds them in his right hand opposite his heart, taking care that no more than a handbreadth of strap extend from his hand, enters, and relieves himself. When he leaves, he should distance himself four cubits from the privy and put them on.[106]

18. When does this apply? In the case of a permanent privy where drops will not spray on him. But he may not enter a temporary privy holding them wrapped; rather, he should remove them and give them to someone else to take care of. Even in a permanent privy

urine will sprinkle unless one is sitting. But if there is powdery dust, it will not sprinkle even while standing. Where the ground is hard, one should stand on an incline so that urine does not sprinkle on him.

19. If while wearing tefillin one has to relieve himself near evening, such that the day would be over by the time he finished, he should not enter with them wrapped in his clothing, even if only to urinate in a permanent privy. Rather, what should he do? He should remove them and place them in their receptacle, if there were a handbreadth's space in it,[107] or in a receptacle which was not theirs, even if it did not have a handbreadth's space in it, hold the receptacle in his hand, and enter. Similarly, if he has to relieve himself at night,[108] he places them in a receptacle, holds the receptacle, and enters.[109]

20. One who has forgotten and entered the privy while wearing tefillin should place his hand on them till he finishes his first movement, go out, remove them, and then reenter and finish relieving himself. For, if he were to interrupt in the middle of his first movement, whether a bowel movement or in urinating, he might suffer very dangerous illness.[110]

21. One who forgot and had intercourse while wearing his tefillin, ought not touch either the strap or the body of the tefillin until he washes his hands and removes them, since the hands are ever busy.[111]

22. It is permissible to put on tefillin in a bathhouse where people stand clothed; but one ought not to put on tefillin or take them off in a place where some people are naked and some clothed. One removes his tefillin in a place where people stand naked, and it goes without saying that he may not put them on there.[112]

23. One should not wear the tefillin of the head while walking in a cemetery. One must remove his tefillin if he is within four cubits of a corpse or grave, and keep them off till he moves away four cubits. One may not wear tefillin until he covers his nakedness and puts on his clothing. A person carrying a load on his head must take off the tefillin of the head till he removes the load. One may not even wear a headscarf with tefillin on, but a turban may be wrapped over them.[113]

24. One may not have sexual relations in a building housing

tefillin or a Torah scroll unless they are removed, or placed within two receptacles, such that the second of them is not theirs. But if it were placed in a second receptacle, or even in a series of receptacles, if they were all designated for them, it would be as if they were in one receptacle.[114] But if they were to be placed within two receptacles,[115] even if his wife were with him in bed, he would be permitted to place them at the head of his bed, between the pillow and the mattress, but not precisely under his head, in order to protect them.[116]

25. The sanctity of tefillin is great since all the while tefillin are on a man's head and arm he is humble and filled with awe, is not attracted to laughter and wasted talk, and does not think bad thoughts; rather, he directs his heart to matters of truth and righteousness. One should therefore strive to have them on him all day long, for that constitutes the commandment concerning them. It was said about Rav, the student of our Holy Rabbi, that in his whole life he was never seen walking more than four cubits without Torah,[117] fringes, or tefillin.[118]

26. Even though the commandment of tefillin is to wear them all day long, it is most important to do so during prayer. The Sages said, "Anyone who recites the Shema without tefillin is like one giving false testimony about himself."[119] One who does not put on tefillin violates eight positive commandments, since in four passages the Torah has commands concerning the tefillin of the head and concerning the tefillin of the arm. Whoever wears tefillin regularly will have a long life, as it says, *Those with the name of the Lord upon them will live* (Isa. 38:16).[120]

CHAPTER FIVE

1. How is a mezuzah to be written? One writes two passages, *Hear* (Deut. 6:4–9) and *If, then, you obey* (Deut. 11:13–21) in a single column on a piece of parchment, leaving about half a fingernail's space at the top and at the bottom. If it is written in two or three columns, it is fit, so long as it is not written like a tail,[121] or a circle, or a tent;[122] but if it is written in one of these fashions, it is unfit. If it has been written out of order—if, for example, one wrote the second passage before the first—it is unfit. If it has been

written on two pieces of parchment, even if they were then sewn together, it is unfit. One does not make a mezuzah from worn-out Torah scrolls or tefillin; nor does one write a mezuzah on the blank parchment in a Torah scroll, since it is not permissible to lower the status of an object from a greater degree of sanctity to a lesser degree of sanctity.[123]

2. It is praiseworthy[124] to make the space between the paragraphs *Hear* (Deut. 6:4) and *If, then, you obey* (Deut. 11:13–21) a closed paragraph,[125] but if the scribe made it open, the mezuzah is fit, because the passages are not next to each other in the Torah. One must take care with the crowns[126] of the letters; here are the crowns in a mezuzah:[127]

3. In the first paragraph there are seven letters, each of which has three little *zayins:* the *shin* and *'ayin* of *shema,* the *nun* of *nafshekha,* the two *zayins* of *mezuzot,* and the two *tets* of *totafot.* In the second paragraph there are six letters, each of which has three little *zayins:* the *gimmel* of *degankha,* two *zayins* of *mezuzot,* the two tets of *totafot,* and the *zadi* of *al ha'arez.* If the scribe did not add crowns to the letters, or added more or fewer than are required, he did not thereby render the mezuzah unfit. But if he wrote it without incising lines, or was not careful with plene and deficient spellings, or added even a single letter in the mezuzah, it is unfit.[128]

4. It is customary to write the word *Shaddai*[129] on the outside of the mezuzah, opposite the space between the paragraphs. Since it is on the outside, it is not objectionable. But those who write the names of angels, holy names, verses, or special shapes on the mezuzah are included in the category of those who have no share in the world to come, since these fools not only cancel the commandment, but make of a great commandment, the unification of the name of the Holy One, blessed be He, His love, and His worship, a charm for their own benefit since they, in their stupidity, think that this is a matter which benefits them concerning worldly vanities.[130]

5. It is praiseworthy to write the words *over the earth* (Deut. 11:21) on the last line alone, either at the beginning of the line, or in its middle. Scribes customarily write mezuzot in twenty-two lines, with *over the earth* at the beginning of the last line. These are the letters[131] at the beginning of each line, in order: *shema, Adonai, ha-devarim, levanekha, u-veshakhbekha, bein, ve-haya, mizvah, bekhol,*

yoreh, 'esev, pen, ve-hishtahavitem, ha-shamayim, ve-avadetem, vi-samtem, attem, ba-derekh, u-ve-she'arekha, asher, 'al ha-arez.[132]

6. In folding the mezuzah, one rolls it from the end of the line toward the beginning, such that when a reader opens it, he reads from the beginning of the line to its end. After rolling the mezuzah it is inserted into a tube of reed or wood or any material and affixed to the doorpost with a nail, or inserted into a groove incised in the doorpost.

7. Before affixing the mezuzah to the doorpost one makes the blessing: "Blessed are You, Lord our God, King of the Universe, Who has commanded us to affix a mezuzah." One does not make the blessing while writing the mezuzah, since affixing it is the commandment.[133]

8. A mezuzah hung on a pole[134] is unfit, since that does not constitute affixing. If one puts a mezuzah behind the door, he has done nothing. If one drills a carpenter's hole in the doorpost and places the mezuzah in it — the way in which the bars of the planks[135] were inserted in rings[136] — it is unfit. A mezuzah inserted more than a handbreadth's deep into the doorpost is unfit. If one were to cut a reed, placed a mezuzah in it, connected the reed to others, and made of this a doorpost, it would be unfit, since the affixing of the mezuzah preceded the making of the doorpost.[137]

9. An individual's mezuzah should be checked twice within every seven years, while a mezuzah affixed to a public building should be checked twice in every fifty years to see whether part of it was torn off or a letter erased. This, since mezuzot are affixed in walls and are thus subject to rot.[138]

10. All are obligated to affix mezuzot, even women and slaves; furthermore, the young are educated to affix mezuzot to their houses.[139] One who rents a house outside the Land of Israel, or one who lives in an inn in the Land of Israel, is exempt for thirty days. But one who rents a house in Israel is obligated to affix a mezuzah immediately.[140]

11. If someone rents a house to another, it is up to the renter to bring a mezuzah and affix it. He is not free of the obligation even were he willing to pay the landlord to affix it, since the obligation of mezuzah devolves on the person who lives in the house, and not on the house itself. But when the renter leaves, he may not take

the mezuzah with him; but if the house belongs to a Gentile, the renter takes the mezuzah with him when he leaves.[141]

CHAPTER SIX

1. Ten conditions must be fulfilled before an inhabitant of a house is obliged to put up a mezuzah; if one of these is missing, there is no obligation to affix a mezuzah:
   - it must have an area of at least four cubits by four cubits
   - it must have two doorposts
   - a lintel
   - roof
   - doors
   - the doorway must be at least ten handbreadths high
   - the house must be profane[142] and intended for permanent and respectable[143] human habitation.[144]

2. A house less than four cubits by four cubits in area is exempt from mezuzah. But if it measures sixteen square cubits, even if it is round or a pentagon, and certainly if it is rectangular, once it measures sixteen square cubits it requires a mezuzah.[145]

3. A porch—that is, a place with three walls and a roof—is exempt from a mezuzah even though it has two columns on the fourth side, since these columns were made to support the roof, and not to serve as doorposts. So also, a roof supported by columns in every corner but without walls is exempt from mezuzah, even though it has the shape of a house, since it has no doorposts, these columns serving only to hold up the roof.[146]

4. A house with two doorposts, but with an arch instead of a lintel, is required to have a mezuzah if the doorposts are at least ten handbreadths high; but if they are not ten handbreadths high, it is exempt, since it has no lintel.[147]

5. A roofless house is exempt from mezuzah. If it is partially roofed it seems to me that if the roofed part is over the entryway, it requires a mezuzah. Doors must be installed before a mezuzah is affixed.[148]

6. The Temple Mount, its chambers and courtyards, and synagogues and study halls which have no living accommodations in them, are exempt since they are holy. Village synagogues in which

visitors lodge are required to have a mezuzah, as are synagogues in cities if they have living accommodations in them. Of all the gates in the Temple, only the Nicanor Gate,[149] the gate within it, and the entrance to the chamber of the Palhedrin[150] had mezuzot, since there were accommodations in that chamber for the High Priest for the seven days of separation.[151]

7. Granaries, barns, lumber rooms, and storehouses are exempt from mezuzah, since it says, *of your house* (Deut. 6:9)—*your* house, which excludes these places and others similar to them. Thus, a cattle barn used by women in which to adorn themselves must have a mezuzah since it is used specifically for human habitation. Guardhouses, porches, covered walkways, gardens, and animal pens are all exempt from mezuzah, since they are not made for habitation. But if houses requiring mezuzot open into these places, they then require a mezuzah as well.

8. Therefore, courtyard gates, alley gates, city gates, and town gates all equally require a mezuzah, since houses which require a mezuzah open on to them. Even in the case of ten[152] entryways, one leading into the other, if the innermost requires a mezuzah, they all do. Thus, they said that the gate opening from a garden to a courtyard requires a mezuzah.[153]

9. Privies, bathhouses, ritual baths, tanneries, and the like are exempt from mezuzah, since they are not made for dignified accommodation. Sukkot made for the holiday on the holiday itself and a cabin on a ship are exempt from mezuzah, since they are not made for permanent habitation. In the case of two sukkot built by an artisan, one leading into the other, the outer one is exempt from mezuzah, since it is not permanent. Shops in a marketplace are exempt, since they are not intended for habitation.[154]

10. In a house that has many entrances, even if only one is used regularly, each requires a mezuzah. The small opening between a house and its attic requires a mezuzah. Internal rooms, even those which open off other rooms, require a mezuzah on the entryway, as do the entryways to the outer rooms and to the house itself, since they are all used for habitation and are permanent.[155]

11. If one has an opening between a study hall or a synagogue and his home, and if he regularly uses it, it requires a mezuzah. In the case of an opening between two houses,[156] we follow the door

hinge, affixing the mezuzah according to the side on which the hinge is seen.[157]

12. Where is the mezuzah to be affixed? Inside the doorway; within a handbreadth of the outside; at the beginning of the upper third of the gate's height[158] — if it is affixed higher, it is fit, so long as it is at least a handbreadth under the lintel; to the right as one enters the house — a mezuzah affixed on the left is unfit. A house owned in partnership requires a mezuzah.[159]

13. One must take great care to fulfill the commandment of mezuzah, since it obliges everyone always. Every time one enters or leaves [his home] he will encounter the unity of God's name, remember His love,[160] awaken from his sleep and from his concentration on temporal vanities, and realize that nothing exists forever and ever but knowledge of the Rock of the Universe; one is immediately restored to one's senses[161] and follows the paths of the upright. The Sages said:[162] one who has Tefillin on his head and his arm, and fringes on his clothing, and a mezuzah on his doorway is assured of not sinning, since he has many reminders; these are the angels which save him from sinning, as it says, *The angel of the Lord camps around those who fear Him and rescues them* (Ps. 34:8).

CHAPTER SEVEN

1. Each and every Jew is commanded to write a Torah scroll for himself, as it says, *Therefore, write down this poem . . .* (Deut. 31:19), that is, write down the Torah which contains this poem, since it is not permissible to write the Torah in separate sections.[163] Even if a person inherited a Torah scroll from his parents, it is still incumbent on him to write his own. If he wrote it himself, it is as if he received it at Sinai. If he does not know how to write it, others may write it for him. Correcting even a single letter in a Torah scroll is considered to be like writing a whole scroll.[164]

2. A king is commanded to write a second Torah scroll for himself as king, over and above the scroll he had while a commoner, as it says, *When he is seated on his royal throne, he shall write* (Deut. 17:18). It is corrected against the scroll in the Temple courtyard under the supervision[165] of the High Court.[166] He stores the scroll he had while he was a commoner, while the one which he wrote or

had written for him as king should be with him always. If he goes out to war, the Torah scroll should be with him; when he enters,[167] it should be with him; when he sits in judgment, it should be with him; when he sits down to eat, it should be opposite him; as it says: *Let it remain with him and let him read in it all his life, so that he may learn to revere the Lord his God, to observe faithfully every word of this Teaching as well as these laws* (Deut. 17:19).[168]

3. If he had no Torah scroll of his own before becoming king, then afterward he must write two Torah scrolls; one he stores; the second must be with him always, except at night, or in the bathhouse, or in the privy, or when he sleeps on his bed.[169]

4. A Torah scroll written without incised lines or written partially on *gevil* and partially on *qelaf* is unfit; rather, it must be written entirely either on *gevil* or on *qelaf*. How is a Torah scroll written? It must be written correctly and beautifully. Blank space the size of a small letter must be left between each word and the size of a line between each line. The length of each line should be thirty letters, enough to write "for your families," [170] three times;[171] this should be the width of each column. Lines should not be shorter than this, so the column does not appear to be like a missive, nor longer than this, so that the eye does not have to wander far across the writing.[172]

5. One should not minimize the size of letters in order to allow for the appropriate space between paragraphs. If the scribe was left with a five-letter word at the end of a line, he should not write two in the column and three in the margin; rather, he should write three in the column and two in the margin. If there is not enough space at the end of the line for three letters, he should leave the space blank and continue on the beginning of the next line.[173]

6. If one comes upon a two-letter word at the end of a line, he should not insert it between the lines, but start a new line. If one comes upon a ten-letter word—more or less—at the end of a line, and there is not enough space to write all of it within the column, if he can write half of it in the column and half in the margin, he does so; otherwise, he leaves the space blank and starts a new line.

7. Between each book of the Pentateuch one leaves exactly four blank lines, beginning the new book on the fifth line. The Torah must be completed in the middle of the last line of a column. If the

scribe sees that many lines will be left, he shortens the lines so that the words *displayed before all Israel* (Deut. 34:12)[174] come out in the middle of the line at the end of the column.[175]

8. One must take special care with the enlarged letters, the miniaturized letters, the letters with dots over them,[176] and the unusually shaped letters — such as the bent-over *peh*s and the crooked letters — as the scribes have copied one from the other.[177] One must also take care with the crowns on the letters, and their number; some crowned letters have one, others have [as many as] seven. All the crowns are shaped like a hair-thin letter *zayin*.

9. All these matters relate only to fulfilling the commandment in the best possible way. If the scribe did not follow the instructions here, or was not careful with the crowns, but wrote all the letters according to their standard form, or brought the lines closer together or spread them further apart, or lengthened them or shortened them, so long as he did not connect two letters, and did not exclude or add letters, and did not alter the shape of any letters, and did not change the open and closed paragraphs, the scroll is fit.

10. There are other practices, not mentioned in the Talmud, which the scribes customarily do according to their traditions:

- that the number of lines in any column be no fewer than forty-eight and no more than sixty
- that the space between paragraph and paragraph be at least nine letters long, so that one could write the word *asher* three times
- that the five lines preceding the Song at the Sea[178] begin with the words *that followed* (Exod. 14:28), *on dry ground* (Exod. 14:29), *the Lord* (Exod. 14:30), *dead* (Exod. 14:30), and *against the Egyptians* (Exod. 14:31)
- that the five lines following the Song at the Sea begin with the words *took* (Exod. 15:20), *after her* (Exod. 15:20), *Horse* (Exod. 15:21), *They went on* (Exod. 15:22), and *They came* (Exod. 15:23)
- that the six lines preceding the song *Give ear* (Deut. 26:1–43) begin with the words *that I may . . . to witness* (Deut. 31: 28), *when* (Deut. 31:29), *the path* (Deut. 31:29), *in time to come* (Deut. 31:29), and *and vexed Him* (Deut. 31:29)
- that the five lines following the song *Give ear* begin with the words *came* (Deut. 32:44), *reciting* (Deut. 32:45), *which* (Deut. 32:46), *this* (Deut. 32:46), *and which* (Deut. 32:47)

All these relate only to fulfilling the commandment in the best possible way; if the scribe has changed them, the scroll is not unfit.

11. But if he has written a plene word as defective, or a defective word as plene, or a word which is read differently from the way it is spelled according to the way it is read — such as *shall sleep with her* instead of *shall copulate with her* (Deut. 28:30) or *with hemorrhoids* instead of *with boils in the anus,* and so on — or wrote an open paragraph as closed, or a closed paragraph as open, or wrote a poetic passage as if it were prose, or wrote a prose passage as if it were poetry, the scroll is unfit. It does not have the sanctity of a Torah scroll at all, but is like any regular Pentateuch from which children are taught.[179]

12. An uncorrected Torah scroll may not be left for more than thirty days in that state; it must be corrected or placed in a *genizah.*[180] A scroll with three mistakes in each column should be corrected; if it has four mistakes in each column it should be placed in a *genizah.* But if most of the scroll has been corrected, and even if the rest have four mistakes in each column, if there is at least one column in that part with fewer than four mistakes, then the scroll ought to be corrected.[181]

13. When does this apply? In a case where the mistakes relate to the writing of plene words defectively, since one has to insert the forgotten letters between the lines. But if he has written defective words plene, even if there are several such mistakes in every column, it is to be corrected, since the correction only involves erasing letters, as opposed to inserting them.

14. A Torah may be written book by individual book; these do not have the sanctity of a complete Torah scroll. One does not write a partial Torah,[182] containing various passages. Nor is a partial Torah to be written for children to study from; this is permissible if the scribe plans to finish out at least one volume of the Pentateuch. It is permissible to write a partial Torah if one writes only three words on each line.[183]

15. It is permissible to bind the Pentateuch, Prophetic Writings, and Hagiographa together in one volume; one must leave between each volume of the Pentateuch four lines, between each prophet three lines — so also, between each of the Minor Prophets, so that if

one wishes to divide the books, one can. This is the order of the Prophetic Writings: Joshua and Judges, Samuel and Kings, Jeremiah
and Ezekiel, Isaiah and the Minor Prophets. This is the order of
the Hagiographa: Ruth, Psalms, Job, Proverbs, Ecclesiastes, Song
of Songs, Lamentations, Daniel, Esther, Ezra, Chronicles.[184]

16. These sacred texts may only be written on incised pages, even
if written on paper. One may write three words without incision,
but writing more is forbidden. The aforementioned volume containing the Pentateuch, Prophetic Writings, and Hagiographa does
not have the sanctity of a Torah scroll, but, rather, that of a volume
of the Pentateuch, because adding something [to the Torah] is like
omitting something.[185]

CHAPTER EIGHT

1. An open paragraph has two forms. If the scribe has finished
the previous paragraph in the middle of a line, he leaves the rest
of the line blank and begins the open paragraph at the beginning
of the following line thusly:

———

————

When does this apply? When there remains enough of a line in
which one could write nine letters. But if only a little space remains,
or if the scribe has finished at the end of the line, he then leaves an
entire line blank and begins the open paragraph at the beginning
of the third line thusly:

————

blank line

————

2. A closed paragraph has three forms. If the scribe has finished
the previous paragraph in the middle of a line, he leaves enough
space [for nine letters] and begins the closed paragraph at the end
of the line, leaving a blank space in the middle thusly:

—————————

—————

But if there is not enough space on the line to leave enough of a
blank space and write at least one letter at the end of the line, he

should leave the whole blank, and leave a little space empty at the start of the next line, starting to write the closed paragraph from the middle of the line, thusly:

———

But if the scribe has finished the previous paragraph at the end of the line, he leaves enough space [for nine letters] at the beginning of the next line and starts writing the closed paragraph from the middle of the line, thusly:

———

It may thus be summarized that an open paragraph always begins at the beginning of a line, and a closed paragraph always begins in the middle of a line.

3. A Torah scroll uncorrected for plene and defective words may be corrected and checked as we have explained.[186] But if the scribe made a mistake concerning the space between the paragraphs, writing a closed paragraph as if it were open, or an open paragraph as if it were closed, or left an open space where a paragraph does not begin, or wrote regularly, without leaving a space where a paragraph begins, or changed the shape of the lines,[187] the scroll is unfit and cannot be corrected without removing every page on which such mistakes are found.[188]

4. Since I have found great inaccuracy in these matters in the Torah scrolls which I have seen, and since the Massoretes who write and compose works to make known which are the closed and which are the open paragraphs are as divided in these matters as are the scrolls on which they rely, I have seen fit to set down here all of the closed and open paragraphs of the Torah and the shapes of the poetic passages so that all Torah scrolls may be corrected and checked against this list.

5. The Torah scroll on which we have relied in these matters is the scroll well known in Egypt containing the twenty-four books,[189] which was in Jerusalem until recently, and which was used to check other scrolls. All relied on it, since Ben Asher corrected it, examined it carefully over many years, and checked it many times, whenever it was copied. I relied on it when I wrote a correct Torah scroll.

Book of Genesis.

[Here Maimonides provides the opening words of all the open and closed paragraphs in Genesis.][190]

The sum of open paragraphs is 43 and of closed paragraphs, 48; together, ninety-one paragraphs.

Book of Exodus.

[Here Maimonides provides the opening words of all the open and closed paragraphs in Exodus.]

The sum of open paragraphs is 69 and the sum of closed paragraphs is ninety-five; together, one hundred sixty-four paragraphs.

Book of Leviticus.

[Here Maimonides provides the opening words of all the open and closed paragraphs in Leviticus.]

The number of open paragraphs is fifty-two, and of closed paragraphs, forty-six; together, ninety-eight paragraphs.

Book of Numbers.

[Here Maimonides provides the opening words of all the open and closed paragraphs in Numbers.]

The number of open paragraphs is ninety-two, and of closed paragraphs, sixty-six; together, one hundred fifty-eight.

Book of Deuteronomy.

[Here Maimonides provides the opening words of all the open and closed paragraphs in Deuteronomy.]

The number of open paragraphs in this book is thirty-four, and of closed paragraphs, one hundred twenty-four; together, one hundred fifty-eight.

The number of open paragraphs in the entire Torah is two hundred ninety, and the number of closed paragraphs is three hundred seventy-nine; together, six hundred and sixty-nine.

6. This is the form of the poem *Give ear* (Deut. 32:1–43): every line has a blank space in the middle, like the shape of a closed paragraph, so that every line is divided in half. It is to be written in seventy-six lines. Here are the words at the beginning of each line: [Maimonides here lists the opening words of the seventy-six lines of the poem.]

7. The Song at the Sea (Exod. 15:1–19) is written in thirty lines.

The first line is normal, while the rest are as follows: one line has an empty space in the middle, while the next line has two empty spaces, so that the line is divided into three and so that there is space opposite each written part, and writing opposite each space. This is its form [as shown in figure 3.][191]

8. In the entire Torah, whether in poetry or the rest of the text, the scribe should strive to write the letters close to each other, but not touching. He must not space the letters such that one word looks like two, but rather leave a hair's breadth between each letter. If he has spaced the letters of a word such that a child unused to reading a Torah scroll would think it was two words, the scroll is unfit until corrected.[192]

CHAPTER NINE

1. One ought not to make a Torah scroll whose height is greater than its circumference, nor one whose circumference is greater than its height.[193] What should its height be? If written on *gevil:* six handbreadths, which are equivalent to the width of twenty-four thumbs.[194] If written on parchment: either less or more, so long as its height equals its circumference. So, too, it is correct to write on *gevil* less than six handbreadths high so long as the script is made smaller, or more than six handbreadths high so long as the script is made bigger, so that its height is equivalent to its circumference.[195]

2. The size of the margins should be as follows: lower margin, four thumb-widths; upper margin, three thumb-widths; and two thumb-widths between each column. One must therefore leave one thumb-width and sufficient room for stitching at the beginning and end of each section of parchment, so that when the sections are stitched together there will remain a space of two thumb-widths between each column through the entire scroll. One must also leave enough parchment at the beginning and end of the Torah scroll to attach to a staff.[196] These measurements are matters of praiseworthiness; if the scribe made them smaller or greater, he did not render the Torah unfit.[197]

3. How can one design the scroll so that its height is equal to its circumference? First, one cuts the pieces of parchment into

equally sized rectangles, the width of each of them being six hand-breadths exactly. He then rolls them very tightly, adding tightly wound pieces of parchment till the circumference of the coiled scroll be six handbreadths, which is the width of the pieces of parchment. He measures with a red thread, which he pulls around the coiled scroll.

4. The scribe then fashions a straight ruler, forty or fifty thumb-widths long. He should then divide one of the thumb-widths of the ruler in half, into thirds, and into fourths, so that he can use it to measure half a finger, a fourth of a finger, and so on. He then measures each piece of parchment with this ruler, so that he may know how many thumb-widths are in each piece of parchment, and so that he may know how many thumb-widths constitute the length of the entire coiled bundle.

5. Afterward, he takes two or three other pieces of parchment to check the size of the script. He uses them to write one column. It is known that a column should be seventeen thumb-widths long, since one leaves blank spaces of three thumb-widths above and four below. The width of the column, however, depends on the size of the script, whether it is thin or thick. So, too, the number of lines in the column depends on the script, since between each line a line must be skipped.

6. After writing as much of the test-column as is desired, the scribe measures its width with the ruler, and adds the two thumb-widths between columns to the column and can then compute how many columns will be in the coiled bundle if he uses the same script as that here tested. Once he knows how many columns there will be, he checks how much of the Torah was written in the test-column, and can then estimate, basing himself on the scroll from which he is copying, and compute if the number of columns will include the whole Torah; if it does, he should continue using this size script. But if there turn out to be too many columns, he should write more words per column so that the number of columns is di-minished, using another test-column. But if the columns are not enough for the whole Torah, he should reduce the number of words per column, so that the number of columns increases, using an-other test-column. So he should do, column after column, till the computations work out.

Figure 3. Laws Concerning Tefellin, Mezuzah, and the Torah Scroll, VIII.7.

7. Once the width of the column and the size of the script are determined, he takes the same coiled bundle and divides the pieces of parchment into incised columns according to the width of the columns which worked out. If he is left with three or four extra thumb-widths after the last column on the section of parchment, he should leave one thumb-width of it, and the space needed for sewing, and cut off the rest, without worrying that in the end he will need extra pieces of parchment to compensate for all the pieces cut off the ends of each parchment. There is no need to compute

this, since the script will keep him to the number of columns [which he originally calculated].

8. If one wishes to make the width of the scroll greater than six handbreadths or less than six, these calculations are to be used and its height will exactly equal its circumference, so long as no mistake was made in the computation.

9. The width of the thumb used in all these measurements, and in the rest of all Torah measurements, is that of an average thumb. We have carefully measured and found it to be the width of seven

average barley-corns placed next to each other tightly, this being equivalent to the length of two barley-corns placed together [end to end] not tightly. A handbreadth in every place equals four of these fingers, and a cubit, six handbreadths.

10. In the Torah scroll which I wrote, each of the columns is four thumb-widths wide, [except for] the Song at the Sea and *Give ear* (Deut. 32:1–43), which are each six thumb-widths wide; there are fifty-one lines in each column; there are two hundred twenty-six columns in the whole scroll, and its length is approximately 1,366 thumb-widths.

11. The six thumb-widths left over according to this computation were used for the blank space at the beginning of the scroll and at its end. I wrote it on ram's skin. If one wishes to write a Torah scroll using these measurements more or less—having one, two, or three columns fewer or more—one need not trouble oneself or engage in computations: its height will automatically equal its circumference.

12. One may not write fewer than three columns on a section of parchment, nor more than eight. If one has a section the size of nine columns, it should divided into pieces for four and for five columns. When does this apply? At the beginning of the scroll or in its middle. But at the end of the scroll, even if only verse remains in one column, it is made a separate column and sewn to the other sections.[198]

13. The sections may only be sewn with the ligaments of a kosher domesticated or wild animal, even from one which has died or been killed,[199] in the same way the tefillin are sewn. This is a law transmitted by Moses from Sinai. Thus, if it were not sewn with ligaments, or with non-kosher ligaments, it is unfit, until it is undone and resewn properly.[200]

14. When sewing the sections together, one does not sew all the way from top to bottom, but leaves a bit at the top and a bit at the bottom without stitches, so that the section will not tear when the Torah scroll is rolled up. Two wooden staves must be prepared, one for the beginning and one for the end; the leather left over at the beginning and at the end is sewn to the staves with ligaments, so that the Torah scroll can be rolled on them. Space must be left between the staff and the writing in the adjacent column.[201]

15. If a section of a Torah scroll was torn to the depth of two lines, it may be sewn up; to the depth of three lines, it may not be sewn up. When does this apply? In the case of a used Torah scroll, when the gallnut treatment is not visible; but if the *gevil* has clearly been treated with gallnut, the tear may be sewn, even if it extends to the third line. Similarly, a tear between columns or between words may be sewn up. All tears may only be sewn with the same kind of ligaments used to stitch together the sections of parchment. With respect to all tears, one must take care that no letter be excised or altered.[202]

CHAPTER TEN

1. We thus find twenty matters which individually render a Torah scroll unfit; if one of them is found, the scroll becomes like the Pentateuchs from which children are taught. It does not have the sanctity of a Torah scroll, and it is not read from publicly. These are

1. If it is written on the skin of a non-kosher animal
2. If it is written on kosher but unprocessed skin
3. If the skin is not processed specifically for a Torah scroll
4. If it is written on an inappropriate side: in the case of *gevil,* on the flesh side; in the case of parchment, on the hair side
5. If it is written partly on *gevil* and partly on parchment
6. If it is written on *dukhsustus*
7. If it is written without incised lines
8. If it is written with impermanent black ink[203]
9. If it is written in other languages
10. If it is written by a Gentile or other unfit person
11. If the scribe writes God's name without correct intention
12. If even one letter is missing
13. If even one extra letter is added
14. If one letter touches another
15. If the shape of a letter is damaged such that it cannot be read at all, or looks like another letter, whether during the original writing, or due to a hole, tear, or smudge
16. If two letters are written too far apart or too close together,

such that one word appears to be two words, or two words appear to be one word

17. If the form of the paragraphs has been changed

18. If the form of the poetic passages has been changed

19. If non-poetic passages are written like poetry

20. If the sections of parchment are not sewn together with kosher ligaments

All other matters are questions of praiseworthiness; they do not impede.[204]

2. A fit Torah scroll is to be treated with extreme sanctity and great respect. It is forbidden to sell a Torah scroll, even if one has nothing to eat, and even if one owns many scrolls, and even in order to replace an old one with a new one. It is never permissible to sell a Torah scroll except for two things: to study Torah with the money or to wed a woman with it. This on condition that one has nothing else to sell.[205]

3. A worn-out or unfit Torah scroll is to be placed in an earthenware pot and buried with a scholar; this is its form of being placed in a *genizah*. Worn out coverings of Torah scrolls are used for shrouds for an unclaimed corpse;[206] this is their form of being placed in a *genizah*.[207]

4. All the following are sacred implements and may not be thrown out—they are to be placed in a *genizah* if they break or wear out: a case prepared for a Torah scroll which has actually been used for that purpose; kerchiefs;[208] the cabinet or tower in which the Torah scroll is placed, even if it is in a case; and a stand prepared for supporting a Torah scroll which has actually been used for that purpose. But the platforms on which those who hold Torah scrolls stand, and the tablets used to teach children, have no holiness. Silver and golden pomegranates, and the like, made to decorate Torah scrolls are sacred implements and may not be made profane, unless they were sold in order to use the money thus realized to purchase a Torah scroll or a Pentateuch.[209]

5. It is permissible to place one Torah scroll on another, and of course it is permissible to place one on a Pentateuch. One may place a Pentateuch on the Prophetic writings and the Hagiographa, but one may not place the prophetic writings and the Hagiographa on

a Pentateuch, nor may one place a Pentateuch on a Torah scroll. None of the sacred writings — not even laws and aggadot — may be thrown out. One may not enter a privy with an amulet containing scriptural passages unless it has been covered with leather.[210]

6. One may not enter a bathhouse, a privy, or a cemetery while holding a Torah scroll in his arms, even if it is wrapped in a kerchief and in its case. One may not read from it unless one is at least four cubits away from a grave, a corpse, or a privy. One may not hold a Torah scroll while naked. One may not sit on a bench that has a Torah scroll on it.[211]

7. One may not engage in marital relations in a building containing a Torah scroll until it is removed or placed in a container within a container, the latter of which was not prepared especially for it. But if it was prepared especially for it, even ten such containers, one within the other, are considered as one. If one has no other building in which to place it, one may erect a barrier ten handbreadths high. But if there is another available building, one may not engage in relations until it is removed.[212]

8. Those ritually impure, even menstruants and Gentiles, may hold a Torah scroll and read from it, since words of Torah cannot become ritually impure. This, on condition that their hands are not soiled or muddy. If they are, they must wash their hands and then they may touch it.[213]

9. Anyone who sees a Torah scroll being carried must stand in its presence. Everyone should remain standing till the person carrying it reaches his destination, or until it is no longer visible to them; then they may sit.[214]

10. It is praiseworthy to set aside a special place for a Torah scroll, to respect that place, and make it very beautiful. The words of the tablets of the covenant are in every Torah scroll.[215] One may not spit in the presence of a Torah scroll, or uncover his nakedness, or stretch out his legs,[216] or carry it on his head like a burden. One may not turn his back on a Torah scroll unless it is ten handbreadths higher than he.[217]

11. If one has gone from place to place with a Torah Scroll, he may not place it in a sack on the back of an ass and ride on the ass. But if he has done so for fear of robbers, it is permitted. But if there is no cause for fear, he holds it near his breast opposite his

heart and rides on the beast. Anyone who sits in the presence of a
Torah scroll must comport himself gravely, in awe and fear, since
the Torah is the trustworthy witness before all the inhabitants of
the world, as it says, *Take this book of Teaching and place it beside the
Ark of the Covenant of the Lord your God, and let it remain there as a
witness against you* (Deut. 31:26). One must respect the Torah to the
utmost of one's capacity. The early Sages said:[218] anyone who pro-
fanes the Torah will be profaned by others, while one who respects
the Torah will be respected by others.[219]

Blessed be the Merciful One Who assists.

TREATISE IV

Laws Concerning Fringes
comprise one positive commandment, to affix fringes
to the corners of one's garment. The clarification of
this commandment is found in these chapters:

CHAPTER ONE

1. A tassel placed on the corner of an article of clothing and made from the same material as the clothing is called a fringe [*ẓiẓit*] since it is similar to the hair [*ẓiẓit*] of the head, as it says, *He stretched out the form of a hand, and took me by the hair [ẓiẓit] of my head* (Ez. 8:3). This tassel is also called "white" since we are not commanded to dye it. The Torah sets no number for the threads of the tassel.[1]

2. One takes a woolen thread dyed the color of the heavens and winds it around the tassel; this thread is what is called "azure." The Torah sets no number for the times this thread is wound.[2]

3. This commandment contains two imperatives: that one make a tassel hanging from the corner and that an azure thread be wound around it, as it says, *Speak to the Israelite people and instruct them to make for themselves fringes on the corners of their garments throughout the ages; let them attach a cord of blue to the fringe at each corner* (Num. 15:38).

4. Absence of the "azure" does not invalidate the "white," and absence of the "white" does not invalidate the "azure." How? If one lacks azure, one makes white fringes only. So also, if one has made fringes of white and azure and the white has broken off near the corner[3] leaving only the azure, it is fit.[4]

5. Even though absence of one does not invalidate the other, they are not two commandments, but one positive commandment. Thus one who wears a tallit having white or azure or both together has fulfilled one positive commandment. The earlier sages said, *"That shall be your fringe* (Num. 15:39)—this teaches that the two

are one commandment."[5] The four fringes invalidate each other, since the four are one commandment.[6]

6. How are the fringes made? One starts at the corner[7] of the tallit, which is where the weave ends, going no more than three fingerbreadths and no less than the length of the first joint of the thumb above it, and inserts there four threads, folding them in the middle. There will thus be eight threads hanging and dangling from the corner. These eight threads must be at least four finger-breadths long. But if they are longer than that—even a cubit or two—they are fit. A fingerbreadth is the width of the thumb. One of the eight threads is to be an azure thread and the other seven white.[8]

7. One winds one of the white threads around the others once near the article of clothing and leaves it. One then takes an azure thread and winds it twice next to the winding of the white thread and ties it. These three coils are called a link. Leaving a little distance, one then makes a second link, using only the azure thread. Leaving a little distance, one then makes a third link, and so forth to the last link, which is wound with two coils of azure and a last of white. Since one begins with white, one ends with it, as one is permitted to add to something's holiness, but not to detract from it. Why does one begin with white? So that the part closest to the corner be of the same kind. In this fashion each of the four corners is done.[9]

8. How many links does one make on each corner? No fewer than seven and no more than thirteen. This is the finest way to fulfill the commandment. But if one has wound only one link, it is fit. If one has wound the azure on most of the fringe, it is fit. Fringes made with azure are considered most beautiful if all the links are in the first third of the dangling threads and two thirds are a tassel. They must be separated so that they are like the fringed hair of the head.[10]

9. In order to make fringes of white without azure, one takes one of the eight threads and winds it around the others for one-third of their length, leaving two-thirds as a tassel. In this winding, it is permissible to make links as one does while winding with azure; this is our custom. If one wishes to wind without links, one may. In general, one should manage things such that the wound part is one-

third of the length, and the tassel two-thirds. There are those who are not careful concerning this with respect to fringes made only of white. If one has wound the white around most of the length of the threads, or has only wound one link, it is fit.

10. Both the white and azure threads may be entwined; even if one has entwined as many as eight threads to make a single strand, it is still considered a single thread.

11. Threads for fringes, whether white or azure, must be spun specifically for fringes. One may not make them from the wool caught in thorns where the sheep lie down, or from tufts pulled off the animal, or from the remains of the woof which the weaver leaves at the end of the cloth; rather, they must be made from wool shorn from the sheep or from linen. One may not make them from stolen wool, or from an apostate city,[11] or from an animal set aside for use in the Temple. If this were done, the fringes would be unfit. If an animal has been worshiped, its wool is unfit for fringes. But if planted flax has been bowed down to, linen made from it is fit since it has been changed.[12]

12. Fringes made by a Gentile are unfit, as it says, *Speak to the Israelite people and instruct them to make for themselves fringes* (Num. 15:38). But if a Jew has made them without correct intention, they are fit. But fringes made from other already existing fringes are unfit.[13]

13. How? If one has sewn a corner of cloth having fringes onto another article of clothing, even if the corner is a square cubit, it is unfit, as it says, *to make for themselves fringes* (Num. 15:38), not from what was already made since it is as if it had come into being by itself.[14] But it is permissible to untie fringes — whether white or azure — from one article of clothing and hang them from another.[15]

14. If one hung threads between two corners from one to the other, tied each in the proper way, and afterward cut them in the middle such that they were separated, it is unfit. This is because while they were being tied they were unfit since the two corners were connected one to the other by the threads between them. When they were cut and thus became two separate sets of fringes, they were in effect made from other already existing fringes.[16]

15. If, having attached fringes on top of fringes, one intends to remove the first set, he may untie it or cut it, and the fringes will

be fit. But if he intends to add, even if he cuts one of the two, it is unfit, since when he makes the addition he renders the whole unfit. When he unties or cuts the additional set what remains will turn out to be made from an already existing set, which when it was first made was unfit.[17]

16. If one attaches fringes to a three-cornered garment and then makes it into a four-cornered garment and then attaches a fourth set, it is all unfit, because of the stipulation *You shall make* (Deut. 22:12)—not from what is already made.[18]

17. One should not take a tallit, fold it in half and attach fringes to the resulting four corners, unless it is sewn up along the entire length of at least one side.[19]

18. If a corner with fringes is detached [from the rest of the garment at least three fingerbreadths from the edge], it may be sewn back in its place; if this occurs within three fingerbreadths of the edge, it may not. If the corner[20] of the article of clothing between the fringe threads and the end of the weave has been diminished, as long as something of the weave remains, it is fit. So, too, if the fringe threads have been diminished, even if only enough remains to tie a loop, it is fit. But if even one thread were parted at the point of attachment, it would be unfit.[21]

CHAPTER TWO

1. Wherever the Torah mentions azure, it refers to wool dyed bluish;[22] this is the color of the clear sky. Fringes dyed azure must be prepared according to the accepted process, such that its beauty is permanent and does not fade. Anything not dyed according to that process is unfit for fringes, even if it is the color of the sky, such as things dyed with woad[23] or other darkening agents; such are unfit for fringes. The wool of the offspring of a ram and a she-goat is unfit for fringes.[24]

2. How is the azure of the fringes prepared? Wool is soaked in lime and then laundered until it is clean. It is then boiled in aloe or similar substances, as dyers customarily do so that it absorbs the color. The blood of the ḥilazon, a fish which is found in the Mediterranean and which is the color of the sea, and whose blood is black as ink, is placed in a barrel with powdered dyes like alkaline

salt[25] and is boiled, as is customarily done by dyers. The wool is then placed in the mixture until it becomes the color of the sky. This is the azure of the fringes.

3. Fringes must be dyed azure for the sake of fulfilling the commandment; if they are not so dyed, they are unfit. If one dyes a small amount of wool in a barrel of dye in order to check if it is satisfactory or not,[26] the entire barrel is rendered unfit. How should one act? One should take dye from the barrel in a small vessel and place a small amount of wool in it to check it. One burns the wool that was checked, since it was dyed only for the purpose of checking it, and pours out the dye in the vessel, since it was used for checking and thus rendered unfit. One then dyes the fringes azure with the rest of the dye, which was not harmed.[27]

4. One may only purchase azure from an expert since one must be sure that it has been dyed for the purpose of fulfilling the commandment. But even if purchased from an expert, if it is checked and found to have been dyed with any impermanent darkening agent other than azure dye, it is unfit.[28]

5. How is the azure wool checked to determine if it is dyed properly or not? One takes a mixture of straw, the secretion of a snail, and urine that has soured for forty days and soaks the azure in the mixture for a twenty-four hour period. If it retains its color without fading, it is fit. But if it fades, one takes barley-dough which has been left to become moldy in order to make fish-brine and places the faded azure in it. The dough is then baked in an oven; the azure is removed from the bread and examined. If it has further faded, it is unfit; but if its color deepened and darkened, it is fit.[29]

6. One may simply purchase azure from a reputable workshop without checking it since the workshop retains its presumption of fitness[30] until there is reason to suspect it. If one leaves azure with a Gentile, it is unfit, since the Gentile is to be suspected of switching it. But if it is in a double-sealed container, such that one seal is within the other, it is fit; if there is only one seal, it is unfit.[31]

7. If one finds azure in the marketplace, it is unfit even if the strands are cut, but if they are twisted together, it is fit. If one purchases a tallit with fringes in the marketplace from a Jew, it is presumed to be fit; if from a Gentile merchant, it is fit;[32] if from a Gentile who is not a merchant, it is unfit.[33]

8. One makes white fringes for a red or green tallit, or made from any other color, such that the fringes are the same color as the tallit: if green, green, if red, red. But if the tallit is all azure in color, one makes its white fringes from any color but black, since it looks like azure, and winds one thread of azure around it, as is done with other fringes which are not colored.[34]

9. The punishment of one who does not affix fringes of white is greater than that of one who does not affix a fringe of azure, since the white is easily found, while azure is not easily found in every place or at any time because of the need for a special dye, as we have specified.[35]

CHAPTER THREE

1. The Torah requires one to attach fringes only to a woolen or linen garment which has four or more corners and is big enough to cover the head and most of the body of a child who is old enough to walk about the marketplace alone.[36]

2. But a tallit of the right size and having four or more corners made of other materials, such as silk or cotton, or camels' wool or rabbit wool or goat hair, and the like, requires fringes only on the authority of the Sages[37] so that we respect the commandment of fringes. This is so since when the Torah mentions an article of clothing simply, it means one made of wool or linen.[38]

3. *You shall make tassels on the four corners of the garment with which you cover yourself* (Deut. 22:12)—a garment with four corners, not one with three. In that case, why does not "four" exclude five? We learn from *with which you cover yourself* even five or more corners.[39] Why do I obligate a garment of five corners, but not one of three, seeing that both do not have four corners? Because five includes four. Thus if one affixes fringes to a garment having five or six corners, one attaches them only to the four corners of those five or six most distant from each other, as it says, *on the four corners of the garment*.[40]

4. A garment made of cloth but having leather corners is required to have fringes, while a leather garment with cloth corners is exempt, since the main part of the garment is determinative. A

garment owned in partnership by two people is required to have fringes, since it says, *Speak to the Israelite people and instruct them to make for themselves fringes on the corners of their garments* (Num. 15:38). Its saying *the garment* (Deut. 22:12) is only meant to exclude a borrowed one,[41] since a borrowed garment is exempt from fringes for thirty days, and after thirty days they are required.[42]

5. One makes the white fringes of a woolen garment from woolen threads, and one makes the white fringes of a linen garment from linen threads; in each case, from the same kind. So also, with other kinds of articles of clothing: the white fringes are made each from the same kind, such as silken threads for a silken garment and goats' hair threads for a goats' hair garment. If one wishes to make white fringes of wool or linen for a garment made of other kinds of cloth, one may, since wool and linen fringes satisfy the requirement whether on a garment of their own kind or not. Other kinds of thread, however, satisfy the requirement with their own kind, but not with other kinds.[43]

6. May one use threads of wool for a linen garment or linen threads for a woolen garment?[44] Even though we are dealing here with white fringes alone, without azure, according to the law it should be permissible, since *sha'atnez* is permitted with respect to fringes, for the azure threads are made of wool and we still affix them to linen garments. In that case, why do we not actually do this? Since it is possible to make white fringes from the same kind of cloth, and in every case where there is a commandment and a prohibition [which might conflict] if they both can be fulfilled, all the better, but if not, then the commandment overrules the prohibition. But in this case, it is possible to fulfill them both.[45]

7. Azure fringes are not affixed to a linen garment; rather, one only makes white fringes of linen for it. This is not because the obligation of fringes is overruled by the prohibition of *sha'atnez;* it is a rabbinic decree lest one cover oneself with the garment at night, when there is no obligation of fringes. In such a case, one would be violating a prohibition without fulfilling a conflicting commandment since the obligation of fringes obtains only during the day, not at night, as it says, *That shall be your fringe; look at it and recall all the commandments of the Lord* (Num. 15:39) — the command-

ment obtains during the time when things may be seen. A blind man is obligated by the commandment of fringes: even though he does not see, others see him.[46]

8. It is permissible to wear fringes at night, whether during the week or on the Sabbath, even though it is not their time, on condition that one makes no blessing over them. From what time in the morning may one make the blessing over the fringes? From the time one can distinguish the azure in them from the white. What is the blessing? "Blessed are You, Lord our God, Who has sanctified us with His commandments and commanded us to wrap ourselves with fringes." Every time one wraps oneself with them during the day, one makes the blessing before doing so. One does not make a blessing over the fringes while making them, since the point of the commandment is to wrap oneself with them.[47]

9. One may enter a privy or a bathhouse while wearing fringes. Torn white or azure threads may be thrown in the garbage, since the commandment bestows no sanctity on the object. One may not sell a tallit with fringes on it to a Gentile unless one unties the fringes first; not because the object has any sanctity, but lest the Gentile wrap himself in it, and accompany a Jew who will think that he is Jewish also, and thus the Gentile will be enabled to kill the Jew.[48]

10. The Torah exempts women, slaves, and minors from the obligation of fringes. From the Sages we learn that a minor capable of wrapping himself is obligated to wear fringes in order to educate him to fulfill the commandments.[49] Women and slaves who wish to wrap themselves with fringes do so without a blessing. So, also, concerning all other positive commandments from which women are exempt: if they wish to fulfill them without a blessing, one does not protest. Persons of doubtful sex and androgynes are obligated to fulfill all the [positive] commandments because of their doubtful status; therefore, they do not make a blessing, but fulfill the commandments without blessings.[50]

11. When is one obligated to fulfill the commandment of fringes? Anyone obligated by this commandment who covers himself with a garment fit for fringes must first affix fringes to it, and only then cover himself with it. If he has covered himself with it without fringes, he has nullified a positive commandment. Articles of cloth-

ing fit for fringes, however, when they are not being worn but are folded and put away, are exempt from fringes, for the obligation is not on the tallit but on the individual who wears it.[51]

12. Even though one is not obligated to purchase a tallit and wrap himself in it, so that he has to affix fringes to it, it is not fitting for a person who is pious to exempt himself from this commandment; rather, such a one should always endeavor to be wrapped in a garment which requires fringes so that he fulfills this commandment. One should be particularly punctilious about this during prayer. It is greatly reprehensible for a scholar to pray while not so wrapped.[52]

13. Let one always take care concerning the commandment of fringes, since Scripture weighed it against all the other commandments and made them all dependent on it, as it says, *That shall be your fringe; look at it and recall all the commandments of the Lord and observe them, [so that you do not follow your heart and eyes in your lustful urge]* (Num. 15:39).[53]

Blessed be the Merciful One Who assists.

TREATISE V

Laws Concerning Blessings
comprise one positive commandment, to bless the
name of the Holy One, blessed be He, after eating.
The clarification of this commandment will be
found in these chapters:

CHAPTER ONE

1. It is a positive commandment from the Torah to make a blessing after eating food, as it says, *When you have eaten and been satiated, give thanks to the Lord your God* (Deut. 8:10). One is only obligated from the Torah if one is satiated, as it says, *been satiated, [and then] give thanks.* But from the Sages [1] we learn that even if one only ate an olive's worth, one must make a blessing after it. [2]

2. The Sages instituted the obligation to make a blessing before eating any food, and only then may one enjoy it. So also, if one smells a pleasant fragrance, one must first make a blessing and then enjoy it. Even if one intended to eat or drink only a small amount, one must first make a blessing and only then may one enjoy it. Anyone who enjoys such things without a blessing is remiss. The Sages also instituted the obligation to make a blessing after eating or drinking anything, provided that one has drunk at least or eaten at least an olive's worth. But if one simply tastes something, [3] there is no requirement to make a blessing before it or after it, unless one has [drunk] a quarter-*hin.* [4]

3. As blessings are to be made over things enjoyed, so also must one make a blessing before the performance of any commandment. The Sages ordained many blessings of praise, thanksgiving, and petition so that one will remember the Creator always, even if one has had no enjoyment or fulfilled any commandment. [5]

4. There are thus three types of blessings: blessings of enjoyment, blessings over the commandments, and blessings of thanks by way

of praise, thanksgiving, and petition so as to remember the Creator always and hold God in awe.

5. Ezra and his court established the text of all the blessings. It is not fitting to change any of them, whether by way of addition or subtraction. Anyone who changes the form of the blessings as established by the Sages errs. A blessing, which does not include God's name and sovereignty,[6] is no blessing, unless it appears immediately next to one which includes them.[7]

6. All the blessings may be recited in any language, so long as one expresses the meaning established by the Sages. If one has changed the form of a blessing, but mentioned God's name and sovereignty and the established meaning of the blessing, one has fulfilled the obligation, even if it has been recited in a profane language.[8]

7. With respect to all the blessings, one must actually hear what he says, but if one has not said them aloud, he has still fulfilled the obligation, whether he has moved his lips or only made the blessing in his thoughts.[9]

8. One may not allow any extraneous concern to come between any of the blessings and the thing over which the blessing has been made. If one has interrupted in that fashion, one must repeat the blessing. But if the interruption has involved matters connected to the thing over which the blessing has been made, there is no need to repeat the blessing. How? If, for example, one has made the blessing over a loaf of bread and then said, "Bring salt," or "Bring food," or "Give so and so food," or "Feed the animal," and so on, there is no need to make the blessing again. And so with anything similar to this.[10]

9. A ritually impure person may make any of the blessings, whether the impurity is one from which one arises that same day or not.[11] But it is forbidden to make a blessing while naked; one must first cover one's exposed private parts. When does this apply? In the case of a man; but a naked woman who is sitting with her private parts against the ground may make a blessing.[12]

10. With respect to all of the blessings, one may make a blessing for others who have not fulfilled their obligation in order to fulfill it for them, even if one has already fulfilled the obligation for himself. This does not obtain with respect to the blessings over things enjoyed which are not commanded, unless one has also enjoyed it

himself with the others. But with respect to blessings over things enjoyed which are matters commanded, such as eating matzah on Passover eve, and the qiddush of the day,[13] one may make the blessing for others who may then eat and drink, even if one does not eat or drink with them.[14]

11. If a person has heard any one of the blessings from the beginning to the end and intended to fulfill his obligation thereby, he has fulfilled the obligation, even if he has not answered, "Amen." If one answers, "Amen," to a blessing, it is as if he has made the blessing himself, on condition that the one making the blessing is obligated to make that same blessing. If the person making the blessing is only obligated on rabbinic authority, while the person answering has an obligation from the Torah, the latter will not have fulfilled his obligation unless he has recited it himself, or heard it from someone having an obligation from the Torah also.[15]

12. If several people gather together to eat bread or drink wine and one makes the blessing while the others answer, "Amen," it is permissible for them to eat and drink. But if they have not planned to eat together, each one coming alone, even if they eat from the same loaf, each must make a blessing. When does this apply? With respect to bread and wine only. But with all other food and drink planning to dine together[16] is not required; rather, if one has made the blessing and the rest have answered, they may then eat and drink, even though they did not plan to dine together.[17]

13. If one hears a Jew make any of the blessings, even if he has not heard it through from beginning to end, and even if he is not obligated to make that blessing, he must answer, "Amen." But if the person making the blessing is a Gentile, or a sectarian, or a Cuthean,[18] or a child being taught, or an adult who has changed the accepted wording of the blessing, one does not respond, "Amen."[19]

14. One should not answer, "Amen," before the person making the blessing finishes,[20] or divide the word into two parts,[21] or abbreviate it,[22] or extend it; rather, it should be said in a normal fashion. Nor should it be said in a voice louder than that in which the blessing has been made. One who is obligated to make a blessing but has not heard it should not answer, "Amen," with the rest.[23]

15. Anyone who makes an unnecessary blessing takes the name of the Lord in vain, just as one who swears falsely, and it is forbid-

den to answer, "Amen." But children are taught the blessings properly. Even though their blessings are in vain, it is permissible, since it is done by way of education. But one does not answer, "Amen," to them. One who has answered, "Amen," to them has not fulfilled his obligation.[24]

16. Answering, "Amen," after one's own blessing is blameworthy. But one who so answers after the last of a series of blessings following an action[25] is praiseworthy, such as after "Who builds Jerusalem" in the grace after meals, or after the last blessing of the recitation of the Shema in the evening. So, after any blessing which is the last of a series of blessings following an action, one answers, "Amen," to his own blessing.[26]

17. Why does one answer, "Amen," after "Who Builds Jerusalem" since the blessing "Who is good and does good" comes after it? Because this blessing was established during the time of the Sages of the Mishnah as a sort of addition, and the last of the essential blessings on food is "Who builds Jerusalem." Why does one not answer, "Amen," after "eternal love"?[27] Because it is the last of a series of blessings which precede an action. So with all similar blessings that are made before something is done, such as the blessings made before the reading of the Scroll of Esther and the lighting of the Hannukah candle—so that one does not interrupt between the recitation of a blessing and the performance of the act over which the blessing has been made.[28]

18. Why does one not answer [himself] after blessings made over fruit and the like? Because such are single blessings and one answers, "Amen," after one's own blessing only in the case of a blessing preceded by other blessings in a series, such as the blessing of a King or a High Priest and so on. By answering, "Amen," to one's own blessing, one announces that he has finished his series of blessings.

19. If one eats something forbidden, whether purposefully or inadvertently, he makes no blessing before it or after it. How? If one eats untithed produce, even if it needs to be tithed only according to rabbinic law,[29] or eats from the first tithe from which the complete heave offering has not been taken,[30] or eats from second tithe[31] or from sanctified foods which have not been properly redeemed, one makes no blessing. There is no need to say that this obtains in a

case where one eats meat from an animal which died on its own, or has not been slaughtered properly, or drinks wine used in an idolatrous service, and similar things.[32]

20. If one eats produce which may or may not have been tithed—which is permissible only to the poor[33]—or eats from the first tithe from which the heave offering has been taken in a case where the heave offering has not been properly calculated because the tithe was taken while the produce was still in sheaves,[34] or eats from the second tithe or from sanctified foods which have been redeemed, without an additional fifth having been added to it;[35] in all such cases one makes a blessing before and after eating.[36]

CHAPTER TWO

1. This is the order of the [blessings in the] grace after meals: the first is the blessing "Who feeds," the second is the blessing over the land, the third is "Who builds Jerusalem," and the fourth is "Who is good and beneficent." Moses instituted the first blessing; Joshua, the second; Solomon and David, his son, the third; while the Sages of the Mishnah instituted the fourth.[37]

2. Laborers working at their craft in the home of their employer do not make a blessing before eating their bread, and make only two blessings after their meal, so that the work of the employer will not be halted: one makes the first blessing as it was instituted, and opens the second with the blessing over the land, includes within it "Who builds Jerusalem," and concludes with the blessing over the land. If their meal constitutes their entire payment, or if they sup with the employer, then they make all four blessings in their proper form like anyone else.[38]

3. One must express gratitude at the beginning and at the end of the blessing over the land, concluding it with [thanks] "for the land and for sustenance." Anyone who does not make reference to a "desirable, good, and broad land" in the blessing over the land has not fulfilled his obligation. One must mention the covenant and the Torah in the blessing, with the reference to the covenant preceding the reference to the Torah, since the covenant referred to in the blessing over the land is the covenant of circumcision, concerning which thirteen covenants were entered into,[39] while for

the entire Torah only three covenants were entered into, as it says, *These are the terms of the covenant which the Lord commanded Moses to conclude with the Israelites in the land of Moab, in addition to the covenant which He had made with them at Horeb* (Deut. 28:69), and *You stand this day, all of you, before the Lord your God—your tribal heads, your elders and your officials, all the men of Israel, your children, your wives, even the stranger within your camp, from woodchopper to water drawer—to enter into the covenant of the Lord your God, which the Lord your God is concluding with you this day, with its sanctions* (Deut. 29:9–11).[40]

4. One opens the third blessing with "Have mercy, Lord our God, on Israel Your people and on Jerusalem Your City," or with "Comfort us, Lord our God, in Jerusalem Your city," and concludes it with "Who builds Jerusalem" or with "Who comforts His People through the building of Jerusalem." That is why this blessing is called "consolation." Anyone who fails to mention the sovereignty of the House of David in this blessing has not fulfilled his obligation, because that is the substance of the blessing, since there can be no complete consolation without the reinstitution of Davidic monarchy.[41]

5. On Sabbaths and holidays one opens [the third blessing] with consolation, concludes it with consolation, and makes reference to the sanctity of the day in the middle. How? One opens with "Comfort us, Lord our God, in Zion Your city," or with "Have mercy, Lord our God, on Israel Your people and on Jerusalem Your City," and ends with "Who comforts His People through the building of Jerusalem" or with "Who builds Jerusalem"; on the Sabbath one says between them: "God, God of our Fathers, may it be Your Will to strengthen us in Your commandments and in the commandment of this seventh day; may we have respite in it and rest in it as Your will commanded; and may there be no trouble or anguish on our day of rest." On holidays one says, "Our God and God of our fathers . . . may remembrance of us . . . ascend and come." So also, on the day of the new moon and on the intermediate days of festivals, one adds "ascend and come" in the middle of the third blessing.[42]

6. On Hannukah and Purim one adds "For the miracles" in the middle of the blessing over the land as one adds it in the *'amidah*. If

a holiday or the day of the new moon falls on a Sabbath, one recites "may it be Your Will to strengthen us" first, and after it "ascend and come." So also, if *Rosh Hodesh* Tevet[43] falls on the Sabbath, one recites "For the miracles" in the blessing on the land and "may it be Your Will to strengthen us" and "ascend and come" in the consolation.[44]

7. God's sovereignty must be mentioned three times in the fourth blessing. When eating in someone else's home, a guest must add a blessing for the host. How does the guest bless the host? He says, "May it be [God's] will that our host suffer no shame in this world and no humiliation in the world to come." One may add to the blessing for the host and make it longer.[45]

8. In the home of a mourner one adds the following to the fourth blessing: "the living, good, and beneficent King, God of truth, true Judge, Who judges righteously, Who rules His world, doing in it as He wills; we are His servants and His nation, and in all we are obligated to thank Him and bless Him." He may plead for mercy for the mourner in order to comfort him as he sees fit, and concludes with "may the Merciful One . . ."[46]

9. In the home of a bridegroom, one adds the blessing over bridegrooms after these four blessings at every meal eaten there. Slaves and minors do not make this blessing. For how long is this blessing added? In the case of a widower who has married a widow, the blessing is recited on the first day only. But if an unmarried man has married a widow, or if a widower has married a virgin, the blessing is made for the whole week of celebration.[47]

10. The blessing added in the home of the bridegroom is the last of the seven wedding blessings. When does this apply? When those who eat the meal are present at the wedding and hear the blessings. But if among those eating are any who did not hear the wedding blessings at the time of the wedding, then the seven blessings are made for them after the grace after meals in the way that they are made at the time of the wedding, on condition that there be at least ten persons present, including the bridegroom.[48]

11. If one has forgotten to mention the special sanctity of the day in the grace after meals on a Sabbath or holiday [in its proper place], but has remembered it before beginning the fourth blessing, then on the Sabbath one says, "Blessed be He Who bequeathed Sab-

bath rest upon His nation Israel, as a sign, and as a sacred covenant. Blessed are You, Lord Who sanctifies the Sabbath."[49]

12. On a holiday, one says, "Blessed is He who gave holidays to His nation Israel, for joy and happiness. Blessed are You, Lord Who sanctifies Israel and the seasons," then begins the fourth blessing and finishes the grace after meals. But if one has remembered after having begun the fourth blessing, one interrupts himself and goes back to the beginning of the blessing "Who feeds."[50]

13. If, on *Rosh Hodesh,* one has forgotten to say "ascend and come," but remembers before beginning the fourth blessing, one says, "Blessed be He Who gave *Rosh Hodeshes* to His nation Israel as a remembrance," does not conclude the blessing,[51] begins the fourth blessing, and finishes the grace after meals. But if one remembers after having begun the fourth blessing, one finishes it without going back. So also, on the intermediate days of the festivals, on Hannukah, and on Purim, if one has forgotten to mention the substance of the day in the grace after meals, one does not go back.[52]

14. If one who has eaten and forgotten to say the grace after meals remembers before the food is digested, he must make the blessing. If he cannot remember if he has made the blessings or not, he must do so, on condition that the food has not yet been digested.[53]

CHAPTER THREE

1. There are five types of grain: wheat, six-rowed barley, rice wheat, two-rowed barley, and spelt.[54] Rice wheat is a type of wheat, while two-rowed barley and spelt are types of barley. When these five types are still in the ear, they are called "produce" in every place. After threshing and winnowing they are called "grain." When any one of them is ground, kneaded [with water] and baked, it is called "bread." Bread made from any one of them is simply called "bread" in every place.[55]

2. One who eats bread is required to make the following blessing beforehand: "Blessed are You, Lord our God, King of the Universe, Who brings forth bread from the earth." If one eats grain boiled in its natural state,[56] one makes the blessing ". . . Who creates the fruit

of the earth"[57] before eating it, and "Who creates many living entities . . ." afterward.[58] If one eats flour, one makes the blessing "that
all" before it and "Who creates many living entities . . ." afterward.[59]

3. If one takes flour made of one of the five types of grain, roasts
it, and mixes it with water or other liquids, if it is thick enough to
eat and chew, then before eating it one makes the blessing "Who
creates diverse kinds of food"; but if it is so soft that it can be drunk,
then one makes the "that all" before it and "Who creates many
living entities . . ." afterward.[60]

4. If one takes flour made of one of the five types of grain, and
boils it in a pot, whether by itself or mixed with other things, such
as dumplings and the like; and, so also, if one takes grain which has
been broken in two or pounded and then boiled in a pot, such as
groats or grits of fresh grain and the like—all this is known as food
prepared in a pot[61]—and, so also, any dish in which any of the five
species of grain have been mixed, whether as flour or bread, before
any of these one makes the blessing "Who creates diverse kinds of
food."[62]

5. When does this apply? When that type of grain constitutes
the main part of the dish for one, and is not secondary to it. But if
one of the five types of grain mixed in the dish are secondary, then
one makes the blessing over the important part, and through that
exempts oneself from the need to make a blessing over the less important part. This is the general rule concerning blessings: in any
case of more and less important foods, one makes a blessing over
the important food, and through it exempts oneself from the obligation to make a blessing over the less important food; this obtains
both when the two are mixed together and when they are not.[63]

6. How might the less important part be mixed? If one has
cooked turnips or cabbage and thickened the dish with flour made
from one of the five types of grain, then one does not make the
blessing "Who creates diverse kinds of food," in that the cabbage is
the important ingredient and the flour secondary to it, since anything added to a dish to make it thicker, or to give it aroma, or to
color it, is secondary to it. But something added in order to determine the flavor of the mixture is considered the important ingredient. Therefore, when one makes different kinds of candies out of

honeys of different types, to which are added grain starch as a thickener, one does not make the blessing "Who creates diverse kinds of food," since the honey is the important part of the dish.[64]

7. How might the less important part not be mixed? One who needs to eat salted fish, and eats bread with it so that the salt does not damage his throat and tongue, makes a blessing on the salty food and thus exempts himself from the need to make a blessing on the bread, since the bread is secondary. And so in all similar cases.[65]

8. If bread has been crumbled and cooked in a pot or kneaded in soup, if there is an olive's worth of crumbs, or if they are recognizably bread, their shape not having been changed, one makes the blessing "Who brings forth" before eating it. But if there is not an olive's worth, or if the bread has lost its shape during the cooking,[66] one makes the blessing "Who creates diverse kinds of food" before eating it.[67]

9. Before eating dough baked in the ground as the desert Arabs do, one makes the blessing "Who creates diverse kinds of food" since it does not have the shape of bread. But if one has made it the central part of one's meal, one makes the blessing "Who brings forth bread." So also, dough kneaded with honey, or with oil, or with milk, or which has been mixed with spices before being baked, this is what is called dessert bread, and even though it is bread, one makes the blessing "Who creates diverse kinds of food" before eating it. But if one has made it the central part of one's meal, one makes the blessing "Who brings forth."[68]

10. One makes the blessing "Who creates diverse kinds of food" before and "Who creates many living entities . . ." after eating cooked rice or rice bread, on condition that it is only rice, and not mixed with anything else. But before eating bread made of millet or other species of pulse, one makes the blessing "that all" and "Who creates many living entities . . ." after it.[69]

11. In any case in which one makes the blessing "Who brings forth bread" before eating, one recites the complete grace after meals consisting of four blessings afterward. In any case in which one makes the blessing "Who creates diverse kinds of food" before eating, except in the case of rice, one recites after it the one blessing which summarizes three.[70]

12. When does this apply? When one eats an olive's worth or

more. But if one eats less than an olive's worth, whether of bread or
of other foods, and if one drinks less than a quarter-*hin,* whether
of wine or other liquids, one makes the blessing appropriate to the
type of food before eating it, and makes no blessing afterward at
all.[71]

13. This is the one blessing which summarizes three:[72] "Blessed
are You, Lord our God, King of the Universe, for food and sustenance and for the precious, good, and broad land in which You
settled our forefathers according to Your will. Have mercy upon
us, Lord our God, and upon Israel Your people, upon Jerusalem
Your city, and upon Zion the abode of Your glory. Cause us to ascend into it, and make us joyful with its reconstruction so that we
may bless You in sanctity and purity. Blessed are You, Lord, for the
land and for sustenance." On Sabbaths and holidays, one includes
in this blessing a reference to the sanctity of the day, as one does in
the grace after meals.[73]

CHAPTER FOUR

1. One must recite the grace after meals and the one blessing
which summarizes three in the place where one has eaten. If one
has eaten while walking, he sits at the spot where he has finished
eating, and makes the blessing. If one has eaten while standing,
he sits down and makes the blessing. If one has forgotten to say
the grace after meals, and remembers before the food has been digested, he makes the blessing at the place where he has remembered. But if one has failed to say it on purpose, he must return
to the place where he has eaten and there make the blessing; but
if one has made the blessing in the place where he remembered,
he has fulfilled his obligation.[74] So also, if one makes the blessing
while standing or walking, he has fulfilled his obligation. But in
the first instance, one should only recite the grace after meals or
the one blessing which summarizes three while seated in the place
where one has eaten.[75]

2. If one is unsure whether or not he has made the blessing "Who
brings forth," he does not make the blessing, since it is not from
the Torah. If one has forgotten to make the blessing "Who brings
forth" but remembers before finishing the meal, then he makes

the blessing, whereas if he remembers after finishing, he does not make the blessing.[76]

3. If one ate in a house, interrupted his meal, and went to another house; or, if one ate, and was called out by someone to talk and left the house and returned, since he has changed his place, he must make the blessing on what he ate[77] and then again make the blessing "Who brings forth" and then finish his meal.[78]

4. Friends who have eaten a meal together and gone out in order to greet a bridegroom or a bride may continue their meal without making a new blessing, if they have left behind an old or sick person.[79] But if they have left no one behind, they must make the concluding blessing[80] and when they resume eating make the blessing necessary before eating.[81]

5. So, too, if people have joined together to drink or eat fruit. Since anyone who changes his place has interrupted his eating, one who does so must make the concluding blessing, and again make the blessing necessary before eating when he has to eat again.[82] But if one moves from place to place in the same house, there is no need to repeat the blessing. [But,] if one has eaten under the eastern edge of a fig tree and then moves to eat under its western edge, one must repeat the blessings.[83]

6. If one has made the blessing over bread, one is exempt from making a blessing over the dips — whether a cooked dish or fruits, and so on — which one eats with the bread. But a blessing on the dips does not exempt one from the blessing over the bread. If one has made a blessing over cooked grains, he is exempt from making a blessing over cooked food, and if one has made a blessing over cooked food, he is exempt from making a blessing over cooked grains.[84]

7. If one has decided that he has finished eating or drinking, and then changes his mind and decides to eat or drink again, he must make the blessing again, even if he has not changed his place. But if one has not decided to finish, but has planned to drink or eat again, he need not make another blessing, even after a full day's interruption.[85]

8. If people who have been drinking say, "Come, let us recite the grace after meals," or, "Come, let us make the qiddush expressing the sanctity of the day," they may not drink until they make the

blessing or make qiddush. If they desire to drink again before reciting the grace after meals or before making qiddush, even though
it is not permitted, they must first make the blessing "Who creates
the fruit of the vine" again before drinking. But if they say, "Come,
let us make Havdalah," they need not repeat the blessing.[86]

9. If people who have gathered to drink wine are given a new
kind of wine, such as if they have been drinking red wine and are
then brought black wine, or if they have been drinking old wine
and are brought new wine, there is no need to make the blessing
over wine a second time. But one makes the blessing "Blessed are
You, Lord our God, King of the Universe, Who is good and beneficent."[87]

10. One makes no blessing over any food or any drink until it
is before him. If one has made a blessing, and then the food is
brought before him, one must make the blessing again. If one takes
food, makes the blessing, and then drops it such that it is burned or
carried away by a river, one takes more food, and makes the blessing over it again, even if it is the same kind of food. And he must
say, "Blessed be the name of His glorious majesty for ever and ever,"
with respect to the first blessing so as not to have uttered the name
of God[88] for naught.[89] But one may stand by an aqueduct, make a
blessing, and drink from it, even though the water which was before him when he made the blessing is not the same water which
he drinks, since that was his original intention.[90]

11. One need not make a blessing before or after parts of a meal
eaten during the meal; rather, the blessing "Who brings forth" before the meal, and the grace after meals exempts one from further
blessings over all the things which are secondary to the meal. But
foods eaten during a meal, which are not parts of the meal, need
a blessing before them, but not one after them. Things eaten after
the meal, whether parts of the meal or not, need blessings before
and after them.[91]

12. On Sabbaths and holidays, or at the meal after a bloodletting,
or on leaving the bathhouse, or at similar meals which begin with
wine,[92] if one has made a blessing over the wine taken before the
food, he is exempt from making a blessing over the wine taken after
the food before the recitation of the grace after meals. But on other
days one must make a second blessing over the wine taken after

the food. If wine is served with the food, each person makes the blessing for himself, since their throats may not be free to answer, "Amen," together after one person. This does not exempt one from making the blessing over the wine taken after the meal.[93]

CHAPTER FIVE

1. Women and slaves are obligated to recite the grace after meals. There is a doubt over whether they are obligated from the Torah, since there is no set time for it;[94] or are not so obligated and, therefore, cannot satisfy the obligation for [male] adults.[95] But children are obligated by the rabbis to recite the grace after meals in order to educate them.[96]

2. Three who have eaten bread together are obligated to recite the invitational blessing before the grace after meals. What is that invitational blessing? If more than three but fewer than ten people have eaten together, one of them makes the blessing, saying, "Let us bless Him of Whose bounty we have eaten." All respond, "Blessed be He of Whose bounty we have eaten and through Whose beneficence we live." He then continues and says, "Blessed are You, Lord our God, King of the Universe, Who feeds . . ." until he completes the four blessings, and the rest answer, "Amen," after each blessing.[97]

3. If those eating are ten or more, one makes the invitational blessing using God's name. How? The one making the blessing says, "Let us bless our God, of Whose bounty we have eaten," and the others respond, "Blessed be our God of Whose bounty we have eaten"; he then begins the grace after meals.

4. When eating in the house of a bridegroom, from the time that preparations are made for the wedding banquet and up till thirty days after the wedding, one makes the blessing "Let us bless He in Whose abode is happiness, and of Whose bounty we have eaten," and the others respond, "Blessed be He in Whose abode is happiness and of Whose bounty we have eaten and thanks to Whose beneficence we live." If there are ten present, one makes the blessing "Let us give blessing to our God in Whose abode is happiness and of Whose bounty we have eaten," and the others respond, "Blessed be our God in Whose abode is happiness and of

Whose bounty we have eaten and thanks to Whose beneficence we live." So, too, at any meal held because of the wedding and up until twelve months after it, one makes the blessing "in Whose abode is happiness."[98]

5. All are obligated to make the invitational blessing as they are obligated to recite grace after meals, even priests who have eaten of the holiest food in the Temple courtyard. So, too, if priests and Israelites have eaten together, the priests eating from the heave offering and the Israelites from profane food, they are obligated to make the invitational blessing. Women, slaves, and minors are obligated to make the invitational blessing as they are obligated to recite the grace after meals.[99]

6. Women, slaves, and minors are not counted toward the number necessary to make the invitational blessing, but make the blessing among themselves. But women, slaves, and minors must not make a group together, for fear of licentiousness, but, rather, women make the blessing by themselves, slaves by themselves, and minors by themselves, save that they not use the name of God in the invitational blessing. An androgyne[100] makes the invitational blessing for others of its kind, but not for women or for men, since its sex is doubtful. One of indeterminate sex never makes the invitational blessing. A minor who knows to Whom blessings are made may be included in the number necessary to make the invitational blessing, even if he is only seven or eight, and is counted toward either the group of three or the group of ten. A Gentile is not so included.[101]

7. The invitational blessing is only made for those who have eaten at least an olive's worth of bread. If seven have eaten bread and three others have eaten vegetables or gravy or something similar with the seven, they join together to recite the invitational blessing with God's name, so long as the one making the blessing is one of those who have eaten the bread. But if six have eaten bread, and four vegetables, they do not join together; those who have eaten bread must be the clear majority. When does this apply? With respect to ten; but with respect to three, each must have eaten an olive's worth of bread, and only then do they recite the invitational blessing.[102]

8. If two have eaten and finished, and are then joined by a third

who has not eaten, if they can eat even a small amount of any food with him, he may join them. The wisest of those eating together makes the blessings for them all, even if he has joined the group last.[103]

9. Three who have eaten together may not divide up;[104] so also, four or five people. A group of between six and ten may divide up,[105] but not a group of ten or more until it reaches twenty. A group may divide up if each subgroup recites the same invitational blessing as the whole group.[106]

10. Three people ought not come together from three other groups of three people each; but if each has already participated in the invitational blessing in his original group, they may divide up and they are not obligated to recite the invitational blessing, since they have already participated in it. Three who have sat down together to eat may not divide up, even if each eats from his own food.[107]

11. If two groups of people eat in the same building and can see one another, they may join together to make one invitational blessing; but if not, each makes the invitational blessing for itself. If one waiter serves both groups, going from one to the other, then they make one invitational blessing together, even if not all the members of each group can see each other, on condition that both groups hear the person making the blessing clearly.[108]

12. If three have eaten together and one has gone out to the marketplace, he is to be called so that he can pay attention in order to hear what they say, and the invitational blessing is made, even while he is in the marketplace; in this way he fulfills his obligation. When he returns to his place, he recites the grace after meals for himself. But if ten have eaten together and one has left, the invitational blessing is not made until he returns and sits in his place with them.[109]

13. If three have eaten together and one has gone ahead and recited the grace after meals for himself, the invitational blessing is made including him, and the other two fulfill the obligation of the invitational blessing, but he does not, since the invitational blessing may not be recited retroactively.[110]

14. If two have eaten, each says the grace after meals for himself. If one knows and the other does not, he who knows recites

the blessing out loud while the second answers, "Amen," after each blessing and so fulfills his obligation. A son may recite the grace after meals for his father, a servant for his master, and a wife for her husband, and they each fulfill their obligation in that fashion. But the Sages said,[111] "Cursed be he whose wife or sons recites the grace after meals for him."[112]

15. In what case do they fulfill their obligation? If they have eaten but are not satiated, and are only obligated to recite the grace after meals by rabbinic authority, and thus may have their obligation fulfilled for them by a minor, a slave, or a woman. But if one has eaten and been satiated, and thus is obligated to recite the grace after meals by the Torah, a woman, a minor, or a slave cannot fulfill the obligation for him. For, in every case where one is obligated to do something by the Torah, one cannot have his obligation fulfilled by any other but one who is likewise obligated by the Torah to do the same thing.[113]

16. If one has entered a place and found people reciting the grace after meals, if the leader has said, "Let us bless, and so on," he responds, "He is blessed and blessed!" If he finds those who have eaten responding with "Blessed . . . we have eaten," he responds with, "Amen."[114]

CHAPTER SIX

1. If one eats bread which requires a "Who brings forth" blessing, he must wash his hands before and afterward, even if it is not sacred bread.[115] This is the case even if his hands are not dirty and even if he does not know them to be impure. One should not eat before washing both hands. So also, before one eats any food dipped in a liquid, one must wash one's hands.[116]

2. When one washes ones hands, whether for eating, reciting the Shema, or praying, one must first recite the blessing "Who has sanctified us with His commandments and commanded us concerning washing the hands." Even though this is a commandment of the Sages, we have been commanded in the Torah to listen to them, as it says, *You shall act in accordance with the instructions given you and the ruling handed down to you* (Deut. 17:11). But one makes no blessing over the washing after the meal, since it is only done

because of the danger;[117] one must therefore take great care concerning it.[118]

3. Washing one's hands between courses is optional; one washes if he wishes, and does not wash if he does not so wish. One need not wash his hands before or after eating non-sacred fruits; anyone who washes his hands before eating fruit is considered arrogant.[119] One must wash his hands after eating any salted bread, lest it contain salt of Sodom, or any other salt of a like nature, since one might rub his eyes and become blind.[120] Because of the salt it was made obligatory to wash one's hands after every meal. In an army camp, one is exempted from the obligation to wash his hands before eating, since he is preoccupied with the war, but is obligated to wash his hands afterward because of the danger.[121]

4. To what point must one wash his hands? To the wrist. How much water must be used? A quarter-*hin* for each pair of hands. Anything which hinders with respect to ritual bathing hinders with respect to washing the hands. Any liquid which may be used for a ritual bath may be counted as part of the quarter-*hin* for washing the hands.[122]

5. Immersing one's hands in the waters of a ritual bath satisfies the requirements of washing the hands. But immersing one's hands in water which does not amount to the minimum needed for a ritual bath or in water drawn but then poured out on the ground counts for nothing. Drawn water only ritually purifies the hands when it is poured over them.[123]

6. In washing the hands, one must take care concerning four things: the water, that it not be unfit for washing hands; the amount of water, that there be at least a quarter-*hin* for each pair of hands; the implement, that the water used be in an implement; the washer, that the water be poured out by human energy.

7. Four things make the water unfit: change in color, exposure, having been used for work, or being so spoiled that an animal would not drink it. How? If the color of water — whether in a utensil or on the ground — has changed, either because of something which fell into it or because of its place, it is unfit. So, too, if the water has been left out for so long that one is no longer permitted to drink it,[124] it is unfit for washing the hands.[125]

8. Any water used for work is considered to be sewage and is

unfit for washing hands. How? Water which had been drawn and then used for washing dishes or soaking bread, and so on, whether in implements or on the ground, is unfit for washing hands. But if one has used the water to rewash already cleaned dishes, or new dishes, it is not thereby rendered unfit. Water in which a baker dipped crackers is unfit, but water which he ladled out with his hands while kneading is fit, since it was the water in his cupped hands with which the work was done, while the water from which he had ladled out remains fit.[126]

9. Water unfit for a dog to drink, such as water so bitter, salty, murky, or smelly that a dog would not drink it, if in an implement, is unfit for washing the hands, but if on the ground may be used to dip one's hand into. One may dip one's hands into water from the hot springs of Tiberias in their place, but if it has been removed in an implement or diverted in an aqueduct to another place, it may not be used for washing before or after the meal, since it is not fit for an animal to drink from.[127]

10. When washing one's hands, one should pour the water a little bit at a time till one reaches the appropriate measure of water. But if one has poured the entire quarter-*hin* in one flow, it is fit. Four or five people may wash their hands together at the same time, with their hands next to each other or above each other, so long as their hands are together loosely so that the water can flow between them, and so long as there is enough water for a quarter-*hin* for each one.[128]

11. One may not pour water on the hands with the sides of broken vessels, or with the handle of a ladle, or with broken pottery, or with the top of a barrel. But if the top has been adjusted so that it is meant for washing the hands, one may do so. A wineskin adjusted so that it is meant for pouring water may be so used. But one may not so use a sack or basket, even if especially adjusted for pouring water. One may not pour water over another's hands with one's cupped palms, since they are not implements. Vessels which have been shattered such that if they were ritually impure they thereby become ritually pure[129] may not be used to pour water over the hands since they are fragments of a vessel.[130]

12. One may wash one's hands with any kind of implement, even of dung or earthenware, so long as it is whole. An implement that

does not hold a quarter-*hin* or does not contain a quarter-*hin* may not be used for pouring water on the hands.[131]

13. All are fit for pouring water, even a deaf-mute, an idiot, and a minor.[132] If there is no one else there, one places the implement between one's knees and pours over his own hands, or tilts the barrel over his hands and washes them, or pours one hand over the other alternately. A monkey may wash one's hands.[133]

14. In a case where a person fills a trough either by hand or by a water wheel, so that the water then streams through an aqueduct to irrigate vegetables or provide water for animals, and then places his hands in the trough so that the water flows over them, the hands are not considered washed, since there was no one pouring the water on his hands. But if one's hands are near the mouth of a pail being spilled out such that the water flows over them because of the force of the person pouring, this washing of the hands suffices.[134]

15. In cases of doubt where one is not sure whether water has been used for work or not, or whether there is enough water or not, or whether the water is ritually pure or ritually impure, or whether or not one has washed one's hands, one's hands are ritually pure, since in every case of doubt concerning ritual purity of the hands, they are considered ritually pure.[135]

16. When washing before a meal, one must lift one's hands such that water does not flow down from the wrists and render the hands ritually impure once again.[136] When washing after a meal, one must lower one's hands so that all the strength of the salt on one's hands is dissipated. One may wash before a meal over a receptacle or onto the ground, but after a meal only onto the ground. Water used to wash before a meal may be heated or cold, but one does not wash one's hands after a meal with hot water. This is only if the water is scaldingly hot, since the filth will only come off if one rubs one's hands;[137] one may use lukewarm water to wash after a meal.[138]

17. If one washes one's hands in the morning and stipulates that it be good for the entire day, he need not wash his hands each time he eats, on condition that he keeps this in mind. But if he does not keep it in mind, he must wash his hands each time it is required.[139]

18. One may wrap one's hands in a cloth and eat bread or food that is dipped, even if one has not washed one's hands. When one

feeds another, he need not wash his hands, but the one eating must wash his hands, even though he does not touch the food and some-one else is feeding him. So, also if one eats with a spoon,[140] he must wash his hands.[141]

19. One may not feed a person who has not washed his hands, even if one puts the food directly into his mouth. It is forbidden to make light of the washing of the hands: the Sages commanded many ordinances and exhortations concerning it. Even if one only has enough water to drink, one should wash one's hands with part of it and then eat and drink with the rest.[142]

20. After washing, one should dry one's hands and only then eat. All who eat without drying the hands are considered as if they were eating ritually impure bread. When one washes one's hands after a meal, one must dry them and only then recite the grace after meals. One should recite the grace after meals immediately after washing one's hands, and not do anything else in between. It is even for-bidden to drink water after having washed the hands after a meal until one has recited the grace after meals.[143]

CHAPTER SEVEN

1. The Sages of Israel observed many customs concerning din-ing, all of them being matters of etiquette. They are as follows: when entering to eat, the greatest among them washes his hands first, and the rest then come in, sit, and recline. The greatest among them reclines at the head of the table, and the second to him fur-ther down the table. If there are three couches, the greatest reclines at the head of the table, the second above him, and the third, below him.[144]

2. The host makes the blessing "Who brings forth bread" and on completing the blessing cuts the bread. A guest recites the grace after meals, so that he blesses the host.[145] But if they are all hosts, then the greatest among them cuts the bread and recites the grace after meals.[146]

3. The one who cuts the bread may not do so until salt and a dip have been placed before each person, unless they had planned to eat dry bread. One should not cut off a small slice, so that he will not appear stingy, or a slice larger than an egg, so that he will not

appear gluttonous. But on the Sabbath one should cut off a large slice. One should only slice where the bread has been well baked.[147]

4. The best way of performing the commandment is to cut from a whole loaf. But if there is a full loaf made of barley and a cut loaf of wheat, one places the cut loaf under the full loaf and cuts them together, so that he cuts from wheat and from a full loaf. On Sabbaths and holidays one is obligated to cut two loaves; he holds both of them and cuts one of them.[148]

5. The individual who cuts the bread gives a slice to each person and keeps one for himself. But one does not place the bread into the hand of the person eating, unless that person is a mourner.[149] The person cutting the bread should be the first person to eat. None of those eating are permitted to taste the food until the person who made the blessing has done so. The person cutting the bread may not taste of the food until the majority of those present have finished saying, "Amen." If the person cutting the bread wishes to behave respectfully toward his teacher or someone else wiser than he and allow him to eat first, he may do so.[150]

6. Two people eating together from the same serving dish wait for each other;[151] but if three are eating together, there is no need to wait. If two have finished eating, the third pauses in his meal while they recite the grace after meals. If one has finished, the other two do not interrupt their meal for him, but continue eating until they finish. One ought not to converse during a meal so as not to come into danger.[152] For this reason, if wine is served during the course of the meal, each one present makes the blessing over the wine for himself, for if one were to make the blessing for all, another might answer, "Amen," while swallowing and endanger himself. One does not stare at a person who is eating, or at another's portion, so as not to cause him embarrassment.[153]

7. The servant waiting upon those who eat does not eat with them, but it is compassionate to let him taste each dish, so that he not be distressed. If they gave him wine to drink, he should make a blessing on each and every cup that they give him, since his drinking is not dependent on his will but on theirs.[154]

8. If someone has left the meal in order to urinate, he must wash the one hand[155] and then return to the meal. If one has spoken to

another for a very long time, he must wash both his hands before returning to the meal. If they have gathered to drink, he should enter,
take his place, wash his hands, and then turn to face the guests.[156]
Why does he wash while sitting in his place? Lest people think that
he did not wash because there was no eating there.[157]

9. Uncooked meat is not placed on bread, nor is a full cup passed
over it. A soup tureen is not leaned on bread, nor is bread to be
thrown. Nor is one to throw pieces of food, nor foods that have
no shell, such as berries, grapes, or figs, because they thus become
disgusting. One may pump wine through pipes at a wedding and
throw parched corn and nuts at the bride and groom during the
summer, but not during the rainy season, lest they become disgusting. One does not wash one's hands with wine, whether unadulterated or mixed with water. So also, one does not discard other food
and drink in a way that shows contempt or ingratitude for them.[158]

10. Guests may not take from what has been served them to give
to the son or daughter of the host, lest he be served all the food he
has and he will become embarrassed when the children accept it
and leave. One should not send someone a barrel of wine with oil
floating on the top, lest someone then send him a barrel full of oil
and he think that it be wine with oil on its top only and he invite
guests[159] and be embarrassed. So, all similar things that embarrass
the host are forbidden.[160]

11. After eating, the table is removed, and the dining area
cleaned. Only then are the hands washed, since crumbs the size of
an olive may have remained, over which it is forbidden to walk or
to wash. But crumbs less than the size of an olive may be destroyed
by hand.[161]

12. When water is brought for washing the hands, he who leads
the grace after meals washes his hands first, so that the greatest
among them[162] does not have to sit with dirty hands while another
washes. The others then wash their hands one after another. Honor
does not determine order in this case, since we do not let honor determine order with respect to dirty hands, to roads, or to bridges;[163]
but it does when entering—but not leaving—an entryway fit for a
mezuzah.[164]

13. Having washed and dried their hands, and having recited the

grace after meals, if incense is brought in, the great one, who led the grace after meals, makes the blessing over the incense and the others answer, "Amen."[165]

14. If wine is available, a cup holding at least a quarter-*log* is brought, as are spices. One holds the wine in his right hand and the spices in his left and recites the grace after meals, and then makes the blessing over the wine and then over the spices. If the spices are mixed with oil, or something similar, he dabs it onto the head of the waiter.[166] But if the waiter is a scholar, he dabs it on the wall, so that he does not go out into the marketplace perfumed.[167]

15. Even though the grace after meals does not require wine, if one has made the blessing over the wine according to the custom we have described, the inside of the cup used for the blessing must be washed and the outside of it rinsed. It may then be filled with unadulterated wine. When he reaches the blessing over the land, a little water is added so that the wine is tasty to drink. Conversation is not permitted over the cup of wine used for the grace after meals, but all are quiet until the grace after meals and the blessings over the wine are completed, and the wine drunk.[168]

CHAPTER EIGHT

1. One makes the blessing "Who creates the fruit of trees" before eating fruit and "Who creates many living entities . . ." afterward. Excepted are fruits of the five species mentioned in the Torah — grapes, pomegranates, figs, olives, and dates — since one makes the one blessing which summarizes three after them. One makes the blessing "Who creates the fruit of the earth" over fruit of the ground and green vegetables and "Who creates many living entities . . ." afterward. Before eating food which does not grow out of the ground, such as meat, cheese, fish, eggs, water, milk, honey, and so forth, one makes the blessing "that all" and "Who creates many living entities . . ." afterward. One who drinks water not to quench his thirst need not make any blessing before or after.[169]

2. Over liquid squeezed from fruit, one makes the blessing "that all" and "Who creates many living entities . . ." afterward. Excepted are the liquid squeezed from grapes and olives: over wine one makes the blessing "Who creates the fruit of the vine" and

afterward the one blessing which summarizes three; over olive oil one makes the blessing "Who creates the fruit of trees." When does this latter apply? In the case where one has a sore throat and drinks the oil with the liquid of boiled vegetables or similar things, since in such a case one has pleasure from his drinking. But if one drinks olive oil alone, or does not have a sore throat, one makes the blessing "that all," since he has had no benefit from the taste of the oil.[170]

3. If fruits or vegetables which are usually eaten raw have been cooked or stewed, one makes the blessing "that all" over them and "Who creates many living entities . . ." afterward. If one eats vegetables which are usually stewed, such as cabbage or turnips, while still raw, he makes the blessing "that all" over them. When one eats things which are ordinarily eaten either raw or cooked, one makes the appropriate blessing over them, whether they be raw or cooked: over fruit one makes the blessing "Who creates the fruit of trees," and over fruit of the ground and green vegetables one makes the blessing "Who creates the fruit of the earth."[171]

4. If one drinks the gravy of vegetables which are usually prepared by stewing, one makes the blessing "Who creates the fruit of the earth" over it, on condition that the vegetables have been stewed in order to prepare gravy for drinking, since the gravy of any food normally stewed is like the food itself. One makes the blessing "that all" over date honey. But if one eats dates which have been mashed by hand and their pits removed such that they are dough-like, one makes the blessing "Who creates the fruit of trees" over them and the one blessing which summarizes three afterward.[172]

5. All[173] of the Ge'onim maintained that when the sap of sweet cane is squeezed out and cooked such that it congeals and appears like salt,[174] one makes the blessing "Who creates the fruit of the earth" over it, while some held that one makes the blessing "Who creates the fruit of trees." They also said that if one sucks those canes, the blessing made over them should be "Who creates the fruit of the earth." But I say that sweet cane is no fruit and the only blessing to be made over it is "that all." The honey[175] of these canes after processing by heat should not be considered more unlike its source than untreated date honey, the blessing over which is "that all."[176]

6. Over heart of palm, which is the topmost stalk of the date

palm and looks like white wood, one makes "that all." One makes
the blessing "Who creates the fruit of the earth" over caper leaves,
since they are not a fruit. But the berries of the caper are a fruit,
since they have the shape of small dates and one makes the blessing
"Who creates the fruit of trees" over them.[177]

7. Over fresh pepper and ginger one makes the blessing "Who
creates the fruit of the earth"; but when they are dried no blessing
need be made, whether before or after, since they are spices and
not food. One need make no blessing before or after food or drink
which is unfit for consumption.[178]

8. But over moldy bread, wine which has developed a scum on its
surface, cooked food gone bad, unripened fallen fruit, beer, vine-
gar, locusts, salt, truffles, and mushrooms, one makes the blessing
"that all came into existence through His word." Over anything
over which one makes the blessing "that all" before eating, one
must make the blessing "Who creates many living entities . . . for
everything which He has created . . . Who lives eternally" after eating. Any food which requires that a blessing be made after eating
it requires a blessing before.[179]

9. If one pours three measures of water over wine sediment and
ends up with four measures of liquid, the blessing made over it is
"Who creates the fruit of the vine" since this is what is called diluted
wine. But if fewer than four measures have come out, even though
it tastes like wine, one makes the blessing "that all" over it.[180]

10. If one has made the blessing "Who creates the fruit of the
earth" over fruits of the tree, he has fulfilled his obligation. But if
he has made the blessing "Who creates the fruit of trees" over fruits
of the earth, he has not. If one makes the blessing "that all came
into existence" over any food, he has fulfilled his obligation, even
over bread or wine.[181]

11. If one holds a glass of beer in one's hand and begins to make
the blessing, intending to say "that all," but errs and says "Who
creates the fruit of the vine" instead, he is not made to repeat the
blessing. So too if there are fruits of the earth in front of him, and
if he begins to make the blessing, intending to say "Who creates
the fruit of the earth" but errs and says "Who creates the fruit of
trees" instead, he is not made to repeat the blessing. So too if a dish
made of grain is before one, and he begins the blessing intending

to say "Who creates diverse kinds of food" but errs and says "Who brings forth bread" instead, he fulfills his obligation, since at the moment he mentions God's name and sovereignty, which are the essential part of the blessing, he actually intends to make the blessing appropriate to the type of food in front of him. Since there was no mistake in the essential part of the blessing, even though he has made a mistake at its end, one is not made to repeat it.[182]

12. If one is unsure whether or not he has made any of these blessings, he does not repeat the blessing, whether before or after eating, since they are all of rabbinic origin. If one has forgotten to make a blessing before putting food in his mouth [and then remembered before swallowing]—in the case of liquids, one swallows and makes the blessing after; if they are fruits which would become disgusting if taken out of the mouth, such as berries and grapes, one should move them to one side of his mouth, make the blessing, and then swallow them; but if they would not become disgusting, such as beans and peas, one should remove them from his mouth and make the blessing with an empty mouth, and then eat.[183]

13. If one has different kinds of food before him and if the blessings on all of them are the same, he makes the blessing over one of them and exempts all the rest. But if the blessings are not the same, he makes the appropriate blessing over each. One may do so in any order. But if he has no preference between them, and one of them is of the seven species, he makes the blessing over that first, in the order in which they appear in the verse. The seven are those mentioned in this verse: *a land of wheat and barley, of vines, figs, and pomegranates, a land of olive trees and honey* (Deut. 8:8); "honey" refers to dates. Dates precede grapes, since they come second after *a land* and grapes come third.[184]

14. The one blessing which summarizes three made after eating the five species of fruit and after drinking wine is the same as that said after eating types of grain, except that over fruit one says "for trees and the fruit of trees, and for the produce of the field, and for the precious land . . ." and over wine one says "over the vine and the fruit of the vine and for the produce of the field, and for the precious land . . ." and concludes each with "for the land and for fruit." If one is in the Land of Israel, one concludes with "for the

land and for its fruit." There are those who add to the one blessing which summarizes three the words "for You are a good and beneficent God" before the conclusion, since they express the substance of the fourth blessing. But there are those who say that the fourth blessing was ordained only for the grace after meals.[185]

15. If one has drunk wine, and eaten dates, and eaten a dish made of one of the five species of grain, he makes the following blessing afterward: "Blessed are You, Lord our God, King of the Universe, for food and sustenance, for the vine and the fruit of the vine, for trees and the fruit of trees, and for the produce of the field, and for the precious, good, and broad land in which You settled our forefathers according to Your will . . ." and concludes "Blessed are You, Lord, for the land and for sustenance and for the fruits."

16. But if one has eaten meat and drunk wine, he makes a blessing after each separately. If one has eaten figs or grapes or apples or pears, and the like, one makes afterward one blessing expressing the substance of three, which includes them all, since they are all fruits of trees, and so in all similar cases.

CHAPTER NINE

1. Just as it is forbidden for a person to enjoy food or drink before making a blessing over it, so it is forbidden to enjoy a pleasant scent before making a blessing over it. What blessing does one make over a pleasant scent? If the fragrant object is a tree or derived from a tree, one makes the blessing "Who creates fragrance-bearing trees." If it is a bush or derived from a bush, one makes the blessing "Who creates fragrance-bearing bushes." If it is derived neither from a tree nor from the ground, such as myrrh, which derives from an animal,[186] one makes the blessing, "Who creates diverse kinds of spices." If it is a fruit fit for eating, such as a citron or an apple, one makes the blessing "Who has placed a pleasing fragrance in fruit." But if one makes the blessing "Who creates diverse kinds of spices" over any of these, he has fulfilled his obligation.[187]

2. One does not make a blessing over incense until its smoke rises. What is its blessing? If the burned incense is derived from a tree, one makes the blessing "Who creates fragrance-bearing trees." If it is derived from a bush, one makes the blessing "[Who cre-

ates fragrance-bearing] bushes"; and if it comes from a species of living thing, one makes the blessing "Who creates diverse kinds of spices."[188]

3. Over persimmon oil[189] and similar things, one makes the blessing "Who creates pleasant oils." But if olive oil were pressed or ground[190] such that it emits a pleasant fragrance, one makes the blessing "Who creates fragrance-bearing trees." Over spiced oil, like anointing oil,[191] one makes the blessing "Who creates diverse kinds of spices." If oil and myrtle are presented to someone, he makes the blessing over the myrtle, and in so doing fulfills his obligation to make a blessing over the oil, since there is one blessing for the two of them: "[Who creates] fragrance-bearing trees."[192]

4. If one has before him fragrances derived from trees and from bushes, the blessing over the one does not exempt him from the other, but, rather, he should make a blessing over each separately. If one is presented with both wine and oil, he should hold the wine in his right hand, the oil in the left, make the blessing over the wine and drink it, and then make the blessing over the oil and smell it and dab it on the head of the waiter. But if the waiter is a scholar, he should dab it on the wall.[193]

5. If one is not sure if a fragrant substance is derived from a tree or from the ground, one makes the blessing "Who creates diverse kinds of spices" over it. If one enters a fragrance store having many different kinds of fragrance in it, one makes the blessing "Who creates diverse kinds of spices." If one spends the whole day there, he only makes one blessing. But if he enters and leaves repeatedly, he makes the blessing each time.[194]

6. One makes the blessing "Who creates fragrance-bearing trees" over lilies and spikenard. Over domesticated narcissus one makes the blessing "Who creates fragrance-bearing trees"; but if it is wild, one makes the blessing "Who creates fragrance-bearing bushes." One makes the blessing "Who creates fragrance-bearing trees" over roses, rose water, frankincense, mastic, and similar substances.[195]

7. There are three sorts of pleasant scent over which no blessing is made: a pleasant scent which it is forbidden to smell, a pleasant scent used to cover an unpleasant smell, and a pleasant scent not made to be smelled itself.

8. How? One makes no blessing over scents used in idolatry, or

on a woman with whom sexual relations are forbidden, since it is forbidden to smell those scents. One makes no blessing over fragrances used on the dead, or in a privy, or in oil used for cleaning, since they are made to cover an unpleasant smell. No blessing is made over incense used to fumigate implements or clothing, since it is not made to be smelled itself. So also, one makes no blessing if one smells fumigated clothing, since there is no actual fragrance there, only the smell without the fragrant substance itself.[196]

9. One makes no blessing over fragrances used at a Gentile party since it is assumed that a Gentile party is devoted to idolatry. If one is walking outside a city and smells a pleasant scent—if the majority of the city are Gentiles, one makes no blessing; but if the majority are Jews, one makes the blessing. If a scent over which one ought to make a blessing becomes mixed with a scent over which no blessing is made, one follows the dominant scent.[197]

CHAPTER TEN

1. The Sages ordained other blessings, like those included in the prayers which we have already listed, and utterances which have no opening or closing formula,[198] by way of praise and thanksgiving to the Holy One blessed be He. They are [as follows]: if one builds a new house, or purchases new utensils, whether he has similar ones or not, he makes the blessing "Blessed are You, Lord our God, King of the Universe, Who has kept us alive and sustained us and brought us to this time."[199]

2. So, too, if one sees a friend for the first time in thirty days, he makes the blessing "Who has kept us alive." If he sees him after an interval of twelve months, he makes the blessing "Blessed are You, Lord our God, King of the Universe, Who resurrects the dead." On first seeing a fruit which is renewed every year, one makes the blessing "Blessed . . . Who has kept us alive."[200]

3. On hearing good tidings one makes the blessing "Blessed are You, Lord our God, King of the Universe, the good, and beneficent." On hearing evil tidings, one makes the blessing "Blessed are You, Lord our God, King of the Universe, the true Judge." One is obligated to make a blessing over evil tidings with graciousness just as one makes a blessing over good tidings with joy, as it says,

You shall love the Lord your God with all your heart and with all your soul and with all your might (Deut. 6:5). Included in this obligation of superabundant love is that even when one is distressed one must thank and praise God with joy.[201]

4. If good fortune occurs to someone, or if he has heard good tidings, even if it seems apparent that these good things will ultimately cause him evil, he makes the blessing "the good and beneficent." Similarly, if evil fortune occurs to someone, or if he has heard evil tidings, even if it seems apparent that these evil things will ultimately cause him good, he makes the blessing "the true Judge," since one makes the blessing not on what will happen in the future but on what has occurred now.[202]

5. If it has rained heavily, and one owns a field, he makes the blessing "Who has kept us alive"; but if he owns the field in partnership with others, he makes the blessing "the good and beneficent." If one owns no field, he makes this blessing: "We thank You, Lord our God, for every drop which You have caused to descend upon us. Even were our mouths as full of song as the ocean [is full of water], and our tongues as full of ringing praise as the multitude of its waves, and our lips as full of praise as the expanse of the firmament, and our eyes illumined like the sun and the moon, and our arms stretched forth like the eagles of heaven, we could not sufficiently thank You, Lord our God, or bless Your name, our King, for one-millionth of the multitude of bounties You have worked for us and our ancestors before us. You redeemed us from Egypt, Lord our God, and delivered us from the house of bondage. You nourished us in times of famine and provided us so that we are satiated. You have rescued us from the sword, enabled us to escape from plague, and saved us from many illnesses. To this point Your mercy has sustained us and Your graciousness has never abandoned us. Thus, the limbs You have implanted in us, and the spirit and soul with which You have inspirited us, and the tongue which You have placed in our mouths, all these will thank and bless Your name, Lord our God. Blessed are You, Lord our God, to Whom is due abounding thanksgiving, the Lord of praise."[203]

6. At what point does one make a blessing over rain? When there is so much water on the ground that the raindrops cause bubbles on the surface of the water, and the bubbles run toward each other.[204]

7. If someone is informed that his father has died and that he is his heir, if he has brothers, he first makes the blessing "the true Judge" and then makes the blessing "the good and beneficent." If he has no brothers, he makes the blessing "Who has kept us alive." In short,[205] for every good thing that happens to a person in conjunction with others, he makes the blessing "the good and beneficent" and for good things that happen to him alone, "Who has kept us alive."[206]

8. Four must give thanks: a sick person who has recovered, a prisoner released from jail, sea travelers when they reach land, and land travelers when they reach a city. One must give thanks in the presence of ten, two of whom must be scholars, as it says, *Let them exalt Him in the congregation of the people, acclaim Him in the assembly of the elders* (Ps. 107:32). How does one give thanks? He stands among the assembled people and makes the blessing "Blessed are You, Lord our God, King of the Universe, Who grants benefits to the undeserving and has granted me good." All those who hear him reply, "May He who granted you good do so in the future, Selah."[207]

9. If a person sees a place at which miracles were done for all Israel, such as the Red Sea or the Jordan River crossings,[208] one makes the blessing "Blessed are You, Lord our God, King of the Universe, Who performed miracles for our ancestors in this place," and similarly when seeing any place where a miracle was done for the multitude. But with respect to a place where a miracle was done for an individual, that individual, his son, and his grandson when seeing the place make the blessing "Blessed are You, Lord our God, King of the Universe, Who performed a miracle for me in this place," or, "Who performed a miracle for my father in this place." One who sees the lions' den[209] or the fiery furnace[210] makes the blessing "Blessed are You, Lord our God, King of the Universe, Who performed a miracle for the righteous in this place." One who sees a place where idols are worshipped makes the blessing "Blessed are You, Lord our God, King of the Universe, Who is long suffering toward those who violate His will." If one sees a place from which idolatry has been uprooted in the Land of Israel, he makes the blessing "Blessed are You, Lord our God, King of the Universe, Who has uprooted idolatry from our land"; if outside the Land, he

makes the blessing "Who has uprooted idolatry from this place." In both cases he says, "As You have uprooted it from this place, so may You uproot it from all places, and may its worshipers worship You."[211]

10. One who sees inhabited Jewish homes[212] makes the blessing "Blessed are You, Lord our God, King of the Universe, Who sets up border markers for the widow."[213] One who sees destroyed Jewish homes makes the blessing "the true Judge." One who sees Jewish graves makes the blessing "Blessed are You, Lord our God, King of the Universe, Who created you in justice, nourished you in justice, sustained you in justice, killed you in justice, and Who in the future will raise you to life in the world to come. Blessed are You, Lord our God, Who resurrects the dead."[214]

11. One who sees six hundred thousand Gentiles together says, "So your mother will be utterly shamed, she who bore you will be disgraced" (Jer. 50:12). If they are Jews in the Land of Israel, one makes the blessing "Blessed are You, Lord, Who understands secrets."[215] One who sees Gentile sages makes the blessing "Blessed are You, Lord our God, King of the Universe, Who gave of His wisdom to human beings." If Jewish sages, one makes the blessing "Blessed are You, Lord our God, King of the Universe, Who gave of His wisdom to those who are in awe of Him." One who sees Gentile kings makes the blessing "Blessed are You, Lord our God, King of the Universe, Who gave of His honor to human beings." If Jewish kings, one makes the blessing "Who gave of His honor to those who are in awe of Him."[216]

12. One who sees a black person or a person with an unusual face or limbs makes the blessing "Blessed are You, Lord our God, King of the Universe, Who has changed His creatures." One who sees a blind person or an amputee, or one afflicted with boils or white blotches, and the like, makes the blessing "Blessed are You, Lord our God, King of the Universe, the true judge." But if they were born thus, one makes the blessing "Blessed are You, Lord our God, King of the Universe, Who has changed His creatures." So also, if one sees an elephant or an ape or a monkey, one makes the blessing "Blessed are You, Lord our God, King of the Universe, Who has changed His creatures."[217]

13. One who sees particularly beautiful and well-formed peo-

ple, and, so also, one who sees beautiful trees, makes the blessing "Blessed are You, Lord our God, King of the Universe, Whose world is thus." One who walks out in fields and gardens in the season of Nisan[218] and sees flowering trees and buds appearing makes the blessing "Blessed are You, Lord our God, King of the Universe, Whose world lacks nothing and Who created in it good and beautiful creatures for human beings to enjoy."[219]

14. One who witnesses storms, lightning, thunder, loud noises in the ground that sound like giant millstones, or the mist in the air which looks like falling stars running from place to place, or which look like stars with tails, makes the blessing "Blessed are You, Lord our God, King of the Universe, Whose power fills the universe." If one prefers, he makes the blessing "Blessed are You, Lord our God, King of the Universe, the Creator."[220]

15. One who sees mountains or hills, or deserts, seas, and rivers after a thirty-day interval makes the blessing "Blessed are You, Lord our God, King of the Universe, the Creator." One who sees the ocean at intervals of thirty days [or less] makes the blessing "Blessed are You, Lord our God, King of the Universe, Creator of the great sea."[221]

16. One who sees a rainbow in a cloud makes the blessing "Blessed are You, Lord our God, King of the Universe, Who is faithful to His covenant and keeps His word." One who sees the moon when it is renewed makes the blessing "Blessed are You, Lord our God, King of the Universe, Who with His word created the cloudy heavens, and with the breath of His mouth all their hosts. He implanted laws and times within them so that they not change their roles. With joy and gladness they do the will of their Possessor; they do truth and their actions are true. To the moon He said that it be renewed to serve as a crown of eminence to those borne in the womb who themselves will, in the future, be renewed like it, to praise their Creator, signifying the glory of His kingdom. Blessed are You, Lord our God, who renews months."[222]

17. One must make this blessing while standing, since all who make the blessing over the new moon at the correct time are as if they received the Divine Presence. If one has failed to make the blessing on the first night, one should make the blessing until the sixteenth day of the month, when it becomes full.[223]

18. If one sees the sun on the day of the vernal equinox at the beginning of the cycle of twenty-eight years when the equinox falls at the beginning of Tuesday evening; then, when he sees it [the sun] on the Wednesday morning, he recites the blessing "the Creator." Similarly, when the moon returns to the beginning of Aries at the beginning of the lunar month, without inclining either to north or to south; and, similarly, when each of the five remaining planets returns to the beginning of Aries without inclining either to north or to south; and, similarly, whenever he sees Aries rise at the eastern limit; in each of these cases he recites the blessing "the Creator." [224]

19. One who sees homes inhabited by non-Jews says, *The Lord will tear down the house of the proud* (Prov. 15:25); if the homes are destroyed, one says, *God of retribution, Lord, God of retribution, appear!* (Ps. 94:1). One who sees graves of non-Jews says, *So your mother will be utterly shamed, she who bore you will be disgraced. Behold the end of the nations — Wilderness, desert, and steppe!* (Jer. 50:12). [225]

20. One who enters a bathhouse says, "May it be Your will, Lord our God, that You bring me in and out safely, and that You save me from this and similar things in the future." On leaving a bathhouse, one says, "I give thanks to You, Lord our God, that You saved me from the fire." [226] On having one's blood let, one says, "May it be Your will, Lord our God, that this procedure heal me, for You heal without reward." On completion of the blood-letting, one says, "Blessed be the Healer of the living." [227]

21. When one goes to measure the grain on one's threshing floor, he says, "May it be Your will, Lord our God, that You bring me in and out safely, and that You bless the work of my hands." While measuring, he says, "Blessed be He Who blesses this heap." But if he first has measured and then beseeches God for mercy, that is a vain prayer. Anyone who cries out in prayer about something that has already happened utters a vain prayer. [228]

22. On entering a study hall, one says, "May it be Your will, Lord our God, that I make no mistake concerning halakhah: that I not call the impure pure or the pure impure, the permitted forbidden or the forbidden permitted. Let me not make a mistake concerning halakhah, so that my friends may be happy with me, and let my friends make no mistakes concerning halakhah so that I may

be happy with them."[229] On leaving the study hall, one says, "I give thanks to You, Lord our God, that You placed my lot among those who sit in the house of study, and not among those who loiter on street corners. I rise in the morning, and they rise in the morning; I rise in the morning to words of Torah; they rise in the morning to vanities. I labor and they labor; I labor and receive reward; they labor and receive no reward. I run and they run; I run to the world to come, and they run to the pit of destruction."[230]

23. On entering a city, one says "May it be Your will, Lord our God, that You bring me into this city in peace." Having entered in peace, one says, "I give thanks to You, Lord our God, for bringing me in peace." On leaving, one says, "May it be Your will, Lord our God, that You bring me out of this city in peace." Having left in peace, one says, "I give thanks to You, Lord our God, for bringing me out of this city in peace; as You have brought me out in peace, so may You cause me to walk in peace, and support me in peace, and guide my footsteps in peace, and save me from the hand of enemies and all that lurks upon the roads."[231]

24. The general principle is that one should cry out in prayer concerning the future and beseech God for mercy and give thanks for what has passed, thanking and praising God, according to his ability. The more one gives thanks to God and praises God always, the more is he praiseworthy.

CHAPTER ELEVEN

1. All blessings open with the word "blessed" and are concluded with a sentence beginning with the word "blessed" with the exception of
- the last blessing of the recitation of the Shema
- one blessing next to another
- blessings over fruit and those similar to it[232]
- a blessing over the performance of a commandment
- those blessings which we have listed here[233] which relate to praise and thanksgiving.

Some of these open with the word "blessed" but do not conclude with it, while some of them conclude with the word "blessed" but do not open with it. A small number of the blessings over the performance of commandments open with the word "blessed" and are sealed with it, such as the blessings over the reading from a Torah scroll.[234] [So also, a small number of blessings] relating to praise and thanksgiving [open with the word "blessed" and are sealed with it] such as the blessing recited by one who sees Jewish graves.[235] But the rest of the blessings over the performance of commandments open with the word "blessed" and are not sealed with it.[236]

2. There are some positive commandments concerning which a person must intensely strive to fulfill, such as phylacteries, sukkah, lulav, and shofar; these are called obligatory since a person must in every case fulfill them. There are other commandments which are not obligatory in this sense, and are similar to optional matters, such as mezuzah and railings around the roof,[237] since no one is obligated to dwell in a building which requires a mezuzah so that he must affix one; rather if he wishes to dwell all his life in a tent or on a boat, he may; nor is one required to build a house so that he must build a railing [around the roof]. One makes a blessing before the fulfillment of every positive commandment which relates to a matter between a person and the Holy One, blessed be He, whether it be obligatory or optional.[238]

3. So also, before fulfilling any of the commandments ordained by the Sages, whether obligatory—such as reading the Megillah, lighting Sabbath candles, or lighting Hanukkah candles—or those which are not obligatory—such as 'eruv[239] and washing the hands —one makes a blessing and says, "Who has sanctified us with His commandments and commanded us to." Where did He command us? In the Torah, since it is written therein: *When they have announced to you the verdict in the case, you shall carry out the verdict that is announced to you from that place that the Lord chose, observing scrupulously all their instructions to you* (Deut. 17:11). The upshot of this matter and its application is as follows: We say, "Who has sanctified us with His commandments," since among those commandments is the command to obey those who ordained the reading of the Megillah, or the lighting of the Hanukkah candles, and so all the other commandments ordained by the Sages.[240]

4. Why does one not make a blessing over washing the hands after a meal? This was only made obligatory because of the danger, and one does not make blessings over things done because of

danger. To what is this similar? To one who strains water before drinking it at night because of the danger of leeches;[241] such a one does not make the blessing "Who has commanded us to strain the water," and so in all similar cases.[242]

5. If one performs a commandment without making a blessing, so long as the performance of the commandment continues, one makes the blessing even after having done it; but if it is already completed, one does not make the blessing. How? If one wraps oneself in fringes, or puts on phylacteries, or sits in a sukkah without first making the blessing, one makes the blessing "Who has sanctified us with His commandments and commanded us to enwrap ourselves with fringes" even after having wrapped himself in the fringes. So, too, one makes the following blessing after putting on [phylacteries], "Who has sanctified us with His commandments and commanded us to don phylacteries," and while sitting [in the sukkah], "Who has sanctified us with His commandments and commanded us to sit in the sukkah," and so in all similar cases.[243]

6. But if one has slaughtered without a blessing, he cannot make the blessing "Who has sanctified us with His commandments and commanded us concerning slaughtering" after the slaughtering has been completed. So, too, if one has covered the blood without making a blessing,[244] or set apart the heave offering or tithe without making a blessing, or immersed oneself in a ritual bath,[245] one does not make a blessing after having done them, and so in all similar cases.[246]

7. There is only one commandment over which one makes the blessing after its performance: the immersion of a proselyte in a ritual bath, since he cannot say "Who has sanctified us ... and commanded us"[247] because he is not sanctified or commanded until he immerses himself. Therefore, after he immerses himself he makes the blessing "on immersion," since at the beginning of the process he was not eligible to make the blessing.[248]

8. In all cases where the performance of a commandment fulfills the obligation entirely, one makes a blessing during the performance of it. But with respect to all commandments which, after their performance, lead to another commandment, one only makes the blessing upon performing the last commandment. How? One who makes a sukkah or lulav or shofar or fringes or phylacteries or

mezuzah does not, while making them, make the blessing "Who has sanctified us with His commandments and commanded us to make a sukkah" or "to write phylacteries" since after making them there is another commandment.[249] When does one make the blessing? At the time one sits in the sukkah, or shakes the lulav, or hears the sound of the shofar, or wraps himself in fringes, or puts on the phylacteries, or puts up the mezuzah. But if one makes a railing around the roof of his house, he makes the following blessing while making it: "Who has sanctified us with His commandments and commanded us to erect a railing," and so in all similar cases.[250]

9. When performing any commandment which occurs annually, such as shofar, sukkah, lulav, reading the Megillah, lighting the Hanukkah candles, and so with every commandment which involves the acquisition of something new, such as fringes, phylacteries, mezuzah, and a railing, and, so also, a commandment which is performed only at irregular intervals and cannot be performed all the time, and in this is similar to commandments which occur annually, such as circumcising a son or redeeming a son, while performing these one makes the blessing "Who has kept us alive and sustained us." If one failed to make the blessing "Who has kept us alive" while making a sukkah, lulav, and so on, one makes the blessing "Who has kept us alive" over them at the time that one fulfills his obligation concerning them, and so in all similar cases.

10. Whether one performs a commandment for himself or for others, one makes a blessing of the following sort before performing it: "Who has sanctified us with His commandments and commanded us to." But one only makes the blessing "Who has kept us alive" over the performance of a commandment which one does for oneself. If one is about to perform several commandments, he does not make the blessing "Who has sanctified us with His commandments and commanded us concerning His commandments . . ." but, rather, makes a blessing for each one separately.[251]

11. If one performs a commandment, whether obligatory or optional, for himself, he makes the blessing "to do." But if he performs the commandment for others, he makes the blessing "concerning."[252]

12. How? If one puts on phylacteries, one makes the blessing "to don phylacteries." If one wraps himself in fringes, he makes the

blessing "to enwrap oneself." If he dwells in a sukkah he makes the blessing, "to dwell in a sukkah." And so one makes the blessings "to light the Sabbath candles" and "to complete the reading of Hallel." So, too, if one puts up a mezuzah in his house, he makes the blessing "to affix a mezuzah." If one makes a railing for the roof of one's home, he makes the blessing "Who has sanctified us with His commandments and commanded us to erect a railing." If one sets apart the heave offering or tithed for himself, he makes the blessing "to set apart." If one circumcises his son, he makes the blessing "to circumcise one's son." If one slaughters his paschal or festival sacrifice, he makes the blessing "to slaughter."

13. But if one puts up a mezuzah for others he makes the blessing "concerning the affixing of the mezuzah." If one makes a roof railing for others, he makes the blessing "concerning the erection of a railing." If one sets apart the heave offering for others, he makes the blessing "concerning the setting apart of the heave offering." If one circumcises another's son, he makes the blessing "concerning circumcision," and so in all similar cases.

14. If one performs a commandment for himself and others together, and it is not obligatory, he makes the blessing "concerning." For this reason, one makes the blessing "concerning the commandment of the *eruv.*" If it is obligatory and he intends to fulfill his own obligation and that of others as well, he makes the blessing "to do." For that reason one makes the blessing "to hear the sound of the shofar."

15. If one takes the lulav, he makes the blessing "on the taking of the lulav," since, as soon as he lifts it, he has fulfilled his obligation. But if one makes the blessing before taking it, one makes the blessing "to take the lulav" like "to sit in the sukkah." From this you learn that one who makes a blessing after performing a commandment without having made a blessing before makes the blessing on the action. But since washing the hands and slaughtering are optional, even if one slaughters for himself, he makes the blessings "on slaughtering and covering the blood" and "on washing the hands." Similarly, one makes the blessing "on the destruction of *hametz,*" whether he is searching for himself or searching for others, since, from the moment that he intends to annul the leaven, the com-

mandment to destroy it has been accomplished, even before the search, as will be explained in its place.[253]

16. No blessing is made over any customary matter, even if it is a custom instituted by the prophets, like the taking of a willow branch on the seventh day of Sukkot, and certainly if it is a custom instituted by the Sages, such as the recitation of Hallel on the days of the new moon and on the intermediate days of Passover. So also, on any matter over which there is a doubt if a blessing is required or not, one does it without the blessing. One must always take care not to make an unnecessary blessing and to make many necessary blessings, and so David said, *Every day will I bless You and praise Your name forever and ever* (Ps. 145 1:2).[254]

Blessed be the Merciful One Who assists.

TREATISE VI

Laws Concerning Circumcision
comprise one positive commandment, it being to circumcise males on the eighth day. The explanation of this commandment is found in these chapters:

CHAPTER ONE

1. Circumcision is a positive commandment, violation of which carries with it the penalty of excision,[1] as it says, *And if any male who is uncircumcised fails to circumcise the flesh of his foreskin, that person shall be cut off from his kin* (Gen. 17:14). The commandment to circumcise his son devolves on the father and in the case of slaves on the master, whether the slave is born into his possession or purchased. If a father or master has not circumcised them, he has nullified a positive commandment but is not excised, since excision applies only to the uncircumcised person himself. The court is commanded to circumcise that son or slave; they may not allow an uncircumcised male to remain among the Jews or their slaves.[2]

2. A man's son is not to be circumcised without the agreement of the father, unless the latter transgresses and refuses to circumcise his son, in which case the court circumcises the son against the father's will. If the son did not come to the court's attention and was never circumcised, he is required to have himself circumcised when he becomes an adult. From the time he becomes an adult, every day in which he does not have himself circumcised he transgresses and nullifies a positive commandment, but he does not incur the penalty of excision unless when he dies he is still deliberately uncircumcised.[3]

3. A master is required to circumcise his slaves, whether they were born into the possession of a Jew or purchased from a Gentile. In the case of a slave born into his state, he is to be circumcised when eight days old, while one who is purchased is circumcised on

the day he is purchased; even if he is purchased on the day he is born, he is to be circumcised on that day.[4]

4. There are some purchased slaves who are circumcised on the eighth day and some born slaves who are circumcised on the day they are born. How? If one purchased a pregnant female slave and also the rights to her fetus, then, when the baby is born, it is to be circumcised on the eighth day. This, even though one purchased the fetus in its own right, and it is thus a purchased slave,[5] since he purchased the mother before she gave birth, the baby is circumcised on the eighth day.[6]

5. If a person has purchased the rights to the unborn babies of a female slave, or purchased a female slave not on condition to immerse her in a ritual bath for servitude,[7] even though her babies are born into his possession, they are to be circumcised on the day of birth, for it is as if this newborn were purchased by itself on the day it was born, since [at the time of its birth] its mother is not in the condition of being owned by a Jew such that her son is considered as one born into servitude. But if the mother immerses herself in a ritual bath after giving birth, the baby is circumcised on the eighth day.[8]

6. If one purchases an adult Gentile slave and the slave does not wish to be circumcised, one puts up with him[9] for a full twelve months. It is forbidden to keep him uncircumcised for longer than that, and he must be sold back to Gentiles. But if while still owned by his Gentile master a condition had been made[10] that he remain uncircumcised, it is permissible to keep him uncircumcised, provided that he accepts the seven commandments and thus is like a resident alien.[11] But if he refuses to accept the seven commandments, he is immediately put to death. Resident aliens are accepted only during periods when the Jubilee is in effect.[12]

7. A proselyte who enters the community of Israel must be circumcised first. If he was circumcised while still a Gentile, a drop of the blood of the covenant must be drawn. So also, if an infant is born circumcised, a drop of the blood of the covenant must be drawn on the eighth day. An androgyne, that being a person born with complete male and female genitalia, must be circumcised on the eighth day. So also someone born by caesarian section. If some-

one is born with two foreskins, both are circumcised on the eighth day.[13]

8. Circumcisions are only performed during the daytime, after the sun has risen, whether it is on the eighth day, which is the proper time, or not in its proper time, that is, from the ninth day forward; as it says, *On the eighth day* (Lev. 12:3)—during the day, and not at night. If one was circumcised after dawn,[14] it is fit. Even though the entire day is fit for circumcision, it is praiseworthy to hasten and do it at the beginning of the day: "the zealous hasten to fulfill the commandments."[15]

9. Circumcision performed at the correct time[16] supersedes the Sabbath, while one performed not at the correct time supersedes neither the Sabbath nor a holiday. But whether at the correct time or not at the correct time, it supersedes leprosy. How? If the skin of the foreskin is afflicted with a bright spot,[17] it is cut off with the foreskin; even though it is prohibited to cut off leprous skin, a positive commandment supersedes a negative commandment.[18]

10. Just as circumcising one's son supersedes the Sabbath, so also the circumcision of slaves on the eighth day supersedes the Sabbath, if their eighth day falls on the Sabbath. This does not include a baby born into servitude whose mother did not immerse herself in a ritual bath before giving birth, for even though such a child is circumcised on its eighth day, that circumcision does not supersede the Sabbath.

11. The following do not supersede the Sabbath, but are circumcised on Sunday, which is their ninth day:

• an infant born circumcised
• a child born in the eighth month of pregnancy, before its development has been completed—such a one is considered like a stillborn, since it will not live
• a child born by caesarian section
• an androgyne
• one born with two foreskins[19]

12. In the case of a child born at twilight,[20] when it is unclear if it is day or night, the eight days are counted from the night and he is circumcised on the ninth day, which is possibly the eighth day. The circumcision of a child born Friday eve at twilight does not super-

sede the Sabbath; he is circumcised on Sunday, since the Sabbath is never superseded in the case of a doubt.[21]

13. A child born in its eighth month with fully formed hair and nails is considered to be a completed fetus in its seventh month, only delayed; it is permissible to move him on the Sabbath since he is not considered to be analogous to a stone,[22] and he is circumcised on the Sabbath. But if he is born with deficient hair and without fully formed nails, then it is definitely an eight-month fetus, that is, a nine-month child born prematurely and uncompleted and is therefore considered to be analogous to a stone and may not be moved on the Sabbath. Despite this, if he has survived thirty days, he is a viable child and is like other infants in every way. A human child who survives thirty days is not a stillborn.[23]

14. A fully formed child born in the seventh month of pregnancy is viable and is to be circumcised on the Sabbath. If it is doubtful whether it is the seventh or eighth month, he is in any event circumcised on the Sabbath, since if he is a fully formed child born in the seventh month his circumcision ought to supersede the Sabbath; while if he is a seven-month infant, then he who performs the circumcision is considered to be analogous to a person simply cutting meat, since an infant born in the eighth month is a stillborn.[24]

15. If the fetus's head was delivered during twilight [on Friday], even though it was not fully delivered till the Sabbath eve itself it is not circumcised on the Sabbath. Any case that does not supersede the Sabbath does not supersede the first day of a holiday but does supersede the second day of a holiday.[25] It does not supersede either of the two days of the festival of Rosh ha-Shanah. So also, a circumcision not carried out in its proper time does not supersede the second day of Rosh ha-Shanah.[26]

16. A sick person is not circumcised until he recuperates. Seven days are counted from the time he gets better, and he is then circumcised. When does this apply? When his belly is hot, and similar illnesses. But if he has painful eyes, he is to be circumcised the moment they are opened and cured, and so in all similar cases.[27]

17. An eight-day-old child who is very greenish is not to be circumcised until his blood develops[28] and he looks like a healthy child. So, too, if he is so reddish that it appears as if he has been

painted, he is not to be circumcised until the blood is absorbed and he appears to be like other infants, since this is a symptom of an illness. Great care must be taken in these cases; only children suffering from no illnesses may be circumcised, since danger to life supersedes everything. While it is possible to circumcise a person after the set time, it is impossible to bring a single Jew back to life.[29]

18. If a woman had her first son circumcised and he died in consequence, the circumcision having weakened him, and so also had her second son circumcised—whether from the same husband or another—and he also died in consequence of the circumcision, she must not circumcise a third son at the appropriate time; we must wait till he grows a bit and gets stronger.[30]

CHAPTER TWO

1. All are fit to perform circumcision; if there is no man, then even an uncircumcised man, a slave, a woman, or a minor may perform circumcision. A Gentile must never circumcise; but if one has done so, there is no need to repeat the circumcision. One may circumcise with anything, including flint, glass, or anything that cuts. But one should not circumcise with a reed sliver because of the danger involved.[31] However, the choicest way of performing the commandment is with metal, whether with a knife or scissors. All Jews customarily use a knife.[32]

2. How is circumcision performed? The skin covering the crown is cut off such that the whole crown is exposed. Then the soft membrane under the skin is peeled off with the nail and pulled to one side and another until the flesh of the crown is visible. The site of the circumcision is then sucked, so that the blood is drawn even from the distant parts so that there will be no danger. A circumciser who does not perform this sucking should be removed from his position. After the sucking, plaster or a bandage, or the like, is place on the wound.[33]

3. There are shreds of skin which invalidate a circumcision, and there are shreds which do not. How? If there remains of the foreskin skin which covers most of the uppermost part of the crown, the person remains uncircumcised as he was; this skin is a shred

which invalidates. But if there remains only a little of it, which does not cover most of the uppermost part of the crown, this is a shred which does not invalidate.[34]

4. If, while still performing a circumcision, the circumciser finds shreds, he must return to his work in order to remove them, whether or not they invalidate the circumcision. But if he has finished the procedure, he goes back only to remove shreds which invalidate circumcision, not those which do not. If one has performed a circumcision but does not remove the soft membrane under the skin, it is as if he has not circumcised at all.[35]

5. In the case of a child whose flesh is soft and hangs loosely, or is fat, such that it appears that he is not circumcised, if he appears circumcised when having an erection, nothing need be done. The flesh on each side must be corrected for appearance's sake. But if when having an erection he appears uncircumcised, the procedure is to be performed again, and the loosely hanging flesh is cut away on the sides such that the crown is visible during an erection. This law is of rabbinic origin; but from the Torah, if one has been circumcised, even if he appears to be uncircumcised he need not be circumcised a second time.[36]

6. Everything that must be done for a circumcision is done on the Sabbath: circumcision, the removal of the membrane, the sucking, returning after having finished the procedure to remove shreds which invalidate, removing shreds which do not invalidate so long as the procedure has not been completed, and applying plaster to the wound. But the tools used for circumcision do not supersede the Sabbath. How? If one has no knife, a knife is not to be made, nor is one to be brought from place to place; it is not to be brought from courtyard to courtyard in an alleyway that does not have an 'eruv. The rabbinic need for an 'eruv is not superseded by the need to bring a knife, since it could have been brought before the Sabbath.[37]

7. So also, one does not grind medicinal herbs or heat water,[38] or prepare the plaster, or mix wine and oil on the Sabbath for a circumcision. If one has not ground cumin[39] before the Sabbath, one may chew it with his teeth and apply it. If one has not mixed wine and oil for the circumcision before the Sabbath, each should be applied separately. This is the rule: anything that could have

been prepared before the Sabbath does not supersede the Sabbath; thus, if one has forgotten to prepare the necessary tools for the circumcision, it is put off till the ninth day.[40]

8. If a child had been circumcised on the Sabbath and the hot water[41] spilled out or the medicinal herbs scattered, anything that needs to be done is done on the Sabbath,[42] because of the danger to the child. In places where it is customary to bathe an infant, he is to be bathed on the Sabbath on the day of his circumcision, whether before the circumcision or after it, or if the third day after the circumcision[43] falls on the Sabbath, whether the whole body is bathed or just the place of circumcision, whether with hot water heated before the Sabbath or with hot water heated on the Sabbath, because of the danger to the child.[44]

9. If those preparing the circumcision forgot to bring a knife before the Sabbath, a Gentile may be told to bring the knife on the Sabbath, provided he does not bring it through a public domain. The general rule is that in order to perform a commandment at its correct time we are permitted to tell a Gentile to do something forbidden to us on the Sabbath because of Sabbath rest,[45] but we may not tell a Gentile to do something forbidden to us if it is actually forbidden work.[46]

10. Holidays are not superseded to prepare the tools necessary for a circumcision, even one being done on the eighth day, since they could have been prepared before the holiday. This is an a fortiori argument: if preparing the tools necessary for circumcision does not supersede the laws of Sabbath rest which are of rabbinic authority, how can they supersede a negative commandment of the Torah? Medicinal herbs, however, may be ground on a holiday for a circumcision, since they may be used for cooking; and so may wine be mixed with oil.[47]

CHAPTER THREE

1. A person circumcising another's son makes the following blessing before performing the circumcision: "Blessed are You, Lord our God, King of the Universe, Who has sanctified us with His commandments and commanded us concerning circumcision." One circumcising his own son makes the blessing "Who

commanded us to circumcise the son." The father of the boy makes another blessing: "Blessed are You, Lord our God, King of the Universe, Who has sanctified us with His commandments and commanded us to bring him into the covenant of our father Abraham." Since a father is more obligated to circumcise his son than are the generality of Jews obligated to circumcise uncircumcised men among them, if the father is not present, no one else makes this blessing. There are those who have instructed that the court make this blessing, or someone else from among those present, but it is not appropriate to do this.[48]

2. If there are others present, they should say, "As you have brought him into the Covenant, so may you bring him to Torah, to marriage, and to good deeds."[49]

3. After that, the father, or the circumciser, or one of those present, should make the following blessing: "Blessed are You, Lord our God, King of the Universe, Who sanctified the beloved while in the womb,[50] and Who placed His law in his flesh, and Who sealed his descendants with the sign of the covenant of holiness. Therefore, in recompense for this, O Living God, be our portion forever. Our Rock, as you commanded the sanctified ones,[51] so also command to save from destruction our remnant's beloved.[52] Blessed are You, Lord, Who enters into the covenant."[53] The father then makes the blessing "Who has kept us alive."[54]

4. One who circumcises proselytes makes the blessing "Blessed are You, Lord our God, King of the Universe, Who has sanctified us with His commandments and commanded us to circumcise proselytes and to draw from them a drop of the blood of the covenant, for without the blood of the covenant, the heavens and earth would not remain, as it says, *As surely as I have established My covenant with day and night—the laws of heaven and earth—so I will never reject the offspring of Jacob and My servant David*" (Jer. 33:25).[55]

5. One who circumcises his slave makes the blessing "Blessed are You, Lord our God, King of the Universe, Who has sanctified us with His commandments and commanded us to circumcise slaves and to draw from them a drop of the blood of the covenant, for without the blood of the covenant, the heavens and earth would not remain, as it says, *As surely as I have established My covenant with day and night—the laws of heaven and earth—so I will never reject the*

offspring of Jacob and My servant David" (Jer. 33:25). If one circumcises someone else's slave, he makes the blessing "on the circumcision of slaves." When an adult is circumcised his genitals must be covered until after the blessing is made; they are then uncovered and circumcised.

6. There is no need to make a blessing when the blood of the covenant is drawn from a proselyte who was circumcised before his conversion or from a child born circumcised. So, too, no blessing is made over the circumcision of an androgyne, because it is not certain that the circumcision is obligatory.

7. A Jew may not remove the foreskin of a Gentile who needs the procedure done because of a wound or a boil, since Gentiles are not to be saved from death or endangered.[56] This is so, even though a commandment is fulfilled with this form of medical treatment, since the Gentile did not intend it. Therefore, if a Gentile intends this procedure to constitute circumcision, it is permissible for a Jew to circumcise him.[57]

8. The foreskin is disgusting, since the wicked are defamed with reference to it, as it says, *Lo, days are coming—declares the Lord—when I will take note of everyone circumcised in the foreskin: of Egypt, Judah, Edom, the Ammonites, Moab, and all the desert dwellers who have the hair of their temples clipped. For all these nations are uncircumcised, but all the House of Israel are uncircumcised of heart* (Jer. 9:25). Great is circumcision, since Abraham our Father was not called "perfect" until he was circumcised, as it says, *Walk in My ways and be blameless. I will establish My covenant between Me and you* (Gen. 17:1–2). Anyone who violates the covenant of Abraham our Father and does not remove his foreskin, or pulls it,[58] has no share in the world to come, even if he has performed many other good deeds.[59]

9. Come and see how serious a matter circumcision is, since Moses our Teacher was given no respite from performing it, even though he was traveling.[60] There were only three covenants made for all the other commandments of the Torah, as it says, *These are the terms of the covenant which the Lord commanded Moses to conclude with the Israelites in the land of Moab, in addition to the covenant which He had made with them at Horeb* (Deut. 28:69); there also he said, *You stand this day . . . to enter into the covenant of the Lord*

your God (Deut. 29:9)—this comes to three covenants. But concerning circumcision, thirteen covenants were made with Abraham our Father, as it says: *I will establish My covenant between Me and you* (Gen. 17:2), *As for Me, this is My covenant with you* (Gen. 17:4), *I will maintain My covenant between Me and you* (Gen. 17:7), *as an everlasting covenant throughout the ages* (Gen. 17:7), *you and your offspring to come throughout the ages shall keep My covenant* (Gen. 17:9), *Such shall be the covenant* (Gen. 17:10), *and that shall be the sign of the covenant* (Gen. 17:11), *Thus shall My covenant* (Gen. 17:13), *an everlasting pact* (Gen. 17:13), *he has broken My covenant* (Gen. 17:14), *I will maintain My covenant with him* (Gen. 17:19), *an everlasting covenant* (Gen. 17:19), *But My covenant I will maintain with Isaac* (Gen. 17:21).

Blessed be the Merciful One Who Assists

The second book has been completed with the help of God. It contains forty-six chapters:

"Laws Concerning the Recitation of the Shema," four chapters
"Laws Concerning Prayer," fifteen chapters
"Laws Concerning Tefillin, Mezuzah, and the Torah Scroll," ten chapters
"Laws Concerning Fringes," three chapters
"Laws Concerning Blessings," eleven chapters
"Laws Concerning Circumcision," three chapters

Blessed be He Who gives strength to the weary.[61]

APPENDIX

Maimonides' "Prayerbook"

As noted in the translator's introduction, Maimonides' order of prayers at the end of the Book of Love contains no surprises and appears to be a reflection of what was commonly accepted in his day in Egypt, carrying no specific or unique normative significance. Throughout his presentation he repeatedly uses expressions like "it is customary" or "the people customarily," emphasizing both that he is reporting on what he has seen and that this report is essentially descriptive as opposed to normative.

Maimonides first presents the order of the morning service. He skips the blessings found in today's prayerbooks, since he holds that these should be said as the appropriate actions are done (see above, "Laws Concerning Prayer, VII) and begins with the text of M. Pe'ah I.1, followed by the preliminaries found in most contemporary prayerbooks (Elbogin, 78–80).[1] He follows this with *Barukh She-Amar,* the verses of song (mentioning that on Sabbaths *Nishmat* is added), and *Yishtabaḥ* (Elbogin, 72–76). Unlike contemporary custom, Maimonides writes that the psalm of the day should be recited after *Yishtabaḥ* (Elbogin, 75). Among the many local variations that he mentions, pride of place is given to different customs relating to the recitation of the Song at the Sea (Ex. 15:1–19; Elbogin, 75).

Maimonides then specifies the two blessings before the recitation of Shema and the blessing after it (Elbogin, 16–24). Having brought up Shema, Maimonides specifies the blessings before and after the evening Shema, and mentions that some have the custom of adding verses to the second blessing.

Next, Maimonides enumerates the blessings of the *'amidah,* with the various additions for various seasons, Saturday night, Rosh Ḥodesh, the intermediate days of festivals, public fasts, the Ninth of Av, Purim, and Hannukah (Elbogin, 24–54).

Maimonides presents only one version of the *qedushah,* with additions for the ten days of repentance (Elbogin, 54–62). He then presents three versions of the kaddish (regular, after the completion of the 'amidah, and after the study of Torah) (Elbogin, 80–84) and describes the various kinds of petitionary prayers customarily said after the 'amidah (Elbogin, 66–72).

Maimonides next presents the text of the 'amidah for Sabbath (Elbogin, 95–99), holidays (Elbogin, 111–117), and days of Awe (Elbogin, 117–129) and mentions the additions "customarily" made during the Days of Awe. This is followed by the text of the confession (Elbogin, 125–126) and the 'amidah of ne'ilah (Elbogin, 127).

The text of the grace after meals is then presented, as well as the blessings made before and after reading the haftarah on Sabbaths and holidays (Elbogin, 143–149). A list of haftarot rounds out the text.

Matters included in contemporary prayerbooks missing from Maimonides include the order of the sacrifices before the morning psalms and the 'aleinu prayer (Elbogin, 71–72).

In the text of the 'Amidah that follows, I cite the translation (freely emended) of Siddur Sim Shalom. Maimonides does not offer the text of the nineteen blessings of the 'amidah; the text presented here represents one contemporary version—it is not meant to be the text that Maimonides himself used (although the variations are likely to be slight). It is presented here to make it easier for the reader to follow the discussions in "Laws Concerning Prayer and the Priestly Blessing."

THE TEXT OF THE 'AMIDAH

1. Blessed are You, Lord our God, God of our ancestors, God of Abraham, of Isaac, and of Jacob, great, mighty, awesome, exalted God, Who bestows lovingkindness, Possessor of all. You remember the pious deeds of our ancestors and will send a redeemer to their children's children because of Your loving nature. You are the king Who helps and saves and shields. Blessed are You, Lord, Shield of Abraham.

2. Your might, O Lord, is boundless. You give life to the dead; great is Your saving power. Your lovingkindness sustains the living, Your great mercies give life to the dead. You support the falling,

heal the ailing, free the fettered. You keep faith with those who sleep in dust. Whose power can compare with Yours? You are the master of life and death and deliverance. Faithful are You in giving life to the dead. Blessed are You, Lord, Who gives life to the dead.

3. Holy are You and Holy is Your name. Holy are those who praise You daily. Blessed are You, Lord, holy God.

4. You graciously endow mortals with intelligence, teaching wisdom and understanding. Grant us knowledge, discernment, and wisdom. Blessed are You, Lord, Who graciously grants intelligence.

5. Our Father, bring us back to Your Torah. Our King, draw us near to Your service. Lead us back to You, truly repentant. Blessed are You, Lord, Who welcomes repentance.

6. Forgive us, our Father, for we have sinned; pardon us, our King, for we have transgressed, for you forgive and pardon. Blessed are You, gracious and forgiving Lord.

7. Behold our affliction and deliver us. Redeem us soon because of Your mercy, for You are the mighty Redeemer. Blessed are You, Lord, Redeemer of the people of Israel.

8. Heal us, O Lord, and we shall be healed. Help us and save us, for You are our glory. Grant perfect healing for all our afflictions, for You are the faithful and merciful God of healing. Blessed are You, Lord, Healer of His people Israel.

9. Lord our God, make this a blessed year for us. May its varied produce bring us happiness. Grant [blessing to/dew and rain to bless] the earth. Satisfy us with its abundance, and bless our year as the best of years. Blessed are You, Lord, Who blesses years.

10. Sound the great shofar to herald our freedom, raise high the banner to gather our exiles. Gather us together from the ends of the earth. Blessed are You, Lord, Who gathers the dispersed of His people Israel.

11. Restore our judges as in days of old, restore our counselors as in former times. Remove from us sorrow and anguish. Reign alone over us with lovingkindness; with justice and mercy sustain our cause. Blessed are You, Lord, King Who loves justice.

12. Frustrate the hopes of all those who malign us; let all evil very soon disappear. Let all the enemies of Your people soon be

destroyed. May You quickly uproot and crush the arrogant; may You subdue and humble them in our time. Blessed are You, Lord, Who breaks the enemy and humbles the arrogant.

13. Let Your tender mercies be stirred for the righteous, the pious, and the leaders of the House of Israel, devoted scholars and proselytes. Reward all who trust in You, cast our lot with those who are faithful to You. May we never come to shame, for our trust is in You. Blessed are You, Lord, Who sustains the righteous.

14. Have mercy, Lord, and return to Jerusalem, Your city. May Your presence dwell there as You have promised. Build it now, speedily in our days, and for all time. Reestablish there the throne of David, Your servant. Blessed are You, Lord, Who builds Jerusalem.

15. Bring to flower the shoot of Your servant David. Hasten the advent of Messianic redemption. Each and every day we hope for Your deliverance. Blessed are You, Lord, Who assures our deliverance.

16. Lord our God, hear our voice. Have compassion upon us, pity us, accept our prayer with loving favor. You listen to entreaty and prayer. Do not turn us away unanswered, our King, for You mercifully heed Your people's supplication. Blessed are You, Lord, Who hears prayer.

17. Lovingly accept Your people and their prayer. Restore sacrificial worship to Your sanctuary. May the burnt offerings and the worship of Your people Israel always be acceptable to You. May we witness Your merciful return to Zion. Blessed are You, Lord, Who restores His presence to Zion.

18. We thank You for being the Lord our God and God of our ancestors throughout all time. You are the Rock of our lives, the Shield of our salvation in every generation. We thank You and praise You morning, noon, and night for Your miracles which daily attend us and for Your wondrous kindnesses. Our lives are in Your hand; our souls are in Your charge. You are good, with everlasting mercy; You are compassionate, with enduring lovingkindness. We have always placed our hope in You. For all these blessings we shall ever praise and exalt You. May every living creature thank You and praise You faithfully, our deliverance and our help. Blessed are You, beneficent Lord to Whom all praise is due.

19. Grant peace to the world, with happiness, and blessing, grace, love, and mercy for us and for all the people Israel. Bless us, our Father, all of us together with the light of Your countenance; for by that light did You give us a Torah of life, love and tenderness, justice, mercy, and peace. May it please You to bless Your people Israel in every season and at all times with Your gift of peace. Blessed are You, Lord, Who blesses His people Israel with peace.

ABBREVIATIONS

NJPS   New Jewish Publication Society (translation of the Bible)

Books of the Bible (in alphabetical order)

Dan.	Daniel
Deut.	Deuteronomy
Exod.	Exodus
Ez.	Ezekiel
Gen.	Genesis
Hab.	Habakkuk
Isa.	Isaiah
Jer.	Jeremiah
Josh.	Joshua
Lam.	Lamentations
Lev.	Leviticus
Neh.	Nehemiah
Num.	Numbers
Prov.	Proverbs
Ps.	Psalms
Sam.	Samuel

Talmudic Tractates

Unless otherwise noted, all references are to the Babylonian Talmud. References to the Mishnah are preceded by "M.," to the Jerusalem Talmud by "J.," and to the Tosefta by "Tos."

'Ar.	'Arakhin
AZ	Avodah Zarah
BB	Bava Batra
Ber.	Berakhot
BK	Bava Kamma
BM	Bava Metzi'a
'Er.	'Eruvin

Giṭ.	Giṭṭin
Ḥul.	Ḥullin
Ket.	Ketubot
Kid.	Kiddushin
Mak.	Makkot
Meg.	Megillah
Men.	Menaḥot
Ned.	Nedarim
Nid.	Niddah
Pes.	Pesaḥim
RH	Rosh Ha-Shanah
Sab.	Sabbath
San.	Sanhedrin
Soṭ.	Soṭah
Suk.	Sukkot
Ta'an.	Ta'anit
Yad.	Yadayim
Yev.	Yevamot
Zev.	Zevaḥot

NOTES

1. Maimonides lists these out of order.
2. In the translation of Shlomo Pines.
3. This may explain why Maimonides includes his discussion of the synagogue in "The Book of Love" and not in "The Book of Temple Service." He apparently chooses to treat the synagogue in its capacity as a venue for worship for all Jews, and not in its capacity as a replacement for the Temple.
4. In the *Guide of the Perplexed* Maimonides groups the laws concerning circumcision with laws regulating sexuality.
5. My thanks to Shmuel Morell for pointing this out to me. Isadore Twersky, *Introduction to the Code of Maimonides,* 260–261, notes that the verse "has an obvious verbal connection with the book's title, but it also plays upon the themes of constancy and continuity and rather subtly links up love expressed through actions with meditation and contemplation. The reciprocity between action and reflection, deeds maintaining as well as manifesting love of God, is thus noted pithily."
6. Translated by Moses Hyamson, *The Book of Knowledge,* 35b.
7. "Laws Concerning Repentance," X.6; Hyamson, 92b.
8. I.39, 89. Maimonides appears to imply that the apprehension of God should be the constant end of all one's actions and not something episodic.
9. There are some passages where Maimonides makes this explicit. "Laws Concerning Character Traits," III.2: "A man should direct all his thoughts and activities to the knowledge of God, alone. All one's activities, even cohabitation, should have this ultimate end in view" (Hyamson, 49b).
10. In "Laws Concerning the Foundations of the Torah," II.1–2, and the fifth of the "Eight Chapters," among other places.
11. Hyamson, 92b.
12. See Steven Harvey, "The Meaning of Terms Designating Love in Judaeo-Arabic Thought."
13. Compare, further, Ehud Benor, *Worship of the Heart,* 56–58. For a very useful discussion of love and knowledge in Maimonides, see Lawrence Kaplan, "Rav Kook and the Jewish Philosophical Tradition."
14. Howard Kreisel, *Maimonides' Political Thought,* 240. Boaz Cohen, "The Classification of the Law in the Mishneh Torah," offers a more prosaic explanation for the contents of "The Book of Love." He is of the opinion that Maimonides "chose the name Love after Deut. 6:4–9. In the three paragraphs of the Shema, most of the subdivisions of the book are alluded to" (534).
15. See Menachem Kellner, *Maimonides on Human Perfection.*
16. Cohen, 534; he cites the end of Tosefta Berakhot.

17. See David Hartman, *Israelis and the Jewish Tradition,* 79. Compare also the passage from *Guide of the Perplexed,* I.39, cited above at n. 8.

18. Kreisel, 240.

19. Twersky, 262, notes: "Book Two is the Book of Love because regular performance of commandments—uninterrupted commitment to, and involvement with, divine law—leads to love of God." Twersky goes on to say (283): "Anticipating potential criticism or skepticism, Maimonides explained at the beginning of the *Mishneh Torah* that 'circumcision is included here because this is a sign in our flesh, serving as a constant reminder, even when phylacteries and fringes, etc., are absent.' While Maimonides is undoubtedly drawing upon Rabbinic statements in Mishnah, Tosefta, and Talmud, which call attention to the permanence and omnipresent reality of circumcision, his reliance upon this insight for purposes of classification is a tour de force."

20. The core text of the liturgy, more popularly known as the *shemonah 'esreh,* or prayer of eighteen (in theory; in practice, nineteen) benedictions.

21. See Daniel Goldschmidt, "Maimonides' Prayer Book According to the Oxford Manuscript"; Moshe Goshen-Gottstein, "The Aleppo Codex and Maimonides' Laws Concerning the Torah Scroll"; and Jordan S. Penkower, "Maimonides and the Aleppo Codex."

22. Compare "Laws Concerning the Foundations of the Torah," I.1–7, esp. paragraph 6. Maimonides here refers to one "basic principle," which implies that affirming God's unity, loving God, and studying God are all essentially the same thing.

23. Num. 15:39: *That shall be your fringe; look at it and recall all the commandments of the Lord and observe them, so that you do not follow your heart and eyes in your lustful urge.* J. Ber. I.5; M. Tamid V.1; M. Ber. II.2.

24. Or perhaps, even, "and study of His Talmud."

25. Hyamson, 94a, translates this as "and studying his words"; Boruch Kaplan, *Maimonides' Mishneh Torah,* 12, has "and the study of Torah"; S. T. Rubenstein (in the Jerusalem 1958 edition) explains the passage as referring to the commandment of Torah study; Nachum Rabinovitch, *Mishneh Torah According to the Bodleian Ms. Huntington 80,* adopts the same position, referring back to Berakhot 2b. These modern translators and interpreters follow the understanding of this term implicitly held by the *Leḥem Mishneh* and *Kesef Mishneh.* I have only found one modern who understands the passage properly, and that is, not surprisingly, Rabbi Joseph Kafiḥ in his edition of the *Mishneh Torah.*

26. So also in "Laws Concerning Idolatry," I.3.

27. In "Laws Concerning Repentance," X.6, Maimonides makes the point that love of God is proportionate to knowledge of God and that one fulfills the commandment in the Shema to love God (Deut. 6:5) only by knowing God. This point finds expression as well in *Sefer ha-Miẓvot,* positive commandment 3 (another text in which Maimonides writes successfully for diverse audiences at the same time). See, further, *Guide of the Perplexed,* I.39, III.28 (512), and especially III.51 (621): "Now we have made it clear several times that love is proportionate to apprehension."

28. *The Authorized Version of the Code of Maimonides (Mishneh Torah), The Book of Knowledge and the Book of Love (Sefer Madda, Sefer Ahabah): Facsimile Edition of Oxford Manuscript Huntington 80.* For an earlier study by Shlomo Zalman Havlin, see "An Autograph Testament of Maimonides," '*Alei Sefer* 18 (1995–96): 171–176 (Hebrew).

29. This edition was published in two volumes: Jerusalem: Maaliot Press, 1994.

30. This edition appeared in one volume: Jerusalem, Makhon Mosheh, 1985; corrected and reissued in 1993.

31. Rabinovitch (9) asserts that this transcription is not to be taken seriously at all. I have not checked myself, but I have no reason to doubt Rabbi Rabinovitch's assessment.

32. The ms. divides each chapter into paragraphs, but does not number them. I have followed the paragraphing in the ms. and have numbered the paragraphs; the paragraph division and numbering in the printed editions often diverge from the ms.

33. See Daniel Goldschmidt, "Maimonides' Prayer Book According to the Oxford Manuscript"; Meir Havazelet, "Traces of the Siddur of Rav Sa'adia Gaon in Maimonides' *Mishneh Torah*"; and Stefan Reif, *Judaism and Hebrew Prayer,* 192–193. J. Kafiḥ, 707–711 in his edition, argues that Maimonides used the Yemenite rite as practiced in his day as his source and saw it as normative for all Jews. This unusual view is criticized by R. Yizḥaq Sheilat in his edition of *Iggerot Ha-Rambam,* 2:701–704. For an excellent summary of the Kafiḥ-Sheilat discussion in English, see Seth Kadish, *Kavvana,* 317–320. Kadish adduces several reasons for rejecting J. Kafiḥ's position and affirms the position taken here, that the description of the prayers appended to "The Book of Love" is not presented as a normative prayerbook for all Israel.

TREATISE I: LAWS CONCERNING THE RECITATION OF THE SHEMA

1. M. Ber. I.6.

2. The biblical text is divided into blocks of verses called *parashot* (sing. *parashah*); it is to these that Maimonides is referring here. See "Laws Concerning Tefillin, Mezuzah, and the Torah Scroll," VIII.

3. Full text of the passage (NJPS): *Hear, O Israel! The Lord is our God, the Lord alone. You shall love the Lord your God with all your heart and with all your soul and with all your might. Take to heart these instructions with which I charge you this day. Impress them upon your children. Recite them when you stay at home and when you are away, when you lie down and when you get up. Bind them as a sign on your arm and let them serve as a symbol on your forehead; inscribe them on the doorposts of your house and on your gates.*

4. Full text of the passage: *If, then, you obey the commandments that I enjoin upon you this day, loving the Lord your God and serving Him with all your heart and soul, I will grant the rain for your land in season, the early rain and the late. You shall*

gather in your new grain and wine and oil—I will also provide grass in the fields for your cattle—and thus you shall eat your fill. Take care not to be lured away to serve other gods and bow to them. For the Lord's anger will flare up against you, and He will shut up the skies so that there will be no rain and the ground will not yield its produce; and you will soon perish from the good land that the Lord is assigning to you. Therefore impress these My words upon your very heart: bind them as a sign on your arm and let them serve as a symbol on your forehead, and teach them to your children—reciting them when you stay at home and when you are away, when you lie down and when you get up; and inscribe them on the doorposts of your house and on your gates—to the end that you and your children may endure, in the land that the Lord swore to your fathers to assign to them, as long as there is a heaven over the earth.

5. Full text of the passage: *The Lord said to Moses as follows: Speak to the Israelite people and instruct them to make for themselves fringes on the corners of their garments throughout the ages; let them attach a cord of blue to the fringe at each corner. That shall be your fringe; look at it and recall all the commandments of the Lord and observe them, so that you do not follow your heart and eyes in your lustful urge. Thus you shall be reminded to observe all My commandments and to be holy to your God. I the Lord am your God, who brought you out of the land of Egypt to be your God: I, the Lord your God.*

6. Most traditionalist interpreters make this refer to the study of Torah. Rabbi Joseph Kafiḥ in his commentary to the *Mishneh Torah* is one of the few properly to understand the import of the phrase.

7. Compare "Laws Concerning the Foundations of the Torah," I.1–7, esp. paragraph 6. Maimonides here refers to one "basic principle," which implies that affirming God's unity, loving God, and studying God are all at root the same thing.

8. Num. 15:39: *That shall be your fringe; look at it and recall all the commandments of the Lord and observe them, so that you do not follow your heart and eyes in your lustful urge.* See J. Ber. I.5; M. Tamid V.1; M. Ber. II.2.

9. In a passage well known from the Passover Haggadah, originating at M. Ber. I.5, the expression *"all* the days of your life" is taken to include the nights.

10. M. Ber. I.9, Ber. 12b.

11. This expression is first found in M. Yoma III.8.

12. After Sifre, piska 31 (to Deut. 6:4) and Pes. 56a.

13. Here and wherever I think it helpful throughout this translation, I cite full verses even if Maimonides only cites the first few words of the verse.

14. Israel being Jacob. See Gen. 32:28 and 35:10.

15. The differences between Maimonides' formulation here and that of his sources (cited in n. 12) are significant. Where the rabbinic sources appear to make the issue one of loyalty to God, Maimonides makes it one of doctrinal orthodoxy.

16. Lit., "daytime."

17. M. Ber. I.8.

18. Ber. 11a–12a.

19. I.e., does not open with the formula "Blessed are You, Lord our God."

Blessings can both open and close with the formula, open but not close with it, or close but not open with it.

20. M. Ber. I.8, Ber. 12a, 33a.

21. Maimonides' precise meaning has been the subject of extended controversy for close to a millennium. The subject is far too complex to be summarized here. Ber. 11b–12a.

22. I.e., halfway from sunset to sunrise.

23. In his commentary on M. Ber. I.1, Maimonides explains "dawn" (*ammud ha-shahar*) as the first light seen in the east, about seventy-two minutes ("one and one-fifth hours") before sunrise.

24. I.e., the Sages (in M. Ber. I.1).

25. Rabinovitch argues that the translation here should read: "in order to keep one from slothfulness." Sources: M. Ber. I.1, VIII.2.

26. M. Ber. VIII.2. *Pesha'* usually connotes avoidable but withal inadvertent transgression.

27. According to Rabinovitch: "who postponed."

28. The "hours" Maimonides is referring to here are relative hours, each being constituted by one-twelfth of the amount of daylight for that day. M. Ber. I.5 (and Maimonides' commentary thereon).

29. M. Ber. VIII.2.

30. M. Ber. I.5.

31. Lit., "directing his heart."

32. I.e., *reading* the passages in order to check them for scribal error.

33. M. Ber. II.1.

34. M. Ber. I.6–7, Ber. 11a, 13b.

35. Lit., "if sleep coerced him."

36. Ber. 13b.

37. As it would be if they recited while working.

38. M. Ber. II.4, Ber. 16a.

39. M. Sab. I.2, Tos. Ber. I.2, II.6.

40. M. Sab. I.2.

41. M. Ber. III.5.

42. I.e., it is forbidden to speak while reciting the Shema; similarly, one should not try to communicate nonverbally.

43. Yoma 19b, M. Ber. II.3.

44. *Be-khol levavkha;* the first word ends with the letter "lamed" and the second begins with it.

45. In Hebrew the two letters transliterated here by "f" and "p" are the same, namely, the letter *peh.*

46. Lit., "the four directions." The point here (based on a discussion in Ber. 13b) is that one ought to extend the word "one" (or its last letter) long enough self-consciously to (re-)accept God's sovereignty over the universe.

47. Which could be construed as meaning "is not one." M. Ber. II.3, P. Ber. II.4, M. Ber. XIII.3.

48. Lit., "holy language." M. Soṭ. VII.1, Ber. 13a.

49. Nor are they in the same order in the Torah as in the recitation of the Shema; that may be Maimonides' meaning here.

50. M. Ber. II.3, Ber. 33b.

51. Meg. 18b.

52. Ber. 21a, M. Ber. II.3.

53. I.e., the word appears in both the first and the second sections of the Shema.

54. Which is recited immediately after the "inscribe them" of "If, then, you obey."

55. Lit., "the habit of his tongue." I.e., he may assume that he recited the Shema in the usual, proper manner. Source: Ber. 16a.

56. M. Ber. II.1, Kid. 30b.

57. M. Ber. II.1.

58. I.e., he may greet those whom he fears and respond to one to whom he is obligated to show respect. Source: M. Ber. II.2.

59. Ber. 14b.

60. Many of the issues raised in this paragraph relate to Deut. 23:10–15: *When you go out as a troop against your enemies, be on your guard against anything untoward. If anyone among you has been rendered unclean by a nocturnal emission, he must leave the camp, and he must not reenter the camp. Toward evening he shall bathe in water, and at sundown he may reenter the camp. Further, there shall be an area for you outside the camp, where you may relieve yourself. With your gear you shall have a spike, and when you have squatted you shall dig a hole with it and cover up your excrement. Since the Lord your God moves about in your camp to protect you and to deliver your enemies to you, let your camp be holy; let Him not find anything unseemly among you and turn away from you.*

61. Sab. 10a.

62. Which has not yet been used.

63. Here and below, perhaps, "owner."

64. Ber. 26a, Sab. 10a.

65. Lit., "in a secular language."

66. AZ 44b, Ber. 24b.

67. See "Laws Concerning the Foundations of the Torah," VI.2.

68. Sab. 10b, 40b.

69. Olives and eggs constitute standard measurements of volume in Halakhah. On "grain" see below, "Laws Concerning Blessings," III.1., Ber. 25a, Suk. 42b.

70. Ber. 25a.

71. M. Ber. III.5.

72. Lit., "at the side of the place."

73. Ber. 25a–b.

74. Either 86.4 milliliters or 149.3 milliliters, depending on the authority consulted. For a table of weights and measures, see "Laws Concerning the 'Erub,"

I.12–13, and the article "Weights and Measures," *Encyclopaedia Judaica,* vol. 16, cols. 376–392.

75. Ber. 25b.
76. Near the anus.
77. I.e., squats to defecate.
78. Ber. 25b.
79. Even less than four cubits.
80. Ber. 25a-b.
81. Ber. 25a, P. Ber. II.3.
82. I.e., if someone breaks wind in your presence, you may continue Torah study, but may not continue the recitation of the Shema, till the odor passes. Ber. 24b.
83. Ber. 25a.
84. Ber. 25b, 24a.
85. I.e., the assumption being that he is reciting while squatting.
86. I.e., one winds the blanket (here in the Hebrew, *tallit*) tightly below the level of the heart, both to cover the private parts and separate the heart from them. Ber. 24b-25a.
87. Ber. 22a.
88. Ber. 24a.
89. Assuming that the marriage took place on Wednesday night (Ket. 2a).
90. M. Ber. III.3, Nazir 29a, M. Ber. II.5.
91. I.e., the commandment to be fruitful and multiply.
92. Parent, spouse, sibling, child.
93. Lit., "his dead."
94. M. Ber. III.1, Ber. 18a, Ber. 14b.
95. So that the funeral not interfere with the recitation of the Shema in its proper time.
96. The entire funeral party is not exempted, only those who have been designated as pallbearers, or their replacements.
97. Ber. 19a, M. Ber. III.1.
98. Ber. 19a.
99. Ber. 17b.
100. M. Ber. II.5.
101. I.e., the bed of a menstruant woman or of one with a vaginal discharge.
102. According to the commentators, the intention is the study of Torah in general, and not just the recitation of the Shema.
103. In "Laws Concerning Prayer," IV.4, Maimonides explains that the intention of this ordinance was to keep scholars from frequent relations with their wives.
104. "Blessed . . . ended" is in Aramaic, not Hebrew.

Treatise II: Laws Concerning Prayer and the Priestly Blessing

1. The Hebrew word *tefillah* means (a) "prayer," (b) the *'amidah* prayer, and (c) a full prayer service. The translation seeks to keep these senses distinct, and where the translation is not clear as to the sense intended, neither is the source.

2. The term here (*le-hitpallel*) can mean "to pray" or "to recite the *'amidah.*"

3. Ta'anit 2a, Sifre sec. 41.

4. M. Ber. III.3, "Laws Concerning Idolatry," XII.3. On the many textual problems in this paragraph, see Ya'akov Blidstein, *Ha-Tefillah be-Mishnato ha-Hilkhatit shel ha-Rambam,* 217–218.

5. *Hishpi'a;* see *Guide of the Perplexed* II.12, p. 279.

6. Ber. 32a.

7. Lit., "uncircumcised lips," based on Exod. 6:12.

8. *Miqdash.*

9. Ber. 30a.

10. From this point on, and in light of Maimonides' historical account, I translate *tefillah* as *'amidah,* unless the context makes it clear that prayer generally is meant.

11. Meg. 17b, Ber. 34a.

12. Although it corresponds to the sacrifice brought as the day waned (*minhah*), this prayer may be recited at any time after midday and before nightfall and is thus usually called the "afternoon" prayer.

13. Ber. 26b.

14. Ber. 27b, 31a.

15. *Nin''alu;* from the same root as *ne''ilah.*

16. J. Ber. IV.1.

17. The order reflects the Jewish tradition that each day begins at sunset. See M. Ber. I.1.

18. I.e., one may recite the *'amidah* as often as one wishes.

19. On which, see "Laws Concerning Vows," I.2.

20. Ber. 21a, 34a.

21. As opposed to individuals.

22. Ber. 21a.

23. Rabban Gamaliel II, who flourished as head of the Sanhedrin around the turn of the first century.

24. Or: "Seeing that responding to this . . ."

25. Or: "Was the greatest of all human needs . . ."

26. Ber. 28b.

27. *Da'at.*

28. M. Ber. IV.3, Ber. 30a.

29. Lit., anoint us.

30. This difficult phrase follows the text of the Jerusalem Talmud, as reported by Rabbenu Yonah in his commentary on Alfasi on Ber. 19b. Maimonides' sources

preserve this clause in a number of different ways, none of which are easy to understand and all of which exercised the commentators.

31. Ber. 29a.

32. The prayer recited at the end of the Sabbaths and holidays. See "Laws Concerning the Sabbath," XXIX. 1,3.

33. Since the "Give us understanding" prayer has no provisions for special additions, when those additions must be said, that prayer may not be used as a substitute for the 'amidah. The additions alluded to here are those for rain in the ninth blessing, "Bless for us, Lord our God, this year and all kinds of its produce . . . ," and commemorating the distinction between holy and profane times in the fourth blessing, "You favor humans with knowledge . . ." Ber. 29a.

34. Tos. Ber. III.12, Pes. 117b.

35. 'Er. 40a, M. RH IV.5.

36. Yoma 87b.

37. Lit., "a fast day." Here and throughout this paragraph.

38. M. RH III.4.

39. M. Ber. IV.2.

40. Sab. 24a.

41. Bezah 17a.

42. Lit., "recites."

43. I.e., one not followed by a holiday on Sunday.

44. The fourth blessing of the 'amidah.

45. Ber. 13b, M. Ber. V.2.

46. As the calendar is structured today, Purim never falls on the Sabbath except in Jerusalem. That may be why the reference to Purim is missing in the printed editions of our text: someone may have excised it as irrelevant.

47. Sab. 24a.

48. I.e., one who is praying alone, not in a congregation.

49. The sixteenth blessing of the 'amidah.

50. The seventh and eighth blessings of the 'amidah.

51. Ta'an. 13b, J. Ta'an. II.2.

52. Ta'an. 3a, M. Ta'an. I.1–2.

53. The third month of the Jewish calendar (which usually corresponds to October/November).

54. The ninth blessing of the 'amidah.

55. In the second blessing; i.e., through the morning ['amidah] prayer of the first holiday of Passover.

56. Babylonia, largely corresponding to present-day Iraq.

57. M. Ta'an. I.3.

58. The sixteenth blessing of the 'amidah.

59. Certain holidays (the first and last days of Passover, the first day of Sukkot, and Shemini 'Azeret) are celebrated for two days, not one, outside of the Land of Israel. On this, see "Laws Concerning Festivals," I.21.

60. At the end of Sukkot.

61. M. Ta'an. I.3.

62. Ber. 12b.

63. Three passages, beginning, "And so, Lord our God, impose Your fear…," "And so, Lord, grant respect…," and "And so, may the righteous see this and rejoice…"

64. M. Ber. IV.1.

65. I.5.

66. Which would make the seder fall on Friday night, on the Sabbath.

67. "Greater" and "lesser" refers to the amount of time left in which the prayer may be recited. M. Ber. V.1, Ber. 26b.

68. I.e., a free-will prayer, not required. See above, I.9.

69. Ber. 26b, Ber. 4a.

70. Ber. 26b, M. Ber. IV.1, Ber. 28a.

71. Ber. 27b.

72. Ber. 26a.

73. Ber. 26a.

74. Ber. 26a.

75. And recite the afternoon service before the additional service even when the special circumstance here described does not obtain. Ber. 28a.

76. In this chapter I usually translate *tefillah* as "prayer" and not as "say the *'amidah* prayer." The latter may be more precisely accurate but, despite that, misleading. Similarly with *le-hitpallel;* its precise meaning is "say the *'amidah* prayer," but in this chapter it is occasionally translated as "pray."

77. Either 3.84 kilometers or 4.8 kilometers; see next note.

78. A cubit (*ammah*) equals six handbreadths (*tefahim*); generally accepted as either 48 or 60 centimeters in today's terms.

79. Compare above, "Laws Concerning the Recitation of the Shema," III.1., Ber. 14b, Pes. 46a.

80. Either .96 kilometers or 1.2 kilometers.

81. Sab. 50b.

82. "Laws Concerning the Recitation of the Shema," IV.8.

83. Ber. 12a, 22a, J. Ber. III.4.

84. Such emission being unconnected in this case with his ailment.

85. Hebrew: *zav*. See Lev. 15:2, 22:4, and Num. 5:2.

86. It was thought that a woman could discharge semen up to three days after intercourse.

87. I.e., the immersion ordained by Ezra.

88. Ber. 12a, 22a, J. Ber. III.4. Compare "Laws Concerning Rebels," II.5–6.

89. Ber. 12a, 22a, J. Ber. III.4.

90. The second of the five reasons for delaying prayer beyond its set time (IV.1 above).

91. See "Laws Concerning the Recitation of the Shema," III.17.

92. Ber. 24b.

93. See "Laws Concerning the Recitation of the Shema," III.4.

94. See "Laws Concerning the Recitation of the Shema," III.

95. Rabbi Kafih reads "saw," which does seem to make better sense.

96. And start again in a pure place. The general point is that whereas one may not move during the recitation of the *'amidah,* which is recited facing east, if one must move, one must remain facing east.

97. Some commentators cite as a reason for this Rashi's explanation in 'Eruvin 65a to the effect that the smell of beer can be intoxicating. Others maintain that beer, like frothing brine, has an offensive odor.

98. Ber. 22b.

99. And thus not prayer.

100. A distance of four "miles" or 8,000 cubits (3,840 or 4,800 meters).

101. Ber. 23a.

102. Ber. 24a, 24b.

103. Ber. 24b.

104. Ber. 24b.

105. And there be a clear interruption between the prayer and the urination. Meg. 27b.

106. Ber. 30b, 'Er. 65a.

107. Lit., "heart."

108. Ber. 31a, San. 22a, J. Ber. V.1.

109. 'Er. 64a.

110. Ber. 31a; my translation here is paraphrastic.

111. This halakhah reflects a reality in which prayerbooks were not used. RH 35a.

112. M. Ber. II.2.

113. In this chapter, *le-hitpallel* always means "say the *'amidah* prayer," even though I occasionally translate it simply as "pray" so as not to make the translation too cumbersome.

114. But not on his back or stomach; see above, "Laws Concerning the Recitation of the Shema," II.2.

115. And not be worried about the animal. M. Ber. IV. 2, VI.2, Tos. Ber. III.17, Ber. 30a.

116. And thus presumably not sure where he is vis-à-vis Jerusalem.

117. Ber. 30a.

118. Ber. 10b.

119. Fearing that he might drop them.

120. On this measurement, see "Laws Concerning the Erub," I.13.

121. Ber. 30b, Suk. 41b, BM 108b.

122. The point being that one may not pray with one's back to the synagogue, since it betokens disrespect for the synagogue. See Maimonides, Teshuvot (= *Responsa*) (Blau), 290, p. 545.

123. Ber. 10b, M. Ber. IV.4, Ber. 6b.

124. This and the following paragraph relate to the requirement (V.6) that one pray in "a low place." Ber. 10b.

125. It appears that in the first case congregational prayer is mandated; in the second it is not allowed. The assumption underlying the last sentence in this paragraph is that there are ten artisans working together.

126. The *havineinu* prayer; see above, II.2–3.

127. Lit., "In either case they do not descend before the ark or lift their hands" (either activity would take more time than is necessary from their work, and thus would cheat their employer). The latter issue only arises if the artisans in question are Priests. M. Ber. II.4.

128. The eighteenth of the nineteen blessings.

129. Lit. (here and in the next paragraph), "says goodbye from his left and then from his right."

130. Ber. 34a.

131. Ber. 28b.

132. Ber. 34b.

133. VI.6–7, based on Lev. 26:1.

134. Lit., "fall on his face."

135. See Josh. 7:10 and Ta'anit 14b.

136. J. Ta'an. II.6.

137. Lit., "pass behind."

138. And, of course, on his arm, but only the phylactery of the head is typically visible to all.

139. Ber. 8b.

140. Ber. 31a.

141. The eighth blessing.

142. The ninth blessing.

143. The sixteenth blessing.

144. Ber. 34a.

145. So that it not be delayed. Ber. 14a.

146. As opposed to the special requirements of the high Priest's haircut; see "Laws Concerning Entering the Temple Compound," I.10.

147. M. Sab. I.2, Sab. 9b-10a.

148. See Ez. 23:15; Babylonians were apparently thought of as individuals who wore tight belts (or sashes). See Sab. 9b-10a and the discussion in Erlich, *Kol Azmotai Tomarna*, 132–135.

149. M. Sab. I.2.

150. Ber. 4b.

151. J. Ber. VIII.1.

152. And still have time to get out of the way.

153. M. Ber. V.1, J. Ber. V.i.

154. M. Ber. III.3.

155. For the expression used here, see Lam. 2:18, Ps. 17:8, Prov. 7:9.

156. Ber. 60b.

157. J. Ber. I.1.

158. Ber. 60b.

159. See Prov. 6:4.

160. Ber. 60b.

161. Ber. 60b.

162. Ber. 60b.

163. Ber. 14b, 11b.

164. Ber. 63b. "Baraitot" are Tannaitic materials not included in the Mishnah, but found in the Tosefta, Tannaitic Midrash, and Gemara.

165. Men. 43b; 86 + 14 = 100.

166. Passage based on Isa. 6:3 and Ez. 3:12.

167. As opposed to a congregation which does recite it.

168. Ber. 42a.

169. See above, V.2.

170. The word *zibbur* derives from the root meaning "to congregate," "to accumulate"; I translate it variously as "communal," "congregational," and "public."

171. Ber. 6a, 8a, 29b, 47b.

172. More literally: "guarding the doorposts of my doors." The minimum plural ("doors") is two; one therefore remains within two door-widths of the entrance to the synagogue. Ber. 6b, 8a.

173. I.e., in the study halls.

174. I.e., not slaves.

175. Hebrew: *shaliah zibbur.* The term literally means agent or emissary of the congregation.

176. M. Meg. IV.3.

177. Hebrew: *pores 'al Shema.* The commentators are divided over what the term literally means. But all agree on how to do it: the leader of the prayer "raises his voice at the beginning to fulfill the obligation on behalf of those who are not knowledgeable, while those standing behind him [and are knowledgeable] pray silently or in a lower voice than his, so as to fulfill their own obligation . . ." These are the words of R. Abraham, son of Maimonides, as quoted by Blidstein, "Maimonides' *Taqqanah* Concerning Public Prayer," 13. Blidstein discusses the *pores 'al Shema* on 13-14. Ismar Elbogin, *Jewish Liturgy,* 24, as opposed to this, explains the term to mean reciting the Shema by dividing it among several speakers. See further Ezra Fleischer, "Towards a Clarification of the Expression *Pores 'al Shema.*"

178. The kaddish prayer has a number of variations, which serve a variety of purposes: dividing segments of the prayer service, marking the end of Torah study, and memorializing the dead. A version of it is always recited after the completion of the *'amidah.*

179. Hebrew: *'edah.*

180. Ten of the twelve spies "muttered" against God; these ten were called a "community."

181. 'Er. 9b.

182. M. RH IV.9.

183. M. Ta'an. II.2, Hul. 24b, M. Meg. IV.6. On reading the Shema aloud, see above, paragraph 5 in this chapter.

184. Which you might think is forbidden, since the prayers should be led by the greatest person present. Meg. 24b.

185. M. Meg. IV.6.

186. Hebrew: *teivah;* chest or box. Maimonides is relating to a reality in which Torah scrolls which were to be used in the service were removed from the *heikhal*

("sanctuary") where they were ordinarily kept and placed in a movable box which also served as a lectern or pulpit for the prayer leader.

187. Ber. 3a, Sab. 119b, M. Ber. VII.3, M. Ta'an. IV.3.

188. I.e., from the beginning of the 'amidah.

189. See above, "Laws Concerning Prayer," VII.17.

190. I.e., before taking the three steps back at the end of the 'amidah.

191. The eighteenth blessing.

192. Since it appears that such a person is praying to two gods. M. RH IV.5, J. Ber. I.5, Soṭ. 40a, M. Ber. V.3.

193. I.e., say the word "holy" three times.

194. Rashi on Soṭ. 49a explains that this refers to the "order" (seder) of the qedushah, recited every day.

195. Deut. 22:6.

196. See Lev. 22:28.

197. On the apparent contradiction between this passage and Guide of the Perplexed III.48, see Stern, "On an Alleged Contradiction," and Weiss, "Maimonides on Shilluah Ha-Qen."

198. See Guide of the Perplexed I.59, pp. 140–141 and Exod. 34:6–7. M. Ber. V. 3.

199. While he and the people are seated.

200. In order to fulfill the obligation of one who cannot make the blessings himself.

201. Which is forbidden; see "Laws Concerning Blessings," XI.16.

202. Sab. 24b.

203. On weekday evenings, there is no repetition of the 'amidah; why on the Sabbath is there one?

204. Having to return from the synagogue alone.

205. I.e., the holiday, the Day of Atonement, or the day of the new moon.

206. I.e., the repetition of the 'amidah in the evening service is unique to the Sabbath; if it is done, for example, on a Sabbath eve which is also a holiday eve, it is done only for the Sabbath. Sab. 24b.

207. Maimonides makes no reference here to the reading of the Torah after the morning service. Rabinovitch is of the opinion that it is simply not relevant in the present context.

208. See above, paragraphs 5 and 6.

209. See above, paragraph 6.

210. See above, "Laws Concerning Prayer," II.4.

211. Lit., "without directing his heart."

212. I.e., the seventeenth blessing of the 'amidah.

213. Ber. 30b, 34a–b.

214. By making them wait for him.

215. M. Ber. V.3.

216. It is customary to decline the honor of leading the services and to accept it only on being importuned.

217. Lit., here and elsewhere in this chapter, "descend before the ark."

218. M. Meg. IV.7. The Talmud ad loc. (Meg. 24b) suggests that such a per-

son is suspected of sectarianism. For discussion, see Blidstein, "Prostration and Mosaics in Talmudic Law," 22.

219. Ber. 21a.

220. Many mss. do not have the negation here.

221. Ber. 21a.

222. J. Taʻan. I.1, Taʻan. 3b.

223. For rain and dew during the wintertime; for blessings during the summertime.

224. The ninth blessing of the 'amidah.

225. The sixteenth blessing.

226. Ber. 29a.

227. A passage added to the 'amidah on Rosh Ḥodesh and the intermediate days of Passover and Sukkot.

228. The seventeenth blessing, to which "[Our God, and God of our fathers, may remembrance of us . . .] arise and come [before You]" is added.

229. Ber. 29b.

230. Ber. 30b.

231. Ber. 30b.

232. Instead of with "the Koly King," the special conclusion of the third blessing during the ten days of repentance.

233. Instead of with "the King of justice," the special conclusion of the third blessing during the ten days of repentance.

234. That he should have concluded the eleventh blessing with "the King of justice."

235. Ber. 12b.

236. The fourth blessing, in which a passage marking the end of the Sabbath is added on Saturday nights.

237. In the eighteenth blessing.

238. Between the seventh and eighth blessings.

239. On a fast day that he had not said "answer us . . ."

240. This last is a prayer of supplication said at the end of the 'amidah proper.

241. To pray the 'amidah. He must still mark the separation of the weekday from the Sabbath or holiday.

242. When one repeats an 'amidah in order to make up a missed prayer, the second is the makeup prayer, not the first. The obligation to say havdalah is thus in the first of the two evening prayers. Reversing the order means that the first 'amidah does not count at all, the second is the one required for that evening, and a third must now be said to make up for the missed afternoon prayer.

243. I.e., in a case where one is praying alone, when they are supposed to be said one right after the other.

244. My translation here reflects Maimonides' apparent source, Ber. 30b.

245. Even if he is ready to say the 'amidah before them. The next sentence takes up the opposite case: where the public has already begun the 'amidah.

246. The ms. says "Kiddush." Both Hyamson and Rabinovitch pass over this in silence.

247. In the Kaddish.

248. I.e., ten adult male Jews.

249. Lit., "place of assembly." The synagogue need not be a building erected for a separate purpose; a room within an already existing building may also be set aside for prayer.

250. I.e., force each other to contribute toward its construction.

251. Tos. BM XI.23.

252. Lit., "courtyard."

253. Maimonides means that the shrine is actually built into the wall of the synagogue. It is the place in which the Torah scrolls are kept when they are not in use.

254. There is a considerable difference of opinion on what this means: in the middle of the building (equidistant from the north and south walls); in the middle between the shrine and the dais; etc.

255. Tos. Meg. III.22.

256. Here and below in this sentence, *qodesh,* not *heikhal.*

257. The prayer leader sits in his regular seat during those portions of the service (such as the Shema) that do not require standing.

258. To keep down the dust.

259. Heb. *Erez ha-zvi,* "land of delight" (after Jer. 3:19).

260. Meg. 28a, Ber. 53a.

261. My translation follows Rashi to Meg. 28b.

262. Meg. 28b.

263. On the basis of the discussion in Meg. 28b, it would seem that the main criterion is whether or not most of the people in the city will come; only in such cases may eulogies be made in the synagogue or study hall.

264. M. Meg. III.4.

265. Meg. 28b.

266. Ber. 62b, Meg. 29a.

267. M. Meg. III.4.

268. I.e., prevented from building the new synagogue and thus be left without any synagogue.

269. BB 3b.

270. *Ḥumash;* the reference is to scrolls of individual books of the Pentateuch, as opposed to a complete Torah scroll.

271. I.e., that it only may be used to purchase things on an equal or higher plane of sanctity than the item sold. Meg. 26b.

272. Hebrew: *aron.*

273. E.g., if they were donated on condition that they could later sold and the money used for a less sanctified purpose, that may be done. Meg. 27a.

274. Presumably since one cannot get permission from all concerned to sell the synagogue. Meg. 26a.

275. M. Meg. III.3.

276. After the purchase of the sacred item.

277. From the sale of the synagogue.

278. Meg. 27a.

279. To handle the matters under discussion here.

280. J. Meg. III.2.

281. Which can be used for another sacred purpose.

282. Meg. 26b.

283. Hebrew: *ma'amadot*. See "Laws Concerning the Temple Implements," VI.5. The Israelites were divided into "watches" which served in the Temple as representatives of all the Israelites.

284. Meg. 26a.

285. Lit., "those who sit on the corners." The term is taken by the commentators to mean either loiterers or busy shopkeepers; in either case, these are people who do not always come to the synagogue on Mondays and Thursdays.

286. Today, customarily, three people are *called* to the Torah, but it is read by someone trained for the task. Maimonides' wording here reflects a reality in which each person called to the Torah read his own portion.

287. BK 82a.

288. M. Meg. IV.1–2, Meg. 31b.

289. Three verses begin with "And the Lord spoke . . ." while 96 begin with "And God spoke . . ."

290. I.e., three people called to the Torah.

291. The text of the Pentateuch is divided into sections, called *parashot* (sing., *parashah*). See "Laws Concerning the Torah Scroll," VIII.

292. The commentators explain that these two laws were set down lest a person come into the synagogue in the middle of the reading and think that fewer than three verses had been read.

293. M. Meg. IV.3.

294. Meg. 21b.

295. Meg. 32a.

296. Soṭ. 39b.

297. Tos. Meg. III.21, M. Yoma VII.1.

298. Maimonides specifies the weekly reading, I presume, in order to distinguish the passage he has in mind from similar passages, Lev. 16:29 and 25:9. The two passages Maimonides cites here deal with the same subject in that on the Day of Atonement the High Priest (as successor to Aaron) enters the shrine. They are also, not coincidentally, the two passages used as an example in Maimonides' source for this law, Meg. 24a.

299. From the first passage before going on the second passage, so as not to burden the congregation. On the translator mentioned here, see below, paragraph 10. M. Meg. IV.4.

300. Soṭ. 39a.

301. Many of the commentators take the adult and the minor here to mean persons of greater and lesser stature (based on Tos. Meg. III).

302. Gen. 35:22: *While Israel stayed in that land, Reuben went and lay with Bilhah, his father's concubine; and Israel found out.*

303. Num. 6:23–26. Verse 26, *The Lord lift up His countenance upon you . . . ,*

might be thought to contradict Deut. 10:17, *Who does not lift up His countenance* . . . See Ber. 20b.

304. M. Meg. IV.8.
305. Lit., "as *maftir.*"
306. Which for this purpose are considered one book.
307. Soṭ. 39b.
308. M. Meg. IV.4.
309. M. Meg. IV.1–2.
310. On this prophetic reading, see Elbogin, 143–149.
311. Meg. 23a.
312. I.e., those listed in the previous paragraphs.
313. M. Giṭ. V.8.
314. Giṭ. 59b.
315. J. RH IV.8.
316. Giṭ. 60a.
317. Most of the commentators on Maimonides and on his Talmudic source (Meg. 32a) explain that one should roll the Torah scroll such that the writing is on the inside. The band which holds the scroll closed should be tied such that the knot faces up when the scroll is laid down to be read.
318. The common explanation offered is that if the stitching between two sections of parchment is centered (i.e., opposite the knot holding the band closed), it is less likely to tear.
319. Meg. 32a.
320. I.e., the portion (*parashah, sidrah*) beginning with this verse; so throughout this chapter.
321. Meg. 29b.
322. Lev. 26:14–46.
323. Deut. 28:15–69.
324. Note the reversal of the order here; see Rabinovitch, ad loc.
325. Meg. 31b.
326. This portion ends with Gen. 6:8.
327. The portion ends with Gen. 11:32.
328. Meg. 31b.
329. The passage in question has eight verses. The first person called to the Torah reads verses 1–3; the second person reads verses 3–5; and the third person reads verses 6–10. See above, XII.13.
330. I follow the commentary of Kafiḥ here and have paraphrased, not translated, the text. For the issue raised here, see above, XII.17, 20.
331. This is actually the last verse of the *haftarah* (passage read from the Prophets), which begins with verse 66:1.
332. Meg. 21b.
333. Even though they include threats and warnings.
334. J. Meg. III.7, RH 21a.
335. For the source of this expression, see Mak. 24a.
336. Without a proper quorum. Men. 30a.

337. 26:14–43.
338. 28:15–69.
339. M. Meg. III.7.
340. When they fall on a Sabbath.
341. From Maimonides' source (Meg. 32a) it is apparent that the meaning of this ordinance is that on each festival we read concerning it from the Written Torah and study its laws from the Oral Torah.
342. 23:4–44.
343. Josh. 5:2–15.
344. Maimonides codifies here the practice of Jews outside of the Land of Israel. See "Laws Concerning Repose on a Festival," I.21.
345. 2 Kings 23:1–25.
346. Meg. III.5–7; Meg. 31a.
347. Deut. 15:19–16:17.
348. 3:1–9. Meg. 31a.
349. The entire passage is 31:2–20. Meg. 31a.
350. Lev. 18.
351. Meg. 31a.
352. Lev. 22:26–23:44.
353. The additional day celebrated outside the Land of Israel.
354. Num. 29:17–34. Meg. 31a.
355. I.e., the first person called to the Torah.
356. Above, paragraphs 8 and 13.
357. Lit., "Book of the Census." The passage referred to is chapters 28 and 29.
358. And not, as is customary today, all at the same time.
359. Above, XII.20.
360. Ez. 37:1–14.
361. Meg. 31a.
362. Num. 6:38–42.
363. Of the consecration of the Tabernacle; Num. 7:17.
364. 7:18–23.
365. Num. 7:89.
366. Zach. 2:14–4:7.
367. 1 Kings 7:40–50.
368. On a Sabbath which falls on Hannukah.
369. Meg. 31a.
370. Meg. 31b.
371. Ex. 30:11–16, to commemorate the custom of assessing the half-shekel Temple tax from the first day of the month of Adar. See "Laws Concerning Shekalim," I.9.
372. 2 Kings 11:17–20, 12:1–17.
373. I.e., just one day before the Sabbath in question.
374. See next paragraph.
375. M. Meg. III.5.

376. M. Meg. III.5.

377. Meg. 30b, 29b.

378. Meg. 29b.

379. Which always occurs during Hannukah.

380. Heb.: *hannukah,* or dedication of the Tabernacle in the wilderness (above, paragraph 17).

381. Meg. 29b.

382. This last sentence is an expanded paraphrase of Maimonides' extremely terse text. Ber. 8a.

383. Lit., "lift their hands." Maimonides uses variants of this expression throughout his discussion here, but I have allowed myself relatively wide latitude in translating these expressions in this chapter.

384. Num. 6:22–27.

385. Ta'an. 26b.

386. According to Ta'an. 26a it was customary to recite *ne'ilah* on public fasts held in response to tribulations.

387. Without reciting the priestly blessing.

388. Ta'an. 26b.

389. I.e., the seventeenth blessing.

390. I.e., with their fists closed.

391. I.e., the eighteenth blessing.

392. The point being that the Priests do not bless the people until they have been prompted to do so.

393. M. Sot. VII.4.

394. Here, *ha-qodesh,* not *heikhal.*

395. M. Sot. VII.4.

396. I.e., the person who prompts the Priests to begin their blessing. This is usually the prayer leader today, but does not have to be.

397. To the eighteenth blessing.

398. Sot. 39b.

399. Sot. 39b, 40a.

400. The concern here is that the mind of the congregant being blessed might wander, not that of the Priest.

401. J. Meg. IV.1.

402. I.e., without being prompted.

403. Sot. 38a.

404. I.e., after the completion of the daily morning sacrifice with its attendant rites. For a description of the platform, see Maimonides, "Laws Concerning the Temple," VI.3.

405. See Ex. 28: 36–38.

406. M. Tamid VI.5, Tos. Sot. VII.8.

407. The first two letters of "Adonai," the word pronounced in place of the explicit name. In citing the first two letters only Maimonides seems to be following the lead of Kid. 71a. Maimonides consistently uses the Arabic *dal* and not the

Hebrew *dalet* when naming the fourth letter of the alphabet. Compare, below, "Laws Concerning Tefillin," I.19.

408. Soṭ. 38a, Yoma 39b.

409. Soṭ. 38a.

410. Soṭ. 38a. I added the emphases in this paragraph.

411. Soṭ. 39a.

412. Soṭ. 15b.

413. See "Laws Concerning the Temple," I.5.

414. Above, paragraph 1.

415. As opposed to Priest or Levite.

416. M. Tamid VI.5.

417. I do not know what Maimonides means by these expressions; and given the various options in the commentaries and translations, it appears that others do not really know, either. Given the parallel expression with respect to hearing in Isa. 59:1, the terms probably refer to types of speech impediments.

418. Meg. 24b.

419. Following Lev. 13:39.

420. This is ambiguous: those staring might be distracted, or the Priest being stared at might be distracted.

421. M. Meg. IV.6, Meg. 24b, Tos. Meg. III.29.

422. The point being that hands stained with crime may not be lifted up to bless. See Isa. 1:15: *And when you lift up your hands, I will turn My eyes away from you; Though you pray at length, I will not listen. Your hands are stained with crime.*

423. Ber. 32b, M. Men. XIII.10, Men. 109a.

424. See the previous paragraph. Priests engaged in the Temple ritual were not permitted to be drunk (see "Laws Concerning Entrance into the Sanctuary," I.1); so also, Priests performing the priestly blessing. See above, XIV.1.

425. Lit., "two fingers and half a finger and a fifth of a finger."

426. The two Hebrew words for "thumb" here are different: *gudal* and *bohen.* Ḥul. 24b, Ta'an. 26b.

427. In a ritually appropriate manner. See "Laws Concerning Blessings," VI.

428. See "Laws Concerning Forbidden Intercourse," chapter 19.

429. Soṭ. 39a, 40a, Ket. 24b.

430. Soṭ. 38b.

431. Soṭ. 38b.

432. The commentators are divided on why Maimonides specifies North and South. R. Kafiḥ, citing Maimonides' grandson, explains that in this fashion all the Jews in the world are included, since most synagogues face East or West (in Babylonia). Thus, the point is that *even* those who live in the North or South are included in the blessing.

433. I.e., in a congregation of eleven.

434. M. Meg. IV.3, Soṭ. 38b, J. Ber. V.4.

435. The nineteenth (and last) blessing of the *'amidah.*

436. M. Ber. V.4.

437. The seventeenth blessing of the 'amidah.

438. RH 28b.

439. Sot. 38b.

Treatise III: Laws Concerning Tefillin, Mezuzah, and the Torah Scroll

1. Not to be confused with Deut. 6:10.

2. These four passages all relate to the commandment of tefillin.

3. In Maimonides' usage, the term "tefillin" applies in some instances only to the passages from the Torah listed here, and not to the leather boxes containing them. This distinction should be borne in mind throughout the discussion.

4. I.e., this is a Torah law, not a rabbinic enactment.

5. M. Men. III.7. Maimonides' source here (and in the next paragraph) is much more general than his discussion.

6. M. Men. III.7.

7. *Halakhah le-Moshe mi-sinai;* in Maimonidean usage, laws having biblical authority, but neither stated explicitly in the Torah nor derived from a Torah text by one of the accepted hermeneutical principles. For the term, see M. Pe'ah II.6, M. 'Eduyot VIII.7, and M. Yadayim IV.3.

8. A type of parchment; see below, paragraphs 6–7. J. Meg. I.9.

9. For background, see Levey, "Some Black Inks in Early Mediaeval Jewish Literature."

10. I.e., lampblack.

11. I.e., instead of smudging, it scrapes off cleanly.

12. I.e., cannot be scraped off, making it impossible to correct a Torah scroll written with such ink.

13. Lit., "kosher." Sab. 23a.

14. Torah, mezuzah, tefillin.

15. Sab. 103b.

16. 'Or; depending on the context, translated as "leather" or as "parchment." For background to the entire discussion here, see Haran, "Bible Scrolls in Eastern and Western Jewish Communities from Qumran to the High Middle Ages."

17. Sab. 79b.

18. I.e., not ritually slaughtered, and thus unfit for consumption.

19. The commentators suggest that the contaminants are bad smells or secretions; compare Maimonides' source, Sab. 108a.

20. Men. 42b.

21. Lines are incised into the parchment with a knife or other sharp implement.

22. And thus sloppy writing will not be seen; mezuzot are often covered as well, but they do not have to be, and even when covered are easily examined.

23. I.e., from memory.

24. And is therefore familiar with them.

25. J. Meg. I.9.

26. Hebrew: *moser;* one who unjustly delivers a Jew into Gentile arms.

27. On the need to put away or bury certain kinds of holy texts respectfully, see "Laws Concerning the Foundations of the Torah," I.8.

28. Thus excluding women, minors, and slaves.

29. I.e., in the obligation to write them, thus excluding Gentiles, apostates, and traitors. "And who believes in it" is not found in Maimonides' source (Giṭ. 45b) and reflects his own agenda.

30. I.e., Torah scrolls, teffilin, and mezuzot. M. Giṭ. IV.6.

31. As in Deut. 6:4, where God's name appears three times in a row.

32. Giṭ. 54b, Ber. 5a.

33. I.e., go over or fill in the previous letter, so as not to begin writing God's name with a pen drenched in ink; such a pen is more likely to lead to an ink blot, which might in turn cause the scribe to erase God's name, which is forbidden.

34. Men. 30b, J. Meg. I.9.

35. When they interrupt their work; it is considered disrespectful to leave the page with the writing exposed. "Sheet of parchment" here translates *yeri'ah.*

36. 'Er. 98a.

37. Or, perhaps, "with the intention that they be written in a holy Torah scroll."

38. See previous note.

39. Giṭ. 54b.

40. I.e., the accepted Hebrew script, as opposed to ancient Hebrew, which used a different alphabet; talmudic literature calls the Hebrew with which the rabbis were familiar "Assyrian script." See San. 21b.

41. Lit., "one who is neither smart nor stupid."

42. M. Meg. I.8, Men. 29a, Sab. 103b.

43. E.g., if a *vav* were broken near the bottom, enough might remain so that it would not be confused with a *yod.*

44. Men. 38a, 29a.

45. See below, III.2–3.

46. Men. 34b, Sifre, Deut. 6:8.

47. The text of a Torah scroll is divided into paragraphs or sections; an "open" paragraph starts at the beginning of the line, with the preceding line wholly or partially blank; a "closed" paragraph begins at any point but the beginning of a line. See below, chapter 8.

48. Sab. 103b.

49. Some Hebrew consonants can also serve as vowels; words written with them are called plene, and those without them, defective.

50. 'Er. 97a.

51. "And," the passage in J. 'Er. X.1 continues, "I have never checked them."

52. The previous chapters dealt with the preparation of the parchments in the tefillin, while this chapter deals with the leather cases of the tefillin. The same word is used for both.

53. Fourth letter of the Hebrew alphabet; today usually called *dalet*. Men. 35a–b, J. Meg. I.9, Sab. 108a.

54. *Ma'aboret.*

55. Or, "would read them in the correct [Scriptural] order thusly."

56. Men. 34b.

57. J. Meg. I.9, Men. 34b.

58. Even if not slaughtered properly; the flesh of such animals may not be eaten.

59. I.e., pounds them.

60. Men. 31a.

61. Hebrew: *halakhah rovaḥat.*

62. Men. 34b.

63. The knot of the tefillin of the head is tied in the middle of the strap, leaving enough left over for both ends to reach the navel; the knot of the tefillin of the arm is tied at the end of the strap, leaving one long strap which must encircle the forearm and reach the hand.

64. But not if they are shorter. Men. 35a–b.

65. I.e., a squarish knot, not today's "square knot."

66. I.e., a knot which looks like the letter *yod.*

67. Sab. 62b, Ḥul. 9a.

68. They are commonly left untreated, while the outer side is covered with black polish.

69. Rashi, Men. 35a, explains that people might think the wearer suffered from a skin ailment and that his straps had been reddened from blood caused by his scratching of his skin.

70. Men. 35a.

71. Or, perhaps, "with the intention that they be written in a holy Torah scroll."

72. I.e., the leather from which the boxes containing the biblical passages are made; these boxes are what are called "tefillin" in ordinary parlance.

73. Rawhide is likened to matzah, "unprocessed bread," in Sab. 79a.

74. San. 47b.

75. Above, III.2.

76. I.e., made the leather box or case in which the tefillin passages are placed.

77. See above, I.13.

78. Sab. 28b.

79. In this passage Maimonides is dealing with the tefillin case or box, not the passages themselves. See "Laws Concerning Prayer," XI.14, on the impermissibility of lowering the status of an article from a greater degree of holiness to lesser degree.

80. I.e., so that it appears to be one compartment.

81. Men. 34b.

82. Men. 35a.

83. In a *genizah*, a place for storing books and objects which may not be simply discarded. See M. Sab. XVI.1, and note 27 above.

84. Men. 35b.

85. Men. 37a–b, Zev. 19a.

86. Men. 36b.

87. Who interpret literally the verse *Bind them as a sign on your arm and let them serve as a symbol on your forehead.*

88. M. Meg. IV.7, Meg. 24b, Men. 37a.

89. M. Men. IV.1, Men. 36a.

90. Men. 36a, Yoma 19b.

91. Suk. 46a.

92. Yoma 33a–b.

93. Ber. 23b, 24a, 26b; Tos. Meg. II.13.

94. ... *At its set time from year to year* may be translated as "from day to day."

95. 'Er. 96a, Ber. 9b, Men. 36a.

96. The concern is that the common run of people may fall asleep while wearing tefillin.

97. The assumption being that the study hall was outside the city.

98. Beẓah 15a.

99. See above, "Laws Concerning the Recitation of the Shema," chapter four.

100. The intent apparently being "the ritually impure are as obligated to put on tefillin as the ritually pure."

101. M. Ber. III.1, 3; Suk. 25b, 26b, 42a; Ber. 11a, 14b, 18a; Nazir 29a; Ḥul. 110a; MK 15a; Zev. 19a.

102. See Exod. 28:36.

103. Men. 36b, Sab. 12a.

104. Sab. 49a, Suk. 26a–b.

105. J. Ber. II.3, Ber. 23b.

106. Ber. 23a.

107. Which renders the receptacle like a "tent."

108. In line with paragraph 12 above.

109. Ber. 23a, 40a.

110. Ber. 25a.

111. One is not always aware of what one's arms touch. Suk. 26b.

112. Sab. 10a.

113. Ber. 18a, J. Ber. II.3.

114. And thus sexual relations are forbidden while they are in the same building.

115. Such that the second was not designated for them.

116. Ber. 25b.

117. I.e., without studying the words of Torah (following Rashi to Meg. 28a).

118. Ber. 30b.

119. Ber. 14b.

120. Maimonides follows Men. 44a. NJPS renders the verse: *My Lord, for all that and despite it My life-breath is revived; You have restored me to health and revived me.* Ber. 14b.

121. I.e., wide on the top, narrow on the bottom.

122. I.e., narrow on the top, wide on the bottom.

123. J. Meg. I.9, Men. 31b, 33a.

124. Hebrew: *mizvah*.

125. See below, chapter 8.

126. Some letters in the Torah scroll are decorated with "crowns" or "tittles" made in the shape of letter *zayin*.

127. Men. 31b.

128. Men. 29b.

129. One of the names of God; for its first appearance in the Bible, see Gen. 17:1. It may also be taken as an acronym for "Guardian of the Religion of Israel" or "Guardian of the doorways of Israel."

130. *Kesef Mishneh* notes that Maimonides here contradicts AZ 11a.

131. Maimonides writes "letters" but actually gives a list of words.

132. Men. 31b.

133. J. Ber. 9:3.

134. Which in turn is placed next to or on the doorpost; but in this case the mezuzah is not affixed to the doorpost.

135. In the Sanctuary (Exod. 26:26–29).

136. I.e., in a hole drilled horizontally into the doorpost.

137. Men. 32b. 33a, 33b.

138. Yoma 11a.

139. Such as in the case of minor orphans who have inherited property.

140. M. Ber. III.3, Men. 44a.

141. BM 101b–102a.

142. I.e., not a synagogue.

143. I.e., not a bathhouse or tannery or the like.

144. These last are three separate conditions. Suk. 3a, Men. 33b–34a, Yoma 11a–b.

145. Suk. 3a.

146. Men. 33b.

147. 'Er. 11b.

148. Yoma 11b. This last sentence applies to all of the previous five paragraphs.

149. See "Laws Concerning the Temple," V.5.

150. Royal advisers. See "Laws Concerning the Temple," V.17.

151. Before the Day of Atonement ("Laws Concerning the Day of Atonement Service," I.3). Yoma 11b, Ber. 47a, Yoma 10a.

152. I.e., many.

153. The precise source is not known. See Men. 33b.

154. Yoma 11b, Suk. 8b.

155. Men. 32a.

156. In such a case, it is impossible to say which direction is in and which direction is out; see the next paragraph.

157. Men. 33a.

158. I.e., the mezuzah must be on the doorpost itself, not on the outer wall,

but within an armbreadth of that wall, and two-thirds of the way up the door-post.

159. Men. 32b, 33a, Yoma 11b.

160. Although the Hebrew is ambiguous, it is likely that Maimonides means human love of God, as opposed to God's love of humans. Throughout his writings, Maimonides emphasizes the obligation of humans to love God (through knowledge), while rarely mentioning God's love of humans (the only passage I know of in all his writings in which God's love for humans is emphasized is "Laws Concerning Idolatry," I.3). It should be remembered that this passage is found in "The Book of [Human] Love [of God]," not in "The Book of [God's] Love [of Humans]" (see Translator's Introduction).

161. I.e., focuses on what is truly important.

162. Men. 43b.

163. See below, paragraph 14.

164. San. 21b, Men. 30a.

165. Hebrew: 'al pi.

166. The court of seventy-one sages. See "Laws Concerning the Sanhedrin," I.3.

167. Possibly, when he returns from war, or when he enters his home, or appears before the royal court; it is not clear.

168. M. San. II.8, J. San. II.6.

169. The commentators are not sure what to make of the distinction between night and when the king sleeps, and neither am I.

170. A nine-letter word found in Exod. 12:21 and 33:54. The word is spelled defectively in both places, while in our ms. Maimonides spells it plene (with a *vav*, and thus the word has ten letters in this fashion).

171. Maimonides actually writes the word out three times.

172. J. Meg. VIII.9, Men. 30a.

173. Men. 30a.

174. The last words of Deuteronomy.

175. BB 13b, Men. 30a.

176. There are ten letters in the Torah with dots over them; for details, see Halivni, *Revelation Restored,* pp. 17, 33–48.

177. I.e., one must follow the established scribal tradition with respect to the exceptional letters.

178. Exod. 15:1–19.

179. Men. 29b, Sab. 103b.

180. Biblical texts, writings containing the name of God, and certain other texts and items may not be simply thrown away, but must be respectfully stored, usually in a place (room, attic, cabinet, etc.) set aside for that purpose. Such a place is called a *genizah.* In some cases, placement in a *genizah* involves burial. For details, see "Laws Concerning Foundations of the Torah," chapter six, and chapter ten below.

181. Ket. 19b, Men. 29b.

182. Here, and in the rest of the paragraph, *megillah.*
183. J. Meg. III.1, Giṭ. 60a. Our ms. has in its margins here a responsum of Maimonides on the permissibility of reciting a blessing over a Torah recitation from a Pentateuch. It corresponds to Blau, #294.
184. BB 13b, 14b.
185. BB 13b.
186. See above, VII.12–13.
187. See below, paragraph 7.
188. Sab. 103b.
189. I.e., it contained the whole Hebrew Bible.
190. The division of the Hebrew Bible into numbered chapters postdates Maimonides; as is therefore customary in traditional Jewish texts, he cites verses by their opening words.
191. Meg. 16b.
192. Men. 30.
193. I.e., the height of the parchment on which the scroll is written should be equal to the circumference of the scroll when it is rolled up. This and other matters dealt with in this chapter relate primarily to considerations of what constitutes a "beautiful" Torah scroll, as opposed to matters which render a scroll fit or unfit.
194. Lit., "twenty-four fingers, each the width of a thumb." In this chapter I translate "finger" as "thumb-width."
195. BB 14a.
196. See below, paragraph 14.
197. Men. 30a.
198. Men. 30a.
199. See above, III.8.
200. Mak. 11a, Meg. 8b.
201. Meg. 19b, BB 14a.
202. Men. 31b.
203. Not that other colors are permissible; see above, I.5.
204. I.e., render the scroll unfit. I have added the numbers to each item here.
205. Meg. 27a.
206. *Met miẓvah;* see "Laws Concerning Mourning," III.8.
207. Meg. 26b.
208. Used to wrap or decorate a Torah scroll.
209. Meg. 26b, J. Meg. III.1.
210. Meg. 27a, Sab. 61b.
211. San. 21b, Ber. 18a.
212. Ber. 25b. The last sentence is apparently Maimonides' own addition.
213. Ber. 22a, Meg. 9a.
214. Kid. 33b.
215. Just as the tablets of the Decalogue were kept in the Ark of the Covenant, so should the Torah be kept in a special cabinet.
216. In a disrespectful manner.
217. Sab. 32a, Soṭ. 40a, J. Ber. III.5.

218. Avot IV.8.

219. Ber. 18a.

Treatise IV: Laws Concerning Fringes

1. Men. 39b, 41a, 42a.

2. Men. 43b.

3. The meaning of this expression is the subject of considerable controversy.

4. M. Men. IV.1.

5. Sifre Zuta to Num. 15:39. The Hebrew translated as "That shall be" is in the singular.

6. M. Men. III.7. The point is that if one places fringes on three corners of a four-cornered garment, he has not fulfilled the commandment.

7. Heb. *zavit*.

8. Men. 41b.

9. Men. 39a.

10. Men. 39a.

11. I.e., from wool obtained in an apostate city; on the latter, see "Laws Concerning Idolatry," chapter IV.

12. Suk. 9a.

13. Men. 42a.

14. And thus the commandment *to make* fringes remains unfulfilled.

15. Men. 41a.

16. Suk. 11a.

17. Men. 40b.

18. Men. 40b.

19. Men. 41a.

20. Heb. *zavit;* everywhere else in this chapter (but paragraph 6), *kanaf.*

21. Men. 41a.

22. On the color here, see "Laws Concerning Vessels of the Sanctuary and Those Who Minister Therein," VIII.13, and "Laws Concerning the Uncleanness of Leprosy," I.4.

23. A blue dye. See "Laws Concerning the Sabbath," XVIII.8.

24. Yev. 4b, Men. 43b.

25. See Maimonides' commentary to M. Sab. IX.5.

26. And thus not for the sake of fulfilling the commandment.

27. Men. 42b.

28. Men. 42b–43a.

29. Men. 42b–43a.

30. Heb. *kashrut.*

31. AZ 39a.

32. A Gentile (*goy*) merchant may be presumed to have purchased it from a reputable source and be unwilling to risk his own reputation (Men. 43a).

33. 'Er. 96b.

34. Men. 41b.
35. Men. 43b.
36. Men. 40b.
37. Who ordained that fringes be affixed to such garments.
38. Men. 39b.
39. I.e., any garment with which we can cover ourselves must have fringes, if as we shall see immediately, it has at least four corners.
40. Zev. 18b.
41. And not, as might be thought, one owned by more than one person (since the Hebrew expression is in the singular).
42. Men. 40b.
43. Men. 39b.
44. And thus, apparently, violate the prohibition of *sha'atnez* (the prohibition against wearing a garment of wool and linen, Deut. 22:11).
45. Men. 40a.
46. Men. 40a.
47. Men. 43b.
48. Meg. 26b, Men. 43a.
49. Suk. 42a.
50. 'Er. 96a.
51. Lit., "who has it." Men. 41a.
52. Men. 41a, Sab. 153a, Sab. 118b, Sab. 10a, Pes. 113b.
53. Men. 43b.

TREATISE V: LAWS CONCERNING BLESSINGS

1. M. Ber. III.1.
2. Ber. 48b.
3. As when cooking.
4. Ber. 35a.
5. Pes. 7b.
6. I.e., the expression "King of the Universe."
7. Ber. 33a.
8. I.e., not Hebrew. Soṭ. 7a.
9. Ber. 15a.
10. Ber. 40a.
11. See "Laws Concerning the Recitation of Shema," IV.8.
12. M. Ber. III.4, J. Ber. I.4, Ber. 24a.
13. On Sabbaths and festivals. See "Laws Concerning the Sabbath," XXIX.1–2.
14. RH 29a.
15. Ber. 45a, M. RH III.5.
16. Lit., "to recline together," reflecting the custom of eating while reclining on couches. See "Laws Concerning Leavened and Unleavened Bread," VII.8.

17. M. Ber. VI.6.
18. See II K 17:24, Ḥul. 6a, and Maimonides' commentary on M. Ber. VIII.8. The Cutheans (often identified with the Samaritans) were thought to keep some of the commandments of the Torah.
19. M. Ber. VIII.8.
20. Or: "pronounce the first vowel as a *hataf-patah* instead of a *qamez.*"
21. Or: "swallow the final *nun.*"
22. By dropping the initial *aleph.*
23. Ber. 47a.
24. Ber. 33a.
25. As Maimonides makes clear in the next paragraph.
26. Ber. 45a.
27. The last blessing before the recitation of the Shema.
28. Ber. 45b.
29. I.e., not according to Torah law itself.
30. For details, see "Laws Concerning Tithes," chapter 1.
31. See "Laws Concerning Second Tithe and Fourth Year's Fruit," chapter 1.
32. Tos. Demai II. 23–24, M. Ber. VII.1.
33. See "Laws Concerning Tithes," chapter 9.
34. See "Laws Concerning Heave Offerings," chapter 3.
35. See "Laws Concerning Second Tithe and Fourth Year's Fruit," chapter 2.
36. M. Ber. VII.1.
37. Ber. 48b.
38. Ber. 16a.
39. See "Laws Concerning Circumcision," III. 9.
40. Ber. 48b.
41. Ber. 48b.
42. Ber. 48b.
43. Which always falls in Hannukah.
44. Sab. 24a.
45. Ber., 49a, 46a.
46. Ber. 46a.
47. Ket. 7b.
48. Ket. 7b.
49. Ber. 49a–b.
50. The first blessing.
51. With the formula "Blessed are You."
52. Ber. 49a–b.
53. M. Ber. VIII.7.
54. In translating these terms I follow the *Encyclopaedia Judaica.*
55. M. Ḥallah I.1, M. Ned. VII.2, Pes. 38a, J. Ned. VII.2.
56. I.e., unshelled.
57. Ordinarily recited over vegetables.
58. The grace after meals ordinarily recited after eating vegetables, meat, and dairy products or drinking any liquid but wine.

59. M. Ber. VI.1, Ber. 37a.
60. Ber. 38a.
61. See M. Ber. VI.5 and "Laws Concerning Vows," IX.7.
62. Ber. 36b, 37a.
63. M. Ber. VI.7.
64. Ber. 39a, AZ 66b,
65. M. Ber. VI.7, Ber. 44a.
66. And was no longer recognizable as bread.
67. Ber. 37a.
68. M. Kelim V.10, Ber. 42b.
69. Ber. 37a.
70. I.e., the abbreviated grace after meals, known as "'al ha-miḥyah." See below, III.13. Tos. Ber. IV.7, Ber. 36b.
71. Ber. 44b.
72. Compare below, VIII.14.
73. Ber. 44a.
74. The meaning here is unclear and the subject of discussion among the commentators. If the case here is where one failed to recite the grace after meals on purpose, how is the issue of remembering relevant?
75. M. Ber. VIII.7, Ber. 53b, Pes. 101b, Ber. 51b.
76. Ber. 51a.
77. I.e., the appropriate grace after meals.
78. Pes. 101b.
79. Who, presumably, could not get up with the others to greet the groom or bride.
80. I.e., the appropriate grace after meals.
81. Pes. 101b.
82. This sentence refers back to paragraph 4 and the first sentence of paragraph 5.
83. J. Ber. VI.8.
84. M. Ber. VI.5.
85. Ber. 42a.
86. Pes. 103a, Pes. 105a.
87. Ber. 59b, J. Ber. VI.8.
88. Lit., "the name of heaven."
89. See "Laws Concerning Vows," XII.11.
90. I.e., his original intention was to drink from whatever water in the aqueduct was before him. J. Ber. VI.1.
91. Ber. 41a.
92. Kove'a se'udato al ha-yayin; beginning the meal with wine stresses its formal nature.
93. M. Ber. VI.5, Ber. 42b.
94. On the principle that women and slaves are exempt from time-bound positive commandments.
95. By reciting it for them. The principle applied here is that only one obli-

gated to fulfill a commandment may, through its performance, exempt someone else obligated to fulfill it.
96. M. Ber. III.3, Ber. 20b.
97. M. Ber. III.1.
98. Ket. 8a.
99. 'Ar. 4a, Tos. Ber. V.14.
100. Defined in "Laws Concerning Circumcision," I.7, as a person born with complete male and female genitalia.
101. M. Ber. VII.1–2, Ber. 45b, Ber. 47a–48a, J. Ber. VII.2.
102. M. Ber. VII.2, Ber. 48a.
103. Ber. 47a.
104. In order to recite the grace after meals individually.
105. Into smaller groups of three or more.
106. M. Ber. VII.4.
107. Ber. 50a.
108. M. Ber. VII.5, Ber. 50b.
109. Ber. 45b.
110. Ber. 50a.
111. Suk. 38a.
112. Because he did not learn how to do it himself, or because, while knowing how, he allows someone of inferior status to do it for him. Ber. 45b, Ber. 20b.
113. Ber. 20b.
114. Ber. 45b.
115. In this chapter, by washing one's hands Maimonides refers to ritually washing the hands by pouring water over them in a prescribed fashion. See below, paragraph 4.
116. M. Ḥag. II.5, Ḥag. 18b, Ḥul. 106a, Sab. 13b.
117. See the next paragraph.
118. Ber. 60a, Ḥul. 105a.
119. Since one does so in order to flaunt the "superior" level of one's observance.
120. See Ḥul. 106b.
121. I.e., the danger of rubbing salt in one's eyes. Ḥul. 105b–106a, M. 'Er. I.10.
122. Ḥul. 106a, 107a.
123. M. Ḥag. II.5, Ḥul. 107a.
124. See "Laws Concerning the Murderer," XI.5–14.
125. M. Yad. I.3, AZ 30b.
126. M. Yad. I.3–5.
127. M. Yad. I.3, Ḥul. 106a.
128. J. Ber. VIII.2, M. Yad. II.1.
129. See Ḥul. 107a.
130. Ḥul. 107a, M. Yad. I.2, M. Kelim II.2, M. Parah V.5.
131. M. Yad. I.2, Ḥul. 107a.
132. Talmudic law sees deaf-mutes, idiots, and minors as having diminished intellectual and hence legal capacity. See Yev. 92b.

133. M. Yad. I.5.

134. Ḥul. 107a.

135. M. Yad. II.4.

136. Since the water carries off the ritual impurity, allowing the water to flow back onto the hands would defeat the purpose of the entire exercise.

137. One will not rub one's hands in scalding water.

138. Soṭ. 4b. Ḥul. 105a–b.

139. Ḥul. 106b.

140. Heb. *magrefah;* see Maimonides, commentary to M. Kelim XIII.4.

141. Ḥul. 107a–b.

142. Ḥul. 107b, 'Er. 21b.

143. Soṭ. 4b, Ber. 42a.

144. Thus, the most important person is in the center. The second-greatest person is placed near his head, the third-greatest near his feet. Ber. 46b.

145. See above, II.7.

146. Ber. 46a.

147. I.e., from the best part of the bread, neither underdone nor overdone. Ber. 40a, 6a, 39b; San. 102b.

148. Ber. 39b.

149. The source of this custom is unknown.

150. Ber. 47a.

151. The commentators disagree about the meaning here.

152. The danger being food becoming lodged in the windpipe.

153. Ber. 47a, 45b; Ta'an. 5b; M. Ber. VI.6.

154. Ber. 48a.

155. With which he had touched his penis.

156. One turns away from the table to wash one's hands.

157. Yoma 30a.

158. Ber. 50b, Sab. 50b.

159. To drink wine with him.

160. Ḥul. 94a.

161. I.e., by crumbling them. Ber. 42a, 52b.

162. Who would be leading the grace after meals.

163. I.e., who passes first in such a case.

164. Ber. 43a, 46b, 47a.

165. M. Ber. VI.6.

166. So as to wipe the perfume off his hands.

167. It is inappropriate for a scholar to appear in public perfumed. Pes. 105a, Ber. 43b.

168. Pes. 105b, Ber. 51a.

169. M. Ber. VI.1, 3, 8; Ber. 40a, 44a–b.

170. Tos. Ber. IV.2, Ber. 38a, Ber. 35b.

171. Ber. 38b.

172. Ber. 39a, 38a.

173. *Kol.* In Maimonidean usage, *kol* often means "many."
174. Maimonides is describing the production of sugar.
175. I.e., the syrup.
176. I.e., if the blessing over unprocessed date honey is "that all" and not the blessing over tree fruit, how much more so should the blessing over sugar be "that all."
177. Ber. 36a.
178. Ber. 36b.
179. Ber. 40b, 12a; M. Nid. VI.11.
180. BB 96b.
181. B. Ber. VI.2, Ber. 40a.
182. Ber. 12a.
183. Ber. 50b.
184. The word "land" is found twice in the verse; wine (grapes) is third in the list after the first occurrence; honey (dates) is second in the list after the second occurrence. Thus, honey is "closer" to the land than wine. M. Ber. VI.4, Ber. 41a.
185. I.e., the full grace after meals. Ber. 44a.
186. See "Laws Concerning the Vessels of the Sanctuary," I.3. "Myrrh" here refers to musk.
187. Ber. 43a–b.
188. Ber. 43a.
189. Balsam.
190. With fragrances.
191. See "Laws Concerning the Vessels of the Sanctuary," 1.2.
192. Ber. 43a.
193. Compare above, VII.14. Ber. 43a.
194. Ber. 43a.
195. Ber. 43b.
196. M. Ber. VIII.6; Ber. 52b, 53a; J. Ber. VI.6.
197. Ber. 53a.
198. Of the form, "blessed are You . . ."
199. M. Ber. IX.3.
200. Ber. 58b, J. Pes. X.5, Ber. 40b, 'Er. 40b.
201. M. Ber. IX. 2, 5.
202. M. Ber. IX. 3.
203. Ber. 59b.
204. Ber. 59b.
205. The ms. reads *kezavo* while the printed editions have *kezaro*. The standard editions of the Talmud (Ber. 59b) read *kezaro,* while Alfasi has *kezavo.*
206. Ber. 59b.
207. Ber. 54b.
208. Josh. 3:17.
209. Dan. 6:17–24.
210. Dan. 3.

211. M. Ber. IX.1, Ber. 57b.
212. There is considerable discussion among the commentators on what this means.
213. The unredeemed Jewish people are likened to widows. For the expression here, see Prov. 15:25.
214. Ber. 58b.
215. Nahmanides explains the source of this as follows: God knows the innermost desires of each Jew.
216. Ber. 58a.
217. Ber. 58b.
218. I.e., in the spring.
219. Ber. 58b, 43b.
220. M. Ber. IX.2.
221. M. Ber. IX.2.
222. Ber. 59a–b.
223. San. 42a, 41b.
224. Ber. 59b. I borrow the translation of this paragraph (with slight emendations to make it consistent with my usage) from Langermann, "Maimonides and Astronomy: Some Further Reflections," p. 12. For commentary on this passage, see Langermann, pp. 12–26.
225. Ber. 58b.
226. There was apparently a real danger of being burned by the fire used to heat the water in ancient bathhouses.
227. Ber. 60a.
228. Ta'an. 8b, BB 42a.
229. Alternatively: "Let me not make a mistake concerning halakhah, so that my friends are happy at my expense, and let my friends make no mistakes concerning halakhah, so that I am happy at their expense."
230. M. Ber. IV.2, Ber. 8b.
231. Or: ". . . and enemies which lurk upon the roads." M. Ber. IX.4.
232. I.e., the blessings of "enjoyment."
233. In chapter 10.
234. "Laws Concerning Prayer," XII.5.
235. Above, X.10.
236. Ber. 46a.
237. See Deut. 22:8 and "Laws Concerning the Murderer," XI.1.
238. J. Ber. VI.1, Pes. 7b.
239. See "Laws Concerning the 'Erub," I.6–7.
240. I.e., of rabbinic authority. Sab. 23a, Ber. 19b.
241. The water needs to be strained since at night one cannot see what is in it. See AZ 12b.
242. Hul. 105a.
243. J. Ber. IX.2, Ber. 60b.
244. See "Laws Concerning Slaughtering," XIV.1.

245. And came out.

246. I.e., in all cases where one should have made the blessing before the act, one cannot make it after the act is completed. J. Ber. IX.2, Pes. 7b.

247. Before performing the commandment.

248. Pes. 7a. Before converting, the then-potential proselyte could hardly say, "Who has sanctified us with His commandments and commanded us to . . ."

249. To sit in the sukkah or put on the phylacteries.

250. Men. 42a.

251. Suk. 46a.

252. Or, "on."

253. "Laws Concerning Ḥameẓ and Matzah," II.l.

254. Suk. 44b, Ta'an. 28b.

Treatise VI: Laws Concerning Circumcision

1. Heb. *karet;* see "Laws Concerning Repentance," VIII.1.

2. M. Keritot I.1, Yev. 70b, Kid. 29a.

3. Yev. 48a, Kid. 29a.

4. Yev. 48b.

5. Which should be circumcised on the day it is born.

6. Sab. 135b.

7. Such immersion would make her obliged to fulfill the same commandments which a Jewish woman is obliged to fulfill.

8. Sab. 135b.

9. Maimonides in his commentary on the Mishnah, Tractate Pe'ah, V.3: "The word *megalgelin* means in their language, 'normalcy,' 'not being especially strict.'"

10. The commentators debate whether the condition was made by the original Gentile owner or by the Jewish purchaser.

11. See "Laws Concerning Idolatry," X.6, and "Laws Concerning Forbidden Intercourse," XIV.7.

12. Yev. 48b. See also 'Arakhin 29a–b, "Laws Concerning Forbidden Intercourse," XIV.9, and "Laws Concerning the Sabbatical Year and Jubilee," X.8.

13. Yev. 47a–b, Sab. 135a.

14. But before the sun had completely risen.

15. M. Meg. II.4, Yev. 72a, Yoma 28b, Pes. 4a.

16. I.e., on the eighth day after birth.

17. See "Laws Concerning Uncleanness of Leprosy," I.2.

18. Sab. 132a–b.

19. J. Yev. IV.2, Sab. 135a-b.

20. "Laws Concerning the Sabbath," V.4: the period between sunset and the appearance of three medium-sized stars.

21. M. Sab. XIX.5.

22. See "Laws Concerning the Sabbath," XXV.6.
23. Yev. 90a–b, Sab. 135a–b.
24. RH 11a.
25. Which is celebrated outside the land of Israel because of historical uncertainty over when the holiday actually falls. See "Laws Concerning Repose on a Festival," I. 21–24.
26. Nid. 42b, M. Sab. XIX.5.
27. Maimonides appears to be distinguishing between generalized and localized infections. M. Sab. XIX.5.
28. *'Ad she-yippol bo damav.* My translation makes the best sense I can of the term and is based on my assumption that Maimonides attributed jaundice to insufficient blood.
29. Sab. 134a, Yev. 64b, Yoma 82a.
30. Yev. 64b.
31. The danger of splinters.
32. AZ 27a, BK 88a.
33. M. Sab. XIX.2, Sab. 133b.
34. M. Sab. XIX.6.
35. Sab. 133b.
36. Sab. 137b.
37. M. Sab. XIX.1, 2, Sab. 130a, Pes. 92a.
38. In order to wash the baby before the procedure.
39. Cumin was used as a medicine to prevent infection.
40. M. Sab. XIX.2.
41. Used to clean the wound.
42. I.e., the water heated and the herbs prepared.
43. When the child was thought to be particularly weak.
44. M. Sab. XIX.3.
45. See "Laws Concerning the Sabbath," VI.9.
46. I.e., one of the thirty-nine categories of "work" forbidden on the Sabbath.
47. Sab. 134a.
48. Pes. 7a.
49. Sab. 137b.
50. A reference to Isaac.
51. Possibly a reference to 'Er. 19a, according to which Abraham saves from Gehinnom all circumcised Jews.
52. I.e., the soul.
53. In my translation here, I follow Maimonides' responsum 214.
54. Sab. 137b.
55. Sab. 137b.
56. Gentiles here are idolaters. See "Laws Concerning Forbidden Foods," XI.8.
57. AZ 26b.
58. So that even though he is circumcised he appears to be uncircumcised.

59. M. Ned. III.10, Avot III.14.
60. See Exod. 4:24.
61. Based on Isa. 40:29.

APPENDIX

1. Here and throughout the appendix, I cite relevant passages from Elbogin's *Jewish Liturgy*. For another overview on the subject, see Reif's *Judaism and Hebrew Prayer*.

GLOSSARY

'amidah. Central prayer of the Jewish liturgy; consists of nineteen
paragraphs ("blessings").

ammah (= cubit). Six handbreadths (*ṭefaḥim,* q.v.); pl.: *ammot.*

baraitot. Tannaitic materials not included in the Mishnah, but
found in the Tosefta, Tannaitic Midrash, and Gemara.

dukhsustus. Hair-side of a *gevil* (q.v.) split in two.

genizah. Place, grave, or cabinet used for the respectful disposal of
texts and items which may not be simply thrown out.

gevil. Hide prepared for use as parchment.

haftarah. Texts from the prophetic books read after the weekly
Torah portion.

halakhah le-Moshe mi-sinai. Laws having biblical authority, but
neither stated explicitly in the Torah nor derived from a Torah
text by one of the accepted hermeneutical principles.

havdalah. (A) Prayer added to the fourth blessing of the *'amidah*
(q.v.) at the end of the Sabbath; (b) ceremony marking the end
of the Sabbath.

kaddish. Prayer with a number of variations, which serve a variety
of purposes: dividing segments of the prayer service, marking
the end of Torah study, and memorializing the dead. A version
of it is always recited after the completion of the *'amidah.*

parashah. Blocks of verses into which the biblical text is divided;
(pl. *parashot*).

parchment. Translates the Hebrew word *'or* when it means a hide
prepared for writing upon and no particular type of parchment
(*qelaf, gevil, dukhsustus,* q.v.) is specified. In other contexts, *'or* is
translated as "leather."

parsah. A distance of four "miles" or 8,000 cubits (3,840 or 4,800
meters).

Pentateuch (= *Ḥumash*). Scrolls of individual books of the Pentateuch, as opposed to a complete Torah scroll; the word does not
mean Genesis, Exodus, Leviticus, Numbers, and Deuteronomy
bound together as a book (its contemporary meaning).

qedushah. Prayer based on Isa. 6:3 and Ez. 3:12.

qelaf. If a *gevil* (q.v.) is split in two, the flesh side is called *qelaf.*

quarter-*hin.* Liquid measurement: either 68 cubic centimeters or 135 cubic centimeters, depending upon the authority consulted.

Shin'ar. Babylonia, largely corresponding to present-day Iraq.

tefah. Handbreadth; one-sixth of an *ammah* (q.v.); pl.: *tefahim.*

WORKS CITED

Secondary Literature

Benor, Ehud. *Worship of the Heart: A Study in Maimonides' Philosophy of Religion*. Albany, N.Y.: SUNY Press, 1995.

Blidstein, Ya'akov. *Ha-Tefillah be-Mishnato ha-Hilkhatit shel ha-Rambam* (Prayer in Maimonides' halakhic thought). Jerusalem: Mossad Bialik, 1994.

————. "Maimonides' *Taqqanah* Concerning Public Prayer," *Maimonidean Studies* 3 (1992–1993): 3–28.

————. "Prostration and Mosaics in Talmudic Law." *Bulletin of the Institute of Jewish Studies* 2 (1974): 19–39.

Cohen, Boaz. "The Classification of the Law in the Mishneh Torah," *Jewish Quarterly Review* 25 (1935): 519–540.

Elbogin, Ismar. *Jewish Liturgy: A Comprehensive History*. Translated and annotated by Raymond P. Scheindlin. Philadelphia and New York: Jewish Publication Society and Jewish Theological Seminary, 1993.

Encyclopaedia Judaica. 16 vols. Jerusalem: Keter, 1972.

Erlich, Uri. *Kol Azmotai Tomarna: Ha-Safah ha-lo-Milulit shel ha-Tefillah* (The nonverbal language of Jewish prayer). Jerusalem: Magnes, 1999.

Fleischer, Ezra. "Towards a Clarification of the Expression *Pores 'al Shema*." *Tarbiz* 41 (1971): 133–144 (Hebrew).

Goldschmidt, Daniel. "Maimonides' Prayer Book According to the Oxford Manuscript." *Studies of the Research Institute for Hebrew Poetry in Jerusalem* 7 (1958): 185–213 (Hebrew).

Goshen-Gottstein, Moshe. "The Aleppo Codex and Maimonides' Laws Concerning the Torah Scroll," in *Jubilee Volume . . . Rabbi Joseph B. Soloveitchik,* ed. S. Israeli and Y. Raphael, 2:871–887 (Hebrew). Jerusalem: Mossad ha-Rav Kook, 1984.

Halivni, David Weiss. *Revelation Restored: Divine Writ and Critical Responses*. Boulder, Colo.: Westview Press, 1997.

Haran, Menahem. "Bible Scrolls in Eastern and Western Jewish

Communities from Qumran to the High Middle Ages." *Hebrew Union College Annual* 56 (1985): 21–62.

Hartman, David. *Israelis and the Jewish Tradition: An Ancient People Debating its Future.* New Haven: Yale University Press, 2000.

Harvey, Steven. "The Meaning of Terms Designating Love in Judaeo-Arabic Thought and Some Remarks on the Judaeo-Arabic Interpretation of Maimonides," in *Judaeo-Arabic Studies,* ed. Norman Golb, 175–196. Amsterdam: Harwood, 1997.

Havazelet, Meir. "Traces of the Siddur of Rav Sa'adia Gaon in Maimonides' *Mishneh Torah,*" *Sinai* 60 (1967): 211–217 (Hebrew).

Havlin, Shlomo Zalman. "An Autograph Testament of Maimonides," *'Alei Sefer* 18 (1995–1996): 171–176 (Hebrew).

Kadish, Seth. *Kavvana: Directing the Heart in Jewish Prayer.* Northvale, N.J.: Jason Aronson, 1997.

Kaplan, Lawrence. "Rav Kook and the Jewish Philosophical Tradition," in *Rabbi Abraham Isaac Kook and Jewish Spirituality,* ed. Lawrence Kaplan and David Shatz, 41–77. New York: New York University Press, 1995.

Kellner, Menachem. *Maimonides on Human Perfection.* Atlanta: Scholars Press, 1990.

Kreisel, Howard. *Maimonides' Political Thought: Studies in Ethics, Law, and the Human Ideal.* Albany, N.Y.: SUNY Press, 1999.

Langermann, Y. Tzvi. "Maimonides and Astronomy: Some Further Reflections," in Langermann, *The Jews and the Sciences in the Middle Ages.* Aldershot, U.K.: Ashgate, 1999.

Levey, Martin. "Some Black Inks in Early Mediaeval Jewish Literature." *Chymia* 9 (1964): 27–31.

Penkower, Jordan S. "Maimonides and the Aleppo Codex." *Textus* 9 (1981): 39–128.

Reif, Stefan. *Judaism and Hebrew Prayer: New Perspectives on Jewish Liturgical History.* Cambridge: Cambridge University Press, 1993.

Siddur Sim Shalom. Ed. Jules Harlow. New York: Rabbinical Assembly and United Synagogue, 1985.

Stern, Josef. "On an Alleged Contradiction between Maimonides' *Guide of the Perplexed* and *Mishneh Torah.*" *Hebrew Law Annual* 14–15 (1988): 283–298 (Hebrew).

Twersky, Isadore. *Introduction to the Code of Maimonides.* New Haven: Yale University Press, 1980.

Weiss, Roslyn. "Maimonides on *Shilluaḥ Ha-Qen.*" *Jewish Quarterly Review* 79 (1989): 345–366.

EDITIONS AND TRANSLATIONS OF *SEFER AHAVAH:*

Havlin, Shlomo, ed. *The Authorized Version of the Code of Maimonides (Mishneh Torah), the Book of Knowledge and the Book of Love (Sefer Madda, Sefer Ahabah): Facsimile Edition of Oxford Manuscript Huntington 80.* Jerusalem and Cleveland: Ofeq Institute, 5757 (1997).

Hyamson, Moses. *The Book of Adoration.* Jerusalem: Boys Town, 1962.

Kafiḥ, Joseph. *Sefer Mishneh Torah Yuza le-Or Pa'am Rishonah 'al pi Kitvei Yad Teiman 'im Perush Maḳif.* Jerusalem: Makhon Mosheh, 1985; corrected and reissued in 1993.

Kaplan, Boruch, and Eliyahu Touger. *Maimonides' Mishneh Torah.* New York: Moznaim, 1989–1992.

Rabinovitch, Nachum L. *Rabbi Mosheh ben Maimon (Maimonides), Mishneh Torah According to the Bodleian Ms. Huntington 80, with a Comprehensive Commentary [Yad Peshuṭah].* Jerusalem: Ma'aliyot Press, 1994.

Rubenstein, Samuel Tanḥum, ed. *Sefer Ahavah.* Jerusalem: Mossad ha-Rav Kook, 1958.

OTHER WRITINGS BY MAIMONIDES

Blau, Joshua, ed. and trans. *Teshuvot ha-Rambam.* 3 vols. Jerusalem: Mekize Nirdamim, 1958.

Chavel, Charles, trans. *The Commandments.* 2 vols. London: Soncino, 1967.

Hyamson, Moses, ed. and trans. *The Book of Knowledge.* Jerusalem: Feldheim, 1974.

Pines, Shlomo, trans. *Guide of the Perplexed.* Chicago: University of Chicago Press, 1963.

Sheilat, Yiẓḥaq, ed. and trans. *Iggerot Ha-Rambam.* 2 vols. Jerusalem: Ma'aliyot Press, 1987.

SCRIPTURAL REFERENCES

2 KINGS

ISAIAH

JEREMIAH

EZEKIEL

HOSEA

ZECHARIAH

PSALMS

PROVERBS

EZRA

DANIEL

6:11, 31

NEHEMIAH

8:3, 56   13:24, 18

INDEX

The Yale Judaica Series consists mainly of translations of ancient and medieval Jewish classics from Hebrew, Aramaic, Ethiopic, and Arabic. The Code of Maimonides, compiled in the latter part of the twelfth century, is the most systematic and exhaustive work of codification in the entire realm of rabbinic literature.

Vol. I. *Saadia Gaon: The Book of Beliefs and Opinions,* translated by Samuel Rosenblatt

Vol. II. *The Book of Civil Laws* (Code of Maimonides, Book 13), translated by Jacob J. Rabinowitz

Vol. III. *The Book of Judges* (Code of Maimonides, Book 14), translated by A. M. Hershman

Vol. IV. *The Book of Offerings* (Code of Maimonides, Book 9), translated by Herbert Danby

Vol. V. *The Book of Acquisition* (Code of Maimonides, Book 12), translated by Isaac Klein

Vol. VI. *Falasha Anthology,* translated by Wolf Leslau

Vol. VII. *Karaite Anthology,* translated by Leon Nemoy

Vol. VIII. *The Book of Cleanness* (Code of Maimonides, Book 10), translated by Herbert Danby

Vol. IX. *The Book of Torts* (Code of Maimonides, Book 11), translated by Hyman Klein

Vol. X. *The Fathers According to Rabbi Hathan,* translated by Judah Goldin

Vol. XI. *Sanctification of the New Moon* (Code of Maimonides, Book 3, Treatise 8), translated by Solomon Gandz

Vol. XII. *The Book of Temple Service* (Code of Maimonides, Book 8), translated by Mendell Lewittes

Vol. XIII. *The Midrash on Psalms,* translated by William G. Braude

Vol. XIV. *The Book of Seasons* (Code of Maimonides, Book 3), translated by Solomon Gandz and Hyman Klein

Vol. XV. *The Book of Asseverations* (Code of Maimonides, Book 6), translated by B. D. Klein

Vol. XVI. *The Book of Holiness* (Code of Maimonides, Book 5), translated by Louis I. Rabinowitz and Philip Grossman

Vol. XVII. *The Tractage "Mourning,"* translated (with Hebrew included) by Dov Zlotnick

Vol. XVIII. *Pesikta Rabbati,* translated by William G. Braude